DATE DUE	
MAR 1 5 1992	
FEB 07 1996	
BRODART, INC.	Cat. No. 23-221

American Furniture 1680-1880

FROM THE COLLECTION OF THE BALTIMORE MUSEUM OF ART

American Furniture 1680-1880

FROM THE COLLECTION OF THE BALTIMORE MUSEUM OF ART

WILLIAM VOSS ELDER III AND JAYNE E. STOKES

with the assistance of
LU BARTLETT
ANN V. CHRISTIE
AUDREY FRANTZ
FAITH M. HOLLAND
M. B. MUNFORD

Library of Congress Cataloging-in-Publication Data

Baltimore Museum of Art.
  American furniture, 1680–1880, from the collection of the
Baltimore Museum of Art.

  Bibliography: p.
  1. Furniture, Colonial—United States—Catalogs.
2. Furniture—United States—History—18th century—
Catalogs. 3. Furniture—United States—History—19th
century—Catalogs. 4. Furniture—Maryland—Baltimore—
Catalogs. 5. Baltimore Museum of Art—Catalogs.
I. Elder, William Voss. II. Stokes, Jayne E. III. Title.
NK2406.B3 1987   749.213'074'01526   86-26518
ISBN 0-912298-62-6

Cover: 76. CYLINDER DESK, (1800–1810). Annapolis or
Baltimore. The Baltimore Museum of Art: Friends of
the American Wing Fund (BMA 1986.12)

Back cover: Detail, cat. no. 76

Contents

49. HIGH CHEST, (1733–1739). Boston
Japanner: Robert Davis
The Baltimore Museum of Art: Purchased as the gift
of Mr. and Mrs. Francis C. Taliaferro, in Memory
of Mr. and Mrs. Austin McLanahan (BMA 1970.37.4)

Foreword

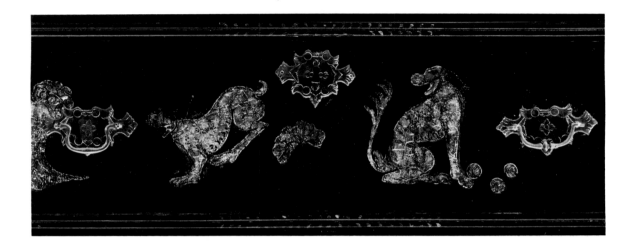

It was in 1925 that the first piece of American furniture entered the permanent collection of The Baltimore Museum of Art. In that year Randolph Mordecai, a Baltimorean living in Paris, gave to the Museum a Baltimore painted chair in the Empire style (BMA 1925.11.1). Tradition suggested that such chairs had been made for the occasion of Lafayette's visit to Baltimore in 1824 to be used at the banquet in the French general's honor. This historic association made the chair uniquely appropriate for the Baltimore Museum collections. The Mordecai chair, a fine example of its kind, initiated a major collection especially noted for its Baltimore and Maryland-related decorative arts. When the new Museum building opened on Art Museum Drive in 1929, half of the building's main floor was dedicated as "The Maryland Wing," featuring paintings by Maryland artists and of Maryland subjects, along with furniture, silver, and architectural elements, dating from the eighteenth and early nineteenth centuries.

The Museum's first substantial commitment to its collection of American decorative arts came with the 1929 acquisition of a high chest of drawers (cat. no. 50), initially acquired as an example of the Philadelphia Chippendale style but in later years determined to be of Maryland origin. In the same year two architectural interiors were also installed in The Maryland Wing, both of which were furnished with borrowed material. The woodwork from the 1750's Maryland house called Eltonhead Manor in Calvert County had been given to the Museum in 1925 and was originally installed in the Museum's town house location at 101 West Monument Street before being moved to the John Russell Pope building in 1929. The beautifully-paneled room of about 1770 from Habre de Venture in Charles County, purchased by the City of Baltimore, was also installed in the Museum's Maryland Wing. And in 1931 the room from the Abbey or Ringgold House in Chestertown became the third period room installed in The Maryland Wing. In 1933 Virginia Purviance Bonsal White (Mrs. Miles White, Jr.) gave to the Museum her major collection of Maryland silver. The gift of the White silver collection was especially notable in the 1930's when so few objects entered the collection, a pattern of slow growth which would continue until at least the 1960's.

In the absence of purchase funds, development of the Museum's collection was almost entirely dependent on the interest and support of a handful of dedicated Baltimore collectors. In 1942 C. Edward Snyder bequeathed several pieces of American furniture, including a major Philadelphia Queen Anne to Chippendale transitional armchair (cat. no. 10). In the early 1950's, J. Gilman D'Arcy Paul (who served as the President of the Museum's Board of Trustees from 1942–1956) succeeded Mrs. Miles White in assuming responsibility for The Maryland Wing and the development of its decorative arts collections. In 1932 Mrs. White had persuaded the Colonial Dames of America, Chapter I, in Baltimore, to purchase for the Museum a splendid sideboard by the Annapolis cabinetmaker John Shaw (cat. no. 109). In turn, Mr. Paul was among the Friends of the Museum who presented a secretary-bookcase to the collection in 1946 (cat. no. 79). This interesting piece of furniture, thought to be of Baltimore origin when purchased, was included in the landmark 1947 exhibition organized by the Museum, *Baltimore Furniture: The Work of Baltimore and Annapolis Cabinetmakers from 1760 to 1810.* This was the first major furniture exhibition sponsored by the Museum and, like all subsequent exhibitions, provided enormous impetus for gifts and bequests. Fifteen pieces of furniture borrowed for the 1947 exhibition have since been given to the Museum (of which thirteen are featured in the present catalogue). Two other pieces and the remarkable thirteen-piece set of painted furniture featured in the same exhibition eventually entered the permanent collection by means of purchase or as partial gift-partial purchase.

By 1956 the combined holdings of American and European decorative arts warranted the appointment of the Museum's first Curator of Decorative Arts. But it was not until 1961 that the collection grew in any way other than by occasional gifts. In that year, members of the Needles family offered the Museum eleven pieces of furniture made from about 1830 to 1860 by their ancestor, the cabinetmaker John Needles of Baltimore. An Empire-style wardrobe (cat. no. 72) and a sofa table in the Gothic Revival style (cat. no. 94) are among the objects from this important collection of locally made furniture included in this catalogue. In 1964 a bequest of Philip B. Perlman, a dedicated and knowledgeable collector who was a former Solicitor General of the United States, added significantly to the American furniture collection. It included a Maryland dressing table (cat. no. 61), a Massachusetts desk (cat. no. 74), and a Philadelphia clock (cat. no. 83), three of the most important pieces owned by Perlman.

In 1966 a late eighteenth-century oval room from Willow Brook, a Baltimore house, was saved from demolition and painstakingly moved to the Museum. Its installation in The Maryland Wing represented the first of many alterations and expansions of Museum space allocated to the American decorative arts. The architectural renovations necessary to install the Willow Brook room were made possible through a public subscription campaign spearheaded by the Museum's good friend Gilman Paul. Numerous gifts came to the collection as a result of the Willow Brook installation, the most important of which was the partial gift of a surviving set of Baltimore painted furniture made in the Federal period (cat. nos. 29, 39, 121). In the following year, 1967, Elizabeth Curzon Hoffman Wing, resident of Charleston but a native of Baltimore, bequeathed to the Museum a collection of eighteenth and early nineteenth-century American furniture and paintings as a memorial to her son, along with funds to create expanded exhibition space. This substantial gift resulted in the construction of additional galleries above the existing Maryland Wing. Mrs. Wing included in her bequest many pieces of furniture from the Baltimore town house designed by American architect Robert Mills in about 1818 for a member of the Hoffman family. As it happened, Mrs. Wing's bequest coincided with the demolition of the Mills-designed Waterloo Row (1817) on Calvert Street in Baltimore. From the ten remaining partially-intact houses of Waterloo Row, the Museum salvaged, restored, and had installed by 1970 in the newly-expanded Maryland Wing an entrance doorway, entrance and stair hall, and double parlors. While this extensive construction was underway, Mr. and Mrs. Francis C. Taliaferro of Baltimore offered to establish at the Museum a suitable memorial to Mrs. Taliaferro's parents, Mr. and Mrs. Austin McLanahan. For this purpose, woodwork from a bedroom from the early eighteenth-century Weston house in Dorchester County was acquired, restored, and installed in The Maryland Wing's upper level and was opened in 1970 with outstanding period furnishings donated by Mr. and Mrs. Taliaferro, including a William and Mary dressing table (cat. no. 58) and a rare Queen Anne japanned high chest (cat. no. 49), both from Massachusetts. The year 1970 also marked the death of the Museum's friend and patron J. Gilman D'Arcy Paul. In addition to the generosity of his lifetime gifts to the American decorative arts collection, Mr. Paul bequeathed to the Museum several choice pieces from his personal collection, chief among which was a rare Philadelphia Queen Anne side table with its original King of Prussia marble top (cat. no. 107), found by Mr. Paul on the island of Montserrat.

The collection of Mrs. Miles White, Jr. had been formed in the late nineteenth century and early years of the twentieth century. She was among the earliest collectors in America and was certainly the first knowledgeable collector of American antiques in Baltimore. At the time of her death in 1955 her Baltimore residence, Kernewood House, and its collection of furniture and other decorative arts passed to her son The Honorable Francis White. His widow, Nancy Brewster White, before her death in 1974, gave to the Museum twenty-eight pieces of American furniture and more than four hundred other decorative arts objects including glass, ceramics, and textiles from her late mother-in-law's collection. At that time this magnificent gift comprised the most significant accession of American decorative arts to be recorded by the Museum.

It has only been in the past fifteen years that the Baltimore Museum's stature as one of the country's foremost repositories of American decorative arts has been nationally acknowledged. In large part this reputation has been forged through the committed activities of a group of Baltimore collectors passionately interested in the field. In the fall of 1970 several of these individuals founded a Museum support group called the Friends of the American Wing. In little more than a decade, the Friends have provided the Museum more than $350,000 in accessions funds for the purchase of major pieces of American furniture. Many of the most outstanding pieces in the collection have come to the Museum through the support of the Friends of the American Wing, including a Massachusetts Chippendale chest-on-chest (cat. no. 55), a Federal-style linen press by John Shaw of Annapolis (cat. no. 71), and, the Friends' most recent purchase, an impressive Baltimore or Annapolis cylinder desk also in the Federal style (cat. no. 76). From time to time the Friends have also provided funds for the purchase of important eighteenth and early nineteenth-century American paintings. A more recently formed group called the Young Friends of the American Wing has also begun to provide accessions funds.

The most extensive and dramatic architectural renovation affecting The Maryland Wing occurred as a result of Dorothy McIlvain Scott's 1978 commitment to the Museum's capital program. Her extraordinary generosity assured the creation of a new ground floor level for The Maryland Wing which almost tripled the amount of space available for American decorative arts. In recognition of the growing diversity of the American decorative arts collection beyond the scope of Baltimore and Maryland makers, the 1982 rededication of these three floors acknowledged the space as The American Wing. At the time of the new American Wing dedication, Miss Scott also announced her intention further to enrich the Museum with the donation of thirty-eight pieces of highly important American furniture from her personal collection. Twenty-three of these promised gifts are included in the catalogue and represent, in addition to the work of Baltimore and Annapolis cabinetmakers, the exceptional handiwork of other major American centers such as Boston (cat. nos. 28, 53, 66), New York (cat. no. 115), and Philadelphia (cat. nos. 7, 13, 57, 63). These and other promised gifts from Miss Scott, such as a Connecticut Chippendale-style chest-on-chest with block-and-shell carved drawer fronts (cat. no. 54), will increase the scope of the Museum's furniture collection. The Museum is also to receive another major private local collection; a separate gallery to house it is included on the ground floor of The American Wing. Several gifts from this collection have already been made, including an unusual gaming table (cat. no. 93), a handsome pier table (cat. no. 120), and a cabriole sofa (cat. no. 43), all made in Baltimore in the Federal period.

From its first gift in 1925, the Museum's collection of American furniture has grown to more than 300 pieces (including the promised gifts of two Baltimore collectors). The 139 pieces published in this catalogue were selected to represent the range of the Museum's collection from the late seventeenth through the last decades of the nineteenth centuries and from as many of America's major cabinetmaking centers as possible. No practical publication could encompass the extraordinary range of the Museum's collection of American furniture, which includes many exceptional objects not catalogued in the present volume (notable among which are fine examples from the twentieth century), but it is hoped that the present volume will provide scholars and the general public alike with a major resource for understanding and appreciating the exceptional collections of American furniture housed at The Baltimore Museum of Art.

No project is as demanding of a museum's resources as that of definitive collection cataloguing. It is not uncommon for such cataloguing projects to extend over decades, as objects accumulated since an institution's founding are retrieved, inventoried, measured and analyzed, newly cleaned or restored, and exhaustively researched to assure the most complete and current cataloguing data. These issues are compounded in logistical complexity when many of the objects in question are large case pieces whose size and weight demand multiple hands. The commitment to such a project therefore carries long-range ramifications for both staffing and financial priorities. The Trustees of The Baltimore Museum of Art are formally committed to publication of the Museum's permanent collections on a regular basis, and in as timely manner as the quality and scope of respective aspects of the permanent collection warrant. Because of the importance of our Museum's American furniture holdings, this collection catalogue was deemed to be of a very high priority despite the fact that it is anticipated that the collection will expand in size and scope in future years. It was also determined that a specific schedule should be assigned to the project to avoid the extended delays that often characterize such publications from the time of their inception until the time of their delivery. Thus, it was only in 1984 that we committed our staff to the American Furniture catalogue.

Confirmation of the catalogue's viability came from the generous support of The Henry Luce Foundation, Inc., which provided a substantial subsidy through the Luce Fund for Scholarship in American Art. We are profoundly grateful to the Luce Foundation for this invaluable support and for the vision which has provided essential financial subsidies for advanced scholarship in American art throughout the country. In addition, significant supplemental financial support for the catalogue was provided by the Kaufman Americana Foundation. I am extremely pleased to express our Board's appreciation to George M. and Linda H. Kaufman of Norfolk, Virginia, and to their Foundation for its endorsement of our publication's importance. The Museum's own Friends of the American Wing added its support to the publication endeavor by a generous matching grant, and we are warmly grateful to all of the Friends and especially to past presidents Bryden B. Hyde and Duncan H. Mackenzie for their substantial commitment to the American furniture collections of the Museum. In addition, funds provided by the Andrew W. Mellon Foundation supported much of the preparatory research for the publication, and we gratefully acknowledge the Mellon Foundation for its ongoing support of collection research in our Museum.

William Voss Elder III came to The Baltimore Museum of Art as Curator of Decorative Arts in 1963 and it is under his guidance that the Museum's collection of American decorative arts has grown to its eminent status. He is largely responsible for the present publication, and it is his professional dedication that has assured the book's realization. In the past three years he has set aside other departmental priorities in order to supervise the exhaustive research and writing needed for this definitive cataloguing of the American furniture collection. In this undertaking he has had the valued assistance of Jayne E. Stokes, who was employed by the Museum to coordinate the daunting assignment of inventory and data research essential for compilation of individual catalogue entries. Elder and Stokes together wrote almost all of the 139 entries for the present volume, and the Museum's most sincere acknowledgment is extended to them for this remarkable achievement. The project also had the constant support of the Department of Decorative Art's Assistant Curator M.B. Munford who, as always, extended herself tirelessly on behalf of the publication's needs while simultaneously maintaining the daily burdens of the department's more routine responsibilities. The Department of Decorative Arts also benefited significantly from the contributions of several volunteers and interns in the course of the publication's preparation: notably, colleague Lu Bartlett contributed her time and energies by cataloguing a number of the pieces for publication; others who were of inestimable assistance included Virginia Ziegaus in the Museum's Library, Terri L. Rosen and Allison E. Letzer of Goucher College, Eleasa J. Sangdahl of Amherst College, Janet Shaw, and, most especially, Georgeanna Linthicum.

The demanding task of cataloguing so many objects in such an exhaustive manner depends on the cooperation of other departments within the Museum. In particular, we would like to acknowledge the critical contributions of our Installation staff (Karen Nielsen, Anthony Boening, Ken Ingels, and Jeff Lewis) in moving and handling the furniture with great care for purposes of examination and photography; our Registrars Melanie Harwood and Frances Klapthor, as well as packer Kim Hallfrisch; Nancy Press, Coordinator of Rights and Reproductions, for assistance with all photography arrangements; Education Director Susan Badder, for assistance in providing interns and volunteers; Librarian Anita Gilden and her former assistant Margaret Prescott; and curatorial secretary Viola Holmes. Martha Parkhurst and Joy Peterson of the Museum's Development Office admirably maintained communication with our several sponsors.

The publication itself is among the most ambitious undertaken by the Museum in its scope and detail. The role of the Museum's Director of Publications Audrey Frantz in this regard cannot be adequately acknowledged in words alone. Her involvement in the book's production has been that of collaborator from the moment of its inception. The quality of this most recent of the Museum's collection catalogues, in short, is a direct reflection of Frantz's rigorous professionalism and caring attention to detail. Publications Assistant Ann V. Christie provided invaluable support over the final months of the book's preparation and her informed and conscientious work on the publication is most sincerely appreciated. Faith M. Holland edited all final manuscript for content and style, working closely with the authors to assure clarity and flow in presentation, and she is to be credited for her sensitivity and dedication in this assignment. As always, the Museum's Assistant Director for Art Brenda Richardson provided impeccable management in overseeing the entire project from its inception.

Outside the Museum, we have been extremely fortunate in being able to rely on a number of highly skilled craftsmen to provide technical analysis and restoration needs. In this regard, we especially want to thank Harry D. Berry, Jr. and his staff at J.W. Berry and Son, Inc., Baltimore; John F. Hardtke, Jr. of Hilgartner Natural Stone, Inc., Baltimore; John Hill, Unionville, Pennsylvania; William R. Hoffman, Baltimore; and William Tillman, Stewartstown, Pennsylvania. Additional technical assistance was generously given by the Radiology Department of Union Memorial Hospital, Baltimore; the Center for Wood Anatomy Research, Forest Products Laboratory, United States Department of

Agriculture, Madison, Wisconsin; and George Reilly and his staff, Analytical Lab, The Henry Francis du Pont Winterthur Museum. To Joel Breger and his associates, who were responsible for almost all of the photography for the catalogue, we extend our deepest appreciation for the skill and painstaking care they brought to bear on this essential component of the publication. And, of course, we are extremely grateful to Alex and Caroline Castro of Baltimore's Hollowpress for their elegant and appropriate graphic design that so distinguishes our book.

Individuals and institutions throughout the country have responded to our research needs with impeccable courtesy and professionalism. Among the many, we would especially like to acknowledge the following:

Robert L. Alexander, Professor, University of Iowa, Iowa City

Nancy Bramucci, Maryland Hall of Records, Annapolis

Stiles Tuttle Colwill, Chief Curator, and Gregory R. Weidman, Curator of Furniture, Museum and Library of Maryland History, Maryland Historical Society, Baltimore

Francie Downing, Decorative Arts Consultant, The New-York Historical Society, New York

Dean Failey, Christie's, New York

Jonathan Fairbanks, Curator of American Decorative Arts and Sculpture, Museum of Fine Arts, Boston

Donald Fennimore, Associate Curator in charge of Metals, Karol Schmiegel, Registrar, and Neville Thompson, Librarian, The Henry Francis du Pont Winterthur Museum, Delaware

J. Michael Flanigan, Administrator, Kaufman Americana Foundation, Norfolk, Virginia

Eugenia Fountain, Reference Librarian, Essex Institute, Salem, Massachusetts

Lynn Dakin Hastings, Curator, Hampton National Historic Site, Towson, Maryland

Morrison H. Heckscher, Curator, Department of American Decorative Arts, The Metropolitan Museum of Art, New York

Ronald Hurst, Curator of Furniture, Colonial Williamsburg Foundation, Williamsburg, Virginia

Brock Jobe, Chief Curator, and Carolyn Hughes, former Registrar, Society for the Preservation of New England Antiquities, Boston

Leslie Keno, Sotheby's, New York

Barry Kessler, Curator, The Peale Museum, Baltimore

Dorothy LaFrance, Head Librarian, Newburyport Public Library, Massachusetts

Milo M. Naeve, Curator of American Arts, The Art Institute of Chicago

Richard H. Randall, Jr., Baltimore

Bradford L. Rauschenberg, Research Fellow, and Luke Beckerdite, Research Associate, Museum of Early Southern Decorative Arts, Winston-Salem, North Carolina

John B. Riggs, Wilmington, Delaware

Harold Sack, Israel Sack, Inc., New York

Robert F. Trent, Curator, and Elizabeth Fox, Assistant Curator, Connecticut Historical Society, Hartford

Susan Tripp, Curator of Collections, The Johns Hopkins University, Baltimore

Nina Zannieri, former Curator, Rhode Island Historical Society, Providence

Phillip Zea, Associate Curator, Historic Deerfield, Massachusetts

Finally, it is with both pride and pleasure that I extend on behalf of every member of the staff of the Baltimore Museum our warmest and most sincere personal appreciation for the sustained faith and support of our Museum's Board of Trustees, and in particular of its current President Margot W. Milch, in making possible the many ambitious achievements that would otherwise be unimaginable. This most recent collection catalogue is yet another example of the Trustees' vision and commitment to Baltimore, its Museum, and its collection.

ARNOLD L. LEHMAN
DIRECTOR

American Furniture 1680-1880

FROM THE COLLECTION OF THE BALTIMORE MUSEUM OF ART

Sequence and Dates
Entries are arranged by form and within form by style. Ascribed dates appear in parentheses.

Materials
Primary woods are those exterior and visible; where more than one is found, their use is specified. Secondary woods are similarly designated. Wood identification was largely done by eye; when microscopic examination was key to the analysis of a piece, that information is noted in the essay.

The term tulip wood, a secondary wood ranging from southern New England through the Southeast, is used here to indicate the species *Liriodendron tulipifera,* commonly referred to as tulip poplar or yellow poplar. This is to distinguish it from true poplar of the species *Populus,* commonly used as a primary wood in early eighteenth-century New England.

Materials are original unless otherwise specified. Only visible hardware is mentioned.

Dimensions
Measurements are given in inches and centimeters, height preceding width preceding depth. Width is measured from side to side, depth from front to back. Overall dimensions are taken from the extreme points of each piece.

Seating Furniture: Chair measurements have been taken at the frame, not to the upholstery. The seat height is to be the highest point of the rails, the seat depth from center front to center back of the seat rails.

Tables: For dropleaf tables the overall width is taken with the leaves extended. A second measurement with leaves down is indicated separately. Card table depth is measured with the fly leaf closed; open measurements can be assumed to be double this dimension.

Case Pieces: Overall height of clocks and case pieces with finials is measured inclusive of the finials. A second measurement for case height is taken from the highest integral element, usually the pediment molding.

Provenance
The earliest known provenance is given, with owners listed in chronological order. Location by city or county and dates of ownership are given when known. Changes of location are also indicated. Unless otherwise noted, the state is Maryland. The Baltimore Museum of Art is abbreviated as BMA.

Footnotes, Exhibitions, and References
Bibliographic references in Notes, Exhibitions, and References when cited more than once have been assigned a bibliography number. Such citations appear as Bibl. number followed by location of the citation within that publication. An alphabetical numbered list of bibliographic material appears on p. 181. Exhibitions and References are listed chronologically and are directly related to the work under discussion. Exhibitions may include catalogues assigned a bibl. number; exhibitions without publications appear in quotation marks. The Baltimore Museum of Art is abbreviated as BMA.

Seating Furniture

I

I. ARMCHAIR (1680–1710)

New England
41¾ × 24¼ × 18¹¹/₁₆ in. (106.1 × 61.6 × 47.5 cm.)
seat h.: 16⅜ in. (41.6 cm.); seat d.: 16⅛ in. (41 cm.)
The Baltimore Museum of Art: Gift from the Estate of
Elizabeth Gilman (BMA 1951.2B)

Slat-back armchairs from New England of this kind
and proportion have long been called "great chairs."
They were produced first in Massachusetts, certainly as early as the mid-seventeenth century.
The earliest great chairs had backs composed of
vertical turned spindles but by the century's end
the slat back came into use. This example from
the Museum's collection reflects the great chair
form as realized about 1700 and produced well into
the eighteenth century. The rather throne-like
appearance of these chairs, their high arm supports
and hand grips or "pommels," as well as their
broad proportions, have contributed to the appel-

lation "great chair." Recent scholarship has suggested that most of these then relatively inexpen-
sive chairs were produced in large quantity in
Charlestown and Boston and then sent to other
areas, both in Massachusetts and beyond.[1] It has
also been suggested that a finial design of two
flanges between the lower part of the urn and the
flame is characteristic of Boston and Charlestown
shops. However, this example has only one such
flange in its turned finials at the top of each stile
of the chair back. Such a construction detail may
point to a Salem cabinetmaker rather than one
working in either Boston or Charlestown. The
Museum's chair is closely related in design to a
great chair in the collection of the Essex Institute.[2]
This thoroughly documented and well-known example, with double flange finials and dated 1680–
1700, has most recently been assigned to Boston
or Salem. Wherever their place of manufacture,
there is a consistency in the use of woods by both
the turner and cabinetmaker. Maple or poplar was
most often used for legs, posts, stiles, and arms;
ash for stretchers, seat lists, and slats. Sometimes,
but not often, ash was used in place of the maple
and poplar. The woods used in this chair follow
the norm. The flattened ball pommels are replacements and the brown stain varnish finish is not
original. Such chairs when first produced were
usually painted black. This armchair was originally
owned by the Gilman family of Exeter, New Hampshire.[3]

NOTES:
1. The late seventeenth and early eighteenth-century chair
   industry of Boston and Charlestown is documented in
   some detail in the following publications: bibl. 21, pp.
   119–124 and *New England Begins: The Seventeenth
   Century*, 3 vols. (Boston: Museum of Fine Arts, 1982),
   vol. 2, pp. 216–217.
2. Margaret Burke Clunie, Anne Farnam, and Robert F.
   Trent, *Furniture at the Essex Institute* (Salem, Massachusetts: Essex Institute, 1980), pp. 10–11, no. 3, ill.
3. According to the late J. Gilman D'Arcy Paul of Baltimore.

MATERIALS: Poplar (stiles), ash (slats). Rush seat (not original)
PROVENANCE: Gilman family of Exeter, New Hampshire; by
descent to Elizabeth Gilman, Baltimore

England chairs of this type, were usually limited to the front and side stretchers. In this example those on the right were replaced with plain stretchers sometime in the late nineteenth century. The present black-painted surface, although not original, duplicates the original finish. This armchair, and several other pieces of furniture in this catalogue (see cat. nos. 5 and 130), were originally owned by the Robbins family of East Lexington, Massachusetts.

MATERIALS: Ash (front legs and arm supports, slats, lower front stretcher, arms), cottonwood (rear stiles), maple (right stretchers). Rush seat (not original)

PROVENANCE: Robbins family of East Lexington, Massachusetts; by descent to Dr. Merrell Langdon Stout, Baltimore; Helen Scarlett Stout (Mrs. Merrell)

2. ARMCHAIR (1720–1750)

New England, probably Eastern Massachusetts
46½ × 22⅝ × 18⅞ in. (118.2 × 57.5 × 48 cm.)
seat h.: 17½ in. (44.5 cm.); seat d.: 15 in. (38.1 cm.)
The Baltimore Museum of Art: Gift of Mrs. Merrell Langdon Stout, in Memory of her Husband, Dr. Merrell Langdon Stout (BMA 1969.46.2)

Such slat-back chairs, in this instance an armchair, were produced in quantity in late seventeenth and early eighteenth-century New England, especially in Massachusetts. They are difficult to date because, like Pennsylvania slat-back chairs, they were in continuous production until the end of the eighteenth century, particularly in rural areas. The bold ball turnings of the front legs and arm supports and the stiles of the chair back, as well as the ball-and-double-reel finials, reflect the art of the turner. Sausage turnings, equally characteristic of New

3. SIDE CHAIR (1730–1770)

New England, possibly Connecticut River Valley
37¾ × 18½ × 15 in. (96 × 47 × 38.1 cm.)
seat h.: 15¼ in. (38.8 cm.); seat d.: 13 in. (33 cm.)
The Baltimore Museum of Art: Gift of Mrs. William George Ewald, in Memory of her Grandmother, Elizabeth Hadley Clark Armistead (BMA 1973.55)

The double serpentine crest rail of this New England side chair suggests an eighteenth-century Connecticut River Valley origin. Such plainly shaped and uncarved crest rails are features of many chairs from this rural area. Other elements of design—the four split banisters of the back, the vase-shaped and ring turnings, and blocking of the back stiles and front legs—are found in Massachusetts and Rhode Island side chairs of the period, and the work of the more urban Boston cabinetmaker would have been the design source. The chair has been black for many years, but there is evidence of both gray and red-brown paints underneath the present surface. The legs have been cut down considerably, removing what were probably ball-shaped front feet. According to the donor, the chair was displayed in 1907 at The Parthenon in Nashville, Tennessee in a belated exhibition celebrating America's Centennial. At that time the chair was said to have been owned originally by Captain Myles Standish (ca. 1584–1656) of Massachusetts. The style of the chair places its manufacture well into the eighteenth century and so refutes the Standish provenance.

MATERIALS: Maple throughout. Rush seat (not original)
PROVENANCE: Mrs. William George Ewald, Baltimore

4

4. ARMCHAIR (1750–1800)

New England, Connecticut River Valley
45¾ × 24 × 19½ in. (116.3 × 61 × 49.5 cm.)
seat h.: 18 in. (45.7 cm.); seat d.: 16¼ in. (41.3 cm.)
The Baltimore Museum of Art: Bequest of John Henry Scarff (BMA 1965.1.2)

Banister-back armchairs like this example were produced in New England's Connecticut River Valley from the mid-eighteenth century through at least the first two decades of the nineteenth century. The more rural, and consequently more conservative the area, the longer the style persisted. The somewhat weak turnings on this armchair, notably on the front stretchers, would seem to indicate it was made near the end of the eighteenth century. A related side chair, owned by Historic Deerfield, is believed to have been made locally.[1] The Museum's armchair and the Deerfield side chair have closely related scalloped crest rails and almost identically shaped bottom rails in the backs. There are also marked similarities in the turnings of the legs, stiles, and stretchers of each chair. The use of five rather than four split banisters in the chair back is unusual (see also cat. no. 5). When received by the Museum, the chair had been stripped of its original painted surface and stain finished.

NOTES:
1. Bibl. 34, p. 31, ill. 42.
MATERIALS: Maple (stiles and arms), ash (seat rails, stretchers, banisters). Rush seat (not original)
PROVENANCE: John Henry Scarff, Baltimore

5

than four split banisters in the chair back is somewhat unusual (see also cat. no. 2). The high placement of the bottom rail of the chair back does not appear to be the result of any cutting down, but may be placed high above the chair's seat to allow for a cushion. The arms are mortised into the stile just below the ball and ring turnings at the base of the vase-shaped turning. More often the arms in such chairs spring from the base of the base turnings. The rush seat of this chair, fortified many years ago with a piece of leather applied to the front rail, would appear to be a very early replacement. A red wash underlies subsequent layers of brown paint and varnish. This chair has the same provenance as cat. nos. 2 and 130. To date the origin of many of the surviving New England banister-back side and armchairs has not been established. Perhaps, as has been recently suggested, much could be learned from studies of the relationships between turned banisters in chair backs and baluster turnings on New England stairways.[1]

NOTES:
1. Bibl. 46, p. 331.
MATERIALS: Maple, ash (seat rails). Rush seat (not original)
PROVENANCE: Robbins family of East Lexington, Massachusetts; by descent to Dr. Merrell Langdon Stout, Baltimore; Helen Scarlett Stout (Mrs. Merrell)

6. SIDE CHAIR (ONE OF TWO) (1740–1760)

Southern Maryland
37¾ × 18¼ × 17⅜ in. (95.9 × 46.4 × 44.1 cm.)
seat h.: 16⅜ in. (41.6 cm.); seat d.: 15⁷⁄₁₆ in. (39.2 cm.)
The Baltimore Museum of Art: Bequest of Lucy Ridgely Seymer, and The Mary Frick Jacobs Collection, by exchange (BMA 1975.36.1)

This side chair and a matching chair are believed to have come from Deep Falls, a house in St. Mary's County in southern Maryland built about the middle of the eighteenth century by Major William Thomas, Sr. (1714–1795).[1] The chairs which may have been part of the original furnishings were bought at a church bazaar in Atlanta, Georgia by a local artist who in turn sold them to a New York dealer. No provenance was available when the chairs were purchased in Georgia but they were undoubtedly part of a set that includes three matching chairs at the Maryland Historical Society.[2] The austere design of these chairs has prompted the suggestion that they were made by a craftsman on the Deep Falls plantation, who may have been a carpenter-joiner rather than a trained cabinetmaker. When compared to other side chairs of the

5. ARMCHAIR (1750–1800)

New England
47½ × 24⅞ × 19 in. (120.7 × 63.2 × 48.3 cm.)
seat h.: 17⅜ in. (44.1 cm.); seat d.: 15¼ in. (38.8 cm.)
The Baltimore Museum of Art: Gift of Mrs. Merrell Langdon Stout, in Memory of her Husband, Dr. Merrell Langdon Stout (BMA 1969.46.3)

The design source for this New England banister-back armchair of the mid-eighteenth century is found in English "great chairs" of the seventeenth century. Many American versions were produced in early eighteenth-century America, and the form was very popular in New England. Like slat-back chairs (see cat. no. 2) these chairs were produced over a long period of time. The use of five rather period, there is a notable absence of turned members. The chairs have an architectural quality in the blocking on the legs, in the shape and design of the chair back, and in their marked verticality. Two previous catalogues of Maryland furniture suggested that the surviving early black haircloth upholstery is original.[3] A recent thorough examination of the slip-seat frame reveals the original covering was black leather.

NOTES:
1. Bibl. 84, p. 48.
2. The three chairs at the Maryland Historical Society had remained at Deep Falls until 1966; it is not known when they were removed from the house.
3. Bibl. 29, p. 17; bibl. 84, p. 48.

6

MATERIALS: Primary: walnut. Secondary: white pine and tulip wood (slip-seat frames). Haircloth upholstery (not original)

PROVENANCE: Probably Major William Thomas, Sr., Deep Falls, St. Mary's County; sale, Atlanta, 1975; Bruce Hafley; The Stradlings, Antiques, New York; BMA, by purchase, 1975

EXHIBITIONS: Bibl. 29, p. 17, no. 1, ill.

7. SIDE CHAIR (1740–1760)

Philadelphia
42¾ × 19⅞ × 20⅛ in. (108.6 × 50.5 × 51.1 cm.)
seat h.: 17¼ in. (43.8 cm.); seat d.: 16½ in. (41.9 cm.)
Collection of Dorothy McIlvain Scott, Baltimore: Promised Gift to The Baltimore Museum of Art

The design of this Queen Anne side chair is typical of the work of Philadelphia cabinetmakers from about 1740–1760: fiddle-shaped back, arched crest rail with shell carving, vase-shaped splat with volute cusps, balloon or "compass" seat, cabriole legs with shell carving on their knees, trifid feet, and rear canted stump legs. This basic form was repeated again and again, often with additions such as carved shells on the front seat rail, carved volutes on the back splat, or the addition of carved volutes in the crest rail. The chair's back is slightly serpentine in profile. The stiles of the back and the crest rail, while flat on the front face, are rounded on the back. The back splat is seated in a shoe with quarter-round and cavetto moldings. The side seat rails are tenoned through the rear stiles. The seat rails are squared on their inner edges and conform to the compass shape on the outside. The original slip-seat frame is made of both yellow pine and walnut. Four vertical chisel marks are found at the inner top of the front seat rail, two on the slip-seat frame. The first owners of the chairs lived near Burlington, New Jersey, across the Delaware River not far from Philadelphia.

MATERIALS: Primary: black walnut. Secondary: yellow pine (slip-seat frame)

PROVENANCE: Samuel Smith (1720–1776), Hickory Grove, Burlington, New Jersey; Richard Smith; Hannah Burling Smith Mott; Richard Field Mott; Amelia Smith Mott Gummere; Richard Mott Gummere; David Stockwell, Inc., Wilmington, Delaware; Dorothy McIlvain Scott, Baltimore, 1981

7

neck, is typical of both Rhode Island and New York design. Another feature found not only on Rhode Island and New York chairs but also on chairs from the Boston area is the carved shell and bellflower-drop motif on the knees of the cabriole legs. New York chairs, however, appear to have knee shells carved with deeper lobes than their Newport or Boston counterparts, as does this example.[2] The elongated C-scrolls flanking the knees, however, have been associated with Newport cabinetmaking. More characteristic of Rhode Island than New York, perhaps, are the turned rear legs and the block and turned stretchers as well as the flat-topped arches of the seat rails.[3] The shell on the crest rail is carved in higher relief than usually seen on Newport chairs and also has incised hor-

8

8. SIDE CHAIR (1750–1770)

Probably New York, possibly Rhode Island (Newport)
39¼ × 22¼ × 21⅝ in. (99.7 × 56.5 × 54.9 cm.)
seat h.: 17½ in. (44.5 cm.); seat d.: 17⅞ in. (45.4 cm.)
The Baltimore Museum of Art: Friends of the American Wing Fund (BMA 1984.49)

Derived from English prototypes, a number of chairs of this form were made in America during the second half of the eighteenth century, and have been variously ascribed to Boston, Newport, and New York. The similarity of their design and construction features has complicated efforts to distinguish regional characteristics. This chair, for example, is closely related to others thought to have been made in Newport and New York.[1] The shape of the back, with projecting crisply carved crest shell and splat pattern with deeply incut

8

6. V. Isabelle Miller, *Furniture by New York Cabinetmakers, 1650–1860*, exhibition cat. (New York: Museum of the City of New York, 1956), p. 25, no. 26, ill.; Dean F. Failey, *Long Island is My Nation* (Setauket, New York: Society for the Preservation of Long Island Antiquities, 1976), p. 52.

MATERIALS: Primary: mahogany. Secondary: sweet gum (slip-seat frame), white pine (glue blocks)

PROVENANCE: C.L. Prickett, Inc., Yardley, Pennsylvania; BMA, by purchase, 1984

REFERENCES: *Antiques*, Mar. 1980, p. 583

izontal striations at the corners that suggest a scallop shell, a New York design preference.[4] Two features also found on chairs with a New York attribution are the rounded flaring of the lower splat and the flattened trifid foot.[5]

In overall appearance this chair is most closely related to a chair in the Museum of the City of New York with a Long Island provenance which probably reflects the influence of Rhode Island cabinetmakers on Long Island furniture.[6] The use of sweet gum as a secondary wood in the framing of the slip seat also suggests a New York rather than a Newport origin for this side chair. The Roman numeral VII is chiseled on both the front seat rail and on the front wooden member of the slip seat.

NOTES:
1. Bibl. 39, p. 62, no. 21, ill.; see also bibl. 46, pp. 358–360, no. 99, ill.
2. Bibl. 39, p. 62.
3. Bibl. 47, pp. 77–78, no. 56, ill.
4. A similar detail is also found on chairs from the set which originally belonged to the Bromfield family of Boston but which are thought to have been made in New York. Bibl. 2, vol. 2, p. 433, no. 1078, ill. Chairs from this set are now in the collections of The Brooklyn Museum, the Museum of Fine Arts, Boston, and Historic Deerfield.
5. This feature is also seen on chairs from the Apthorp family of New York. See bibl. 49, p. 113, fig. 130; bibl. 39, pp. 63–65, no. 22, ill.; bibl. 2, vol. 5, p. 1166, no. P4027, ill.

9

9. SIDE CHAIR (ONE OF TWO) (1740–1770)

Rhode Island
40¼ × 21¼ × 20¼ in. (102.3 × 54 × 51.5 cm.)
seat h.: 16¾ in. (42.6 cm.); seat d.: 17¼ in. (43.8 cm.)
Collection of Dorothy McIlvain Scott, Baltimore: Promised
Gift to The Baltimore Museum of Art

Although the stiles of its back are squared, not
rounded, this balloon-seated side chair exhibits
most of the other accepted characteristics of the
Rhode Island, rather than Boston, Queen Anne
chair. The splat waist shaping, narrow when compared to Boston examples, is found on chairs attributed to Newport cabinetmakers.[1] The back
splat is chamfered on its rear edges, as are the rear
legs between the seat rails and the side stretchers.
The unusually thick flat arched seat rails have
straight inner sides. The back splat is seated in a
shoe above the rear seat rail. The chair illustrated
is chisel-marked I on the upper interior of the front
seat rail; its mate is marked V.

NOTES:
1. Bibl. 46, pp. 349–351, no. 95, ill. and pp. 356–357, no.
    98, ill.

MATERIALS: Primary: walnut. Secondary: maple (seat frame)

PROVENANCE: David Stockwell, Inc., Wilmington, Delaware;
Dorothy McIlvain Scott, Baltimore, 1973

10. ARMCHAIR (1750–1780)

Pennsylvania
41¼ × 29¼ × 23⅝ in. (104.8 × 74.3 × 60 cm.)
seat h.: 17½ in. (44.5 cm.); seat d.: 17⅞ in. (45.4 cm.)
The Baltimore Museum of Art: Bequest of C. Edward
Snyder (BMA 1942.86)

The serpentine of the earred crest and the squared
seat rails of this amply proportioned armchair
denote the developed Chippendale style of the
1760's and 1770's as found in Philadelphia, while
the solid splat and trifid feet are both elements
common to the Queen Anne style of that region.
The crest rail's pronounced serpentine and the
narrowness of the splat indicate a certain naiveté
on the part of the maker in his imitation of the
proportions of the Philadelphia form. The front
seat rail is shaped with a pointed ogee arch, the
side rails have a square headed ogee arch, and even
the rear rail is shaped with a deep chamfer. All
seat rail tenons are secured with two pins. The
side rails are tenoned through the rear stump legs.
An old break at the joint of the splat into the crest
resulted in the replacement of the lower third of
the shell.

MATERIALS: Primary: walnut. Secondary: yellow pine (slip-
seat frame, shoe glue block)

PROVENANCE: C. Edward Snyder, Baltimore

10

11. SIDE CHAIR (1750–1770)

Philadelphia
41¼ × 23¾ × 20¾ in. (104.8 × 60.3 × 52.7 cm.)
seat h.: 17¼ in. (43.8 cm.); seat d.: 16¾ in. (42.6 cm.)
The Baltimore Museum of Art: Gift of Mrs. Francis
White, from the Collection of Mrs. Miles White, Jr.
(BMA 1973.76.213)

The broad splat of this side chair is in sharp contrast
to the chair in the preceding entry. Here the maker's
design sensibility is more sophisticated but clearly
influenced by a taste for the earlier solid space-
filling splat of the Queen Anne style. The eared
serpentine crest with its predominant ruffled shell,
a rocaille ornament—a feature commonly found
on Philadelphia furniture in the Chippendale style—
clearly links this chair to the later period rather
than to the Queen Anne style. This feature appears

on two other side chairs (see cat. nos. 12 and 13).
The carved shells on the front legs are elements
retained from an earlier period. The side seat rails
are tenoned through the rear stump legs, which
have flat side faces; all seat rail tenons are double
pinned. Both the front seat rail and that of the slip
seat are chisel-marked V.

MATERIALS: Primary: walnut. Secondary: tulip wood (slip-
seat frame); glue blocks (not original)

PROVENANCE: Mrs. Miles White, Jr., Baltimore; Francis White;
Nancy Brewster White (Mrs. Francis)

REFERENCES: Bibl. 55, vol. 1, p. 146, no. 90, ill. p. 147

11

11

12

the crest rail and its strongly lobed ears (accented with three pairs of incised crescents and divided into three parts by the continuation of the bead edges of the upper crest rail and the rear stiles) contrasts sharply with the unvaried surface of the preceding chair's crest. Though the two have a similar central ornament, this chair is more elaborately and less stiffly carved. The talonless ball-and-claw feet have an unusually straight rear claw. Rounded stump rear legs receive the visible tenon of the side seat rails which, on their bottom edges, repeat the flat-headed arch of the front seat rail.

MATERIALS: Primary: mahogany. Secondary: yellow pine (slip-seat frame), white cedar (blocks under shoe)
PROVENANCE: Mrs. Miles White, Jr., Baltimore; Francis White; Nancy Brewster White (Mrs. Francis)
REFERENCES: Bibl. 55, vol. 1, p. 146, no. 92, ill. p. 147

13. SIDE CHAIR (ONE OF TWO)   (1750–1780)

Philadelphia
39 × 23¼ × 22¾ in. (99.1 × 59.1 × 57.8 cm.)
seat h.: 17⅛ in. (43.5 cm.); seat d.: 16⅝ in. (42.2 cm.)
Collection of Dorothy McIlvain Scott, Baltimore: Promised Gift to The Baltimore Museum of Art

The scrolled strapwork back splat of this side chair was one of the most popular patterns made in Philadelphia during the latter part of the eighteenth century. Produced from a template, the splat design is found, with slight variations, on a large number of surviving chairs. Many are more elaborately carved than this example. Here the carving on the splat is confined to leafage at the top and carved volutes flanking the central oval void. The crest, however, is ornamented with crisply carved rope and tassel motifs extending from the deeply scrolled ears across the arch on each side of the central rocaille shell, also a favorite element in the Phil-

12

12. SIDE CHAIR   (1755–1780)

Philadelphia
40⅝ × 23½ × 21 in. (103.2 × 59.7 × 53.4 cm.)
seat h.: 16⅞ in. (42.8 cm.); seat d.: 16⅞ in. (42.8 cm.)
The Baltimore Museum of Art: Gift of Mrs. Francis White, from the Collection of Mrs. Miles White, Jr. (BMA 1973.76.210)

The solidity of this chair is enlivened by the modeling of the crest, the feet, and the sharp cusps of the lower splat. Modulation of the thickness of

13

remembered as an avid collector. According to one authority, the chairs were first owned by Ellicott's Pennsylvania ancestors.[1]

NOTES:
1. Bibl. 55, vol. 1, p. 154, no. 123, ill. p. 155.
MATERIALS: Primary: mahogany. Secondary: yellow pine (slip-seat frame)
PROVENANCE: Possibly the Miller family of Avondale, Pennsylvania; Mary Miller Ellicott; William Miller Ellicott, Baltimore; Ann Murray Ellicott; Ann Murray Ellicott Madeira; Joseph A. Hennage; Israel Sack, Inc., New York, 1979; Dorothy McIlvain Scott, Baltimore
REFERENCES: Bibl. 55, vol. 1, p. 154, no. 123, ill. p. 155

14. SIDE CHAIR (1760–1780)

Philadelphia
39 × 22⅝ × 21¼ in. (99.1 × 57.5 × 54 cm.)
seat h.: 17 in. (43.2 cm.); seat d.: 17¾ in. (45.1 cm.)
Collection of Dorothy McIlvain Scott, Baltimore: Promised Gift to The Baltimore Museum of Art

The "Gothic" back splat of this side chair represents a well-known type found on a number of chairs by Philadelphia cabinetmakers in the Chippendale style. Its design has been defined as "a synthesis of a number of motifs found in plates X, XI, XIII, and XVI of Chippendale's *Director*" (London, 1762).[1] The quatrefoil piercing at the base of the back splat is found on side chairs bearing the label of Philadelphia cabinetmaker James Gillingham (1736–1781), and consequently over the years Gillingham attributions have been erroneously assigned to many Philadelphia side chairs like this example.[2] A similar quatrefoil-pierced Gothic-tracery splat on a chair labeled by yet another Philadelphia cabinetmaker, Thomas Tufft (ca. 1738–1788), has fostered further erroneous attributions.[3] This is a pleasing example of a Philadelphia type often more fully carved on back splat,

13

adelphia carver's vocabulary (see cat. nos. 11 and 12). The knees of the front legs are also carved in typical Philadelphia fashion with symmetrical acanthus leaves. The rear legs are ovoid in shape; the stiles are chamfered on their back edges. The side seat rails are tenoned through the stiles. Both chairs retain their original but renailed corner seat blocks. In 1937 the chairs were owned by William Miller Ellicott of Baltimore. Descended from the Miller family of Avondale, Pennsylvania, Ellicott inherited many pieces of furniture, but is also

14

14

15. ARMCHAIR (1770–1780)

Baltimore
Maker: attributed to Gerrard Hopkins
39¾ × 29¼ × 23 in. (101 × 74.3 × 58.4 cm.)
seat h.: 16¼ in. (41.3 cm.); seat d.: 18⅜ in. (46.7 cm.)
The Baltimore Museum of Art: Gift of William C.
Whitridge, Baltimore (BMA 1977.59.2)

One of Maryland's early collectors, Mrs. Breckinridge Long, acquired this armchair early in this century from descendants of Governor Robert Bowie (ca. 1750–1818) of Prince George's County. It was sold at auction in 1959 with a New York attribution, but in more recent times has become part of a growing group of furniture attributed to the Baltimore cabinetmaker Gerrard Hopkins (1742–1800; working in Baltimore 1767–1800).[1] Of an old Anne Arundel County family, Hopkins was apprenticed in 1757 to the Philadelphia cabinetmaker Jonathan Hopkins.[2] The key to the Gerrard Hopkins attributions is a high chest of drawers in the Chippendale style (fig. 15a) that bears his printed label on which Philadelphia and the street address are inked out and Baltimore written in ink at the top.[3] When Hopkins returned to Baltimore from Philadelphia in 1767, he apparently used the same sign, that of a tea table and chair, for his cabinetmaking shop on Gay Street. He worked in Baltimore for over thirty years, until his death in 1800.[4] The carved shell on the skirt of the high chest of drawers (fig. 15b) and that on the front seat rail of the Museum's armchair are of the same design and seemingly by the same hand.[5] The leaf carvings on the knees and knee brackets of the front cabriole legs are also the same design as similarly placed carving on the high chest. All these carved decorative elements can also be found on a dressing table (present whereabouts unknown),[6] another

crest rail, and front seat rail.[4] The two rear legs are canted and chamfered, squared in section and slightly rounded; the back edges of the splat are also chamfered. The front corner blocks of the seat are replacements but the rear blocks are original. The rear seat rail is chisel-marked on the inside with the Roman numeral VI and the rear slip-seat rail with numeral III.

NOTES:
1. Bibl. 39, p. 103, no. 57.
2. Bibl. 21, p. 7, fig. 6.
3. Charles F. Hummel, *A Winterthur Guide to American Chippendale Furniture* (New York: Crown Publishers, 1976), pp. 66–67, figs. 58 and 58A.
4. Bibl. 39, pp. 103–105, nos. 57 and 58, ill.

MATERIALS: Primary: mahogany. Secondary: yellow pine (rear corner blocks of seat)

PROVENANCE: David Stockwell, Inc., Wilmington, Delaware; Dorothy McIlvain Scott, Baltimore

15

armchair,[7] and a set of six side chairs, the latter now in the collection of the U.S. Department of State.[8] In other elements of design and decoration there are some slight variations, but essentially all of the chairs now attributed to Hopkins share the design concept illustrated by this armchair.

The rather simple openwork back splat with carved volutes is mounted in an unusual high cove molded shoe. The elaborately carved serpentine crest rail contains a distinctive and well-executed ruffle decoration above an area of hatching and stipplework like that found as background for the carved shell on the front seat rail and on the knees of the front legs. The molded arm supports curve outward at their bases rather than inward, as found in Philadelphia chairs as well as in the privately-owned armchair cited above and attributed to Hopkins. The latter also differs from the example here in that its arm supports have a spiral beading at their center as do the scrolled terminations of the armrests. The tops of the armrests are not shaped like those on the Museum's example. The balls of the feet are "squashed" in the Philadelphia manner and the claws are thin and without talons. The side rails are not tenoned through into the rear stump legs. Originally strips were nailed inside the seat rails to support the slip seat.

NOTES:

1. *Antiques, Rare American Furniture, and Decorative Arts from the Estates of the late Honorable and Mrs. Breckinridge Long*, sale cat. (William D. Morley, Inc., Philadelphia, 29 Sept.–7 Oct. 1959), p. 62, lot 508, ill.
2. Samuel Gover Hopkins Genealogical Collection, G5025, Book 4, Maryland Historical Society, Manuscript Collection.
3. Privately owned; presently on loan to The Baltimore Museum of Art. Although some of the label's printed text is missing or is too faded to read, from what remains it can be seen that the text was like that used by

15

Fig. 15a. High Chest. Gerrard Hopkins, Baltimore, 1767–1780. Mahogany and yellow pine; 93⅛ × 44⅜ × 24⅝ in. (236.6 × 112.8 × 62.6 cm.); case h.: 89 in. (226.1 cm.). Private Collection, on extended loan to The Baltimore Museum of Art (R.10529).

Hopkins in his first advertisement in the *Maryland Gazette* in 1767. See bibl. 29, p. 120.

4. For more information on Gerrard Hopkins, see bibl. 84, pp. 46 and 73–74.

5. Luke Beckerdite relates these carvings to a chimneypiece in the Brice House of Annapolis, attributed to William

15

Fig. 15b.

Bampton. However, it is the opinion of the authors that the Brice House carving is at such variance with the furniture carving that they cannot all be attributed to Bampton. Bibl. 9, pp. 21–26.

6. Bibl. 28, pp. 358–359, ill. p. 358, fig. 4.
7. *Antiques*, Sept. 1951, p. 149; Helen Comstock, "American Furniture in California," *Antiques*, Jan. 1954, p. 56, fig. 15; *Antiques*, May 1972, inside front cover.
8. Bibl. 32, p. 152, ill. See also bibl. 35, p. 165, fig. VIII-19.

MATERIALS: Primary: mahogany. Secondary: tulip wood (glue blocks, slip-seat frame)

PROVENANCE: Bowie family of Prince George's County; The Honorable and Mrs. Breckinridge Long, ca. 1930; Breckinridge Long Sale, 1959 (see note 1); Joseph Kindig, Jr., Antiques, York, Pennsylvania; William C. Whitridge, Baltimore

EXHIBITIONS: Bibl. 29, p. 21, no. 5, ill.; bibl. 11, p. 69, no. 53, ill.

REFERENCES: Bibl. 28, p. 359, ill. p. 358, fig. 5; bibl. 9, pp. 31–34, figs. 4, 4a, 4b, and 4c

16

16

16. SIDE CHAIR (ONE OF TWO) (1770–1780)

Annapolis
37½ × 22¾ × 24 in. (95.3 × 57.8 × 61 cm.)
seat h.: 16¼ in. (41.3 cm.); seat d.: 19⅞ in. (50.5 cm.)
The Baltimore Museum of Art: Gift of Dorothy McIlvain Scott, Baltimore (BMA 1974.7.2)

This side chair belonged at the beginning of the nineteenth century to Henry Banning Chew of Epsom in Baltimore County near Towson. Chew was a descendent of the Chew family of Anne Arundel County; his father and grandfather, Chief Justice Benjamin Chew of the Pennsylvania Supreme Court, lived in Philadelphia. Epsom, however, became the summer home of Henry through marriage into the Ridgely family of nearby Hampton, so the chair may well have both a Ridgely and Chew provenance. Because both families had early ties with Anne Arundel County, and because of the chair's relationship to other pieces of furniture thought to be the work of Annapolis cabinetmakers, it seems likely that this side chair was made in Annapolis rather than Baltimore. Chair backs of similar design are found on chairs of known English origin, but Annapolis cabinetmaking before the Revolution can be very English in character. The carved anthemion in the top center of the openwork back splat is found in differing forms on the backs of other chairs now believed to have been made in Annapolis. One of these chairs has a saddle seat equally as broad as the seat of this example and characteristic of Annapolis and Baltimore Chippendale chairs.[1]

When this pair was acquired by the Museum in 1972, the brackets at the top of the front legs were missing. Fortunately there remained under the upholstery glue blocks shaped to fit behind the brackets, thus enabling reproduction of similarly shaped facings. The carved faces of the restored brackets are based on the logical continuation of the leg moldings as they turn at the top of the leg.[2] The back splat is behind a modern shoe that replaces the lost original. An unusual construction feature is found in a single piece of wood nailed to the inside of the rear rail and tenoned into the side rails. The pair was extensively repaired in 1974, at which time the legs were extended to their original length, and the carved leg brackets replaced. The use of brass nails in the fully upholstered seat follows an original nail pattern.

NOTES:
1. See exhibition catalogue, bibl. 4, p. 175, no. 112, ill. and p. 180, no. 117, ill.
2. A table also with a likely West River Chew family provenance has similarly molded legs and has also lost its original brackets. Bibl. 29, p. 48, no. 31, ill.

MATERIALS: Primary: mahogany. Secondary: red oak (seat rails), sweet gum (rear rail bracing strip), beech (open diagonal front seat braces)

PROVENANCE: Chew family of Anne Arundel County; Henry Banning Chew; Miss Harriet R. Chew; Miss Bessie Chew Green; Dorothy McIlvain Scott, Baltimore

EXHIBITIONS: Bibl. 4, p. 174, no. 111, ill.

REFERENCES: Bibl. 55, vol. 1, p. 138, no. 74, ill. p. 139 and p. 158, no. 136, ill. p. 159; bibl. 28, p. 358, ill. p. 355, fig. 3

17

17. SIDE CHAIR (ONE OF TWO) (1770–1800)

Southern mid-Atlantic states
37¾ × 21 × 20½ in. (95.9 × 53.4 × 52.1 cm.)
seat h.: 16¾ in. (42.5 cm.); seat d.: 17⅜ in. (44.1 cm.)
The Baltimore Museum of Art: Bequest of Elizabeth Curzon Hoffman Wing, in Memory of Hanson Rawlings Duval, Jr. (BMA 1967.30.9B)

This pair of transitional-style side chairs are of a type generally associated with the Southern mid-Atlantic states. Although often designated Virginia chairs, they could as well have been made in Maryland. The donor was a member of a family long resident in Maryland that intermarried with other equally long-established Maryland families, any one of which could have been the source for the chairs. The crest rail design and simple splats,

18

18

as well as the proportions and overall dimensions are quite similar to a chair owned by Colonial Williamsburg, thought to be Southern, possibly from Virginia.[1] The seat frame contains four triangular glue blocks each further secured by two nails. The slip-seat frame of the chair illustrated is original, that of its mate has been replaced.

NOTES:
1. Bibl. 49, p. 155, fig. 210. Two other side chairs at Williamsburg, related in design, are also believed to be Southern in origin. See bibl. 49, p. 152, fig. 205 and p. 153, fig. 207.

MATERIALS: Primary: walnut. Secondary: yellow pine (glue blocks, inside rear seat rail facing, slip-seat frame)

PROVENANCE: Dallam, Hoffman, Duvall, or Thomas families of Maryland; by descent to Elizabeth Curzon Hoffman Wing, Charleston

18. SIDE CHAIR (ONE OF TWO) (1760–1790)
Rhode Island
38 × 21 × 19 1/16 in. (96.6 × 53.4 × 48.4 cm.)
seat h.: 16 7/8 in. (42.9 cm.); seat d.: 16 3/4 in. (42.6 cm.)
The Baltimore Museum of Art: Gift of Mr. and Mrs. Dudley I. Catzen, and Mr. and Mrs. Robert W. Catzen, in Memory of Hortense B. Catzen (BMA 1972.17.1)

The design of the splat of this Newport side chair is possibly derived from the published work of the eighteenth-century London cabinetmaker Robert Manwaring and was used in modified forms by Boston, Salem, Newport, Providence, and New York cabinetmakers.[1] Here the splat is a rather original interpretation of the prevalent design.[2] However, the crosshatching of the crest rail lunette and the stop-fluting on the front legs are typical of the work of Newport cabinetmakers. There are

19

also elaborately carved raised moldings on the crest rail ears. The unusually heavy stretchers add to the chair's overall impression of strength and stability. The inside front seat rail of this side chair is chisel-marked III, the companion chair IIII. The wooden seat frames are marked VI and I respectively.

NOTES:
1. Bibl. 53.
2. Bibl. 46, pp. 409–410, no. 122, ill.

MATERIALS: Primary: mahogany. Secondary: maple (slip-seat frame, replaced glue blocks)

PROVENANCE: John Walton, Antiques, Jewett City, Connecticut

19. SIDE CHAIR (1770–1800)

Hartford, Connecticut area
38½ × 22¹³⁄₁₆ × 20½ in. (97.8 × 58 × 52.1 cm.)
seat h.: 16⅝ in. (42.2 cm.); seat d.: 16½ in. (41.9 cm.)
Collection of Dorothy McIlvain Scott, Baltimore: Promised Gift to The Baltimore Museum of Art

Although a number of chairs of this pattern have been attributed to the shop or school of Eliphalet (1741–1807) and Aaron (1753–1835) Chapin of East Windsor, Connecticut, this example is probably a product of an as yet unknown maker influenced by the Chapin shop, perhaps one of the large extended family of artisans that grew up around it.[1] Although possessing the overall form and the distinctive Gothic interlace splat design imposed on a large X motif seen on some pieces attributed to the Chapins, the Museum's chair does not have the construction details that would link it to them.[2] Furthermore, the chair lacks the through tenons uniting the seat rails to the rear posts and the inner construction of the seat frame reminiscent of Philadelphia techniques also found on Chapin chairs. It has been upholstered over the seat rails at some time and the tack marks from this upholstering are still visible on the exterior of the rails. The present slip seat is a replacement. VI is incised on the inside rear seat rail. The splat is seated inside the shoe which is in turn nailed to the seat rail at the rear. The medial stretchers are half dovetailed into the side seat rails. The legs are chamfered on their inside edges and have a bead on the outer corners at the front. The rear legs are pieced out approximately three inches from the bottom. The chair has been refinished.

NOTES:
1. For a discussion of the Chapins, see Emily M. Davis, "Eliphalet Chapin," *Antiques*, Apr. 1939, pp. 172–175; bibl. 47, pp. 138–142; Henry Maynard, "Eliphelet Chapin, the resolute Yankee, 1741–1807," *Connoisseur*, Feb. 1969, pp. 126–129; bibl. 49, pp. 146–149; Joseph Lionetti and Robert F. Trent, "New information about Chapin chairs," *Antiques*, May 1986, pp. 1082–1095.
2. Foremost among features which are indicative of the Chapin shop is the use of rounded mortise and tenon joints at the crest rail and upright stiles. Because this joint is not visible to the naked eye, radiographic examination was necessary to discern the type of joint used on this chair which was found to have rectangular rather than rounded mortise and tenons at the crest rail juncture.

MATERIALS: Primary: cherry. Secondary: white pine (slip-seat frame, glue blocks)

PROVENANCE: David Stockwell, Inc., Wilmington, Delaware, 1976; Dorothy McIlvain Scott, Baltimore

20

book was used by Philadelphia cabinetmakers and it is now thought that many of them made these so-called "Trotter-type" chairs.[1] The honeysuckle pattern refers to the carved anthemion often found in an oval at the center of crest rails and horizontal splats. This armchair features a five-branched plume, a carved motif often used instead of the anthemion. Other carved decorations are the eight-petaled rosettes at the top of each stile and the scrolled and voluted handholds at the ends of the arms. The lower two inches of the rear legs have been pieced out, and three splats have cracked at the center due to inherent weakness.

NOTES:
1. Bibl. 62, p. 149, no. 117, ill.
MATERIALS: Primary: mahogany. Secondary: yellow pine (slip-seat frame, glue blocks)
PROVENANCE: J. Gilman D'Arcy Paul, Baltimore
REFERENCES: Bibl. 55, vol. 1, p. 238, no. 390, ill. p. 237; Milo M. Naeve, "Daniel Trotter and his ladder-back chairs," *Antiques*, Nov. 1959, p. 445, figs. 6 and 7

20. ARMCHAIR (1780–1800)

Philadelphia
36¼ × 26⅝ × 20⅝ in. (92.1 × 67.7 × 52.4 cm.)
seat h.: 15½ in. (39.4 cm.); seat d.: 17⅞ in. (45.4 cm.)
The Baltimore Museum of Art: Gift of J. Gilman D'Arcy Paul (BMA 1970.6)

For many years late eighteenth-century American side and armchairs with such pierced-swag crest rails and horizontal slats have been attributed to the Philadelphia cabinetmaker Daniel Trotter. Trotter did indeed make six chairs of this type for Stephen Girard of Philadelphia in 1786, and such chairs are described in *The Cabinetmaker's Philadelphia and London Book of Prices* (Philadelphia, 1796) as having "A Splat Back . . . Honeysuckle Pattern . . . with mahogany rails. . . . " The price

21. SIDE CHAIR (ONE OF TWO) (1790–1810)

Baltimore
37⅛ × 19½ × 18⅛ in. (94.3 × 49.5 × 46 cm.)
seat h.: 16⅜ in. (41.6 cm.); seat d.: 16¼ in. (41.3 cm.)
The Baltimore Museum of Art: Anonymous Gift (BMA 1983.332)

A popular chair design of Baltimore cabinetmakers of the Federal period featured an oval back with three pierced vertical splats, the larger center splat being inlaid with bellflowers. There are, however, many variations in the treatment of the chair seats and front legs of oval-back chairs. This chair has a bowed front seat rail and the seat is upholstered over only the upper half of the rails, a peculiarly Baltimore treatment. The lower edges of the mahogany-veneered seat rails are neatly finished on

21

Fig. 21a. Side Chair, Baltimore, 1790–1810. Mahogany with walnut and yellow pine; 37¾ × 20⅝ × 20¼ in. (95.9 × 52.4 × 51.5 cm.); seat h.: 17¼ in. (43.8 cm.), seat d.: 17⁹⁄₁₆ in. (44.6 cm.). The Baltimore Museum of Art: Gift of Mrs. Francis White, from the Collection of Mrs. Miles White, Jr. (BMA 1973.76.216).

Fig. 21b. Side Chair, Baltimore, 1790–1810. Mahogany with oak and yellow pine; 37⅝ × 19⅞ × 19⅞ in. (95.6 × 50.5 × 50.5 cm.); seat h.: 17¼ in. (43.8 cm.), seat d.: 16⅝ in. (42.2 cm.). Halsted Collection of The Johns Hopkins University, on extended loan to The Baltimore Museum of Art (L.23.13.24).

the front and sides with an inlaid band of dark and light blocks. In the Museum's collection is another variation of the chair base with a serpentine front seat rail and inlaid legs (fig. 21a). A chair on loan to the Museum from The Johns Hopkins University (see fig. 21b) illustrates the incorporation of a saddle seat and molded front legs in the oval-back chair design. Here the side rails have a straight inner face with the outside curve cut from the solid, while the front rail inner face follows that of the outer bow shaping. Four open diagonal braces strengthen the seat rails. The spade feet of the tapering front legs are cut from the solid on the sides but the spade is completed with applied pieces on the front and rear faces.

MATERIALS: Primary: mahogany, mahogany veneers, light and dark wood inlays. Secondary: tulip wood (seat rails)
PROVENANCE: Private Collection, Baltimore

22

Fig. 22a. Side Chair, Baltimore, 1790–1810. Mahogany and oak; 38¼ × 18⅞ × 19¼ in. (97.2 × 48 × 48.9 cm.); seat h.: 16¼ in. (41.3 cm.), seat d.: 16¼ in. (41.3 cm.). The Baltimore Museum of Art: Bequest of Margaret Maund (BMA 1931.18.6).

22. SIDE CHAIR (1790–1810)

Baltimore
37⅛ × 19½ × 18⅛ in. (94.3 × 49.5 × 46 cm.)
seat h.: 16⅜ in. (41.6 cm.); seat d.: 16¼ in. (41.3 cm.)
The Baltimore Museum of Art: Gift of Mrs. Francis White, from the Collection of Mrs. Miles White, Jr. (BMA 1973.76.214.2)

Derived from designs by Hepplewhite, chairs with shield-shaped backs were made in Philadelphia, New York, and New England as well as Baltimore.[1] However, the arrangement of the back splats and the carving on this chair are typical of Baltimore, found on many other surviving examples. According to family tradition, this chair, one of two owned by the Museum (see also cat. no. 23), was first owned by Charles Carroll of Carrollton (1737–1832), and used at Doughoregan Manor.[2] Matching chairs from the same set still belong to Carroll

descendants. Unlike the more elaborate side chair illustrated in cat. no. 23 (perhaps the result of a special order placed by Charles Carroll), this side chair in an identical or slightly variant form is found in some number in the Baltimore area. In fact, the Museum owns eight more similar Baltimore side chairs: a set of six chairs (see fig. 22a) of slightly differing dimensions lacks the intermediate leaf carving on the three back splats of this example;[3] two others have the same back design as this chair but with beaded and molded front legs and saddle seats.[4] This same popular Baltimore chair back is found on two chairs of otherwise different design in the Maryland Historical Society.[5] This example has been reupholstered and finished with a double row of brass nails, in the fashion of the original as suggested by nail marks on the rails. The half-round leaf motif carved at the base of the splats is applied, while the other

23. SIDE CHAIR (1795–1810)

Baltimore
36½ × 21⅛ × 22 in. (92.7 × 53.8 × 55.9 cm.)
seat h.: 17 in. (43.2 cm.); seat d.: 18¾ in. (47.6 cm.)
The Baltimore Museum of Art: Gift of Dorothea Harper
Pennington Nelson, Baltimore (BMA 1979.46)

The quality of carving on this chair is characteristic of the finest found on late eighteenth-century Baltimore chairs. A direct descendant of Charles Carroll of Carrollton (1737–1832) gave the chair, one of five with the same family provenance, to the Museum in 1979.[1] These chairs would have been expensive in 1800, but the Carrolls would have easily afforded them, being among the richest families in America at the time. The shield-shaped back design is taken from Thomas Sheraton's *Drawing-Book* of 1793.[2] Five beautifully carved plumes extend from the top of the tapered center splat into the top center of the crest rail. The carved drapery swags strengthen the thinner reeded members of the back splat, whose elements all spring from a pedestal base with acanthus carving. Like the legs of a card table in the Museum's collection (cat. no. 100), the chair's front legs are carved on two sides with bellflower drops and half-floral rosettes instead of the more usual inlaid bellflow-

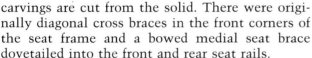

carvings are cut from the solid. There were originally diagonal cross braces in the front corners of the seat frame and a bowed medial seat brace dovetailed into the front and rear seat rails.

NOTES:
1. Bibl. 40, pl. 5.
2. Mrs. Miles White, Jr. purchased the chairs from Carroll descendants (see also cat. no. 110). These two chairs, with the three others from the same set, were lent by Carroll descendants for an exhibition held at The Baltimore Museum of Art in 1937, bibl. 15.
3. BMA 1931.18.1–.6, Bequest of Margaret Maund.
4. BMA 1960.41.8–.9, Bequest of Philip B. Perlman.
5. Bibl. 84, p. 102, no. 44, ill. p. 103.

MATERIALS: Primary: mahogany. Secondary: mahogany (rear seat rail), oak (side and front seat rails); medial seat brace and seat corner blocks (not original)

PROVENANCE: Charles Carroll of Carrollton (1737–1832), Baltimore; by descent to Charles Carroll of Homewood, Howard County; Faris C. Pitt, Antiques, Baltimore; Mrs. Miles White, Jr., 1921; Francis White; Nancy Brewster White (Mrs. Francis)

EXHIBITIONS: Bibl. 15, p. 52, ill. p. 53

ers.[3] The rosette and quarter fans carved on the front and outer side of the chair stiles are repeated on a larger scale on the card table's legs. This side chair and the four other surviving examples have at the bottom edge of their veneered half-upholstered seat rails a band of light wood inlay that is also found on the card table skirt. Despite their many shared design elements the chairs and card table are not now considered to be a matching set. Characteristic of Baltimore Federal-style chairs is the half, rather than fully, upholstered seat. The spade feet of the front legs are cut from the solid. The fact that the carved half-rosette and bellflower drop of the left leg are set slightly lower than the similar carving on the right leg, resulting in a quarter inch uncarved strip at the top of the left leg, cannot be explained. The seat frame, as in most Baltimore chairs of the period, originally had diagonal corner braces.

NOTES:
1. Three chairs are said to have been acquired from members of the Carroll family of Maryland by the late Louis Guerineau Myers of New York, an early collector of American furniture, prior to 1929 when he exhibited one in the Girl Scouts exhibition (bibl. 51, no. 717, ill.) [letter of Joseph Kindig, Jr., 1 June 1957, BMA]. The chairs were sold at public auction with the rest of his collection in 1932, possibly to Mrs. Hamilton Fish of New York from whom they were purchased by Joseph Kindig, Jr. of York, Pennsylvania (bibl. 17, p. 158, no. 542, ill. p. 159). Kindig in turn sold two of the chairs to Winterthur, and the third (BMA 1957.43) was acquired by the Baltimore Museum in 1957 (Kindig advertised three chairs in *Antiques*, Aug. 1941, inside front cover. One of the two chairs owned by Winterthur is illustrated in bibl. 56, p. 149, no. 9). All four legs of the mate to this entry have been pieced at the bottom. The fourth chair is in a private Baltimore collection, and the fifth is discussed here.
2. Bibl. 73, no. 5, pl. 36.
3. One design source for the carved bellflowers may be Plate 2 of Hepplewhite, bibl. 40. Two side chairs at the Maryland Historical Society have similarly carved front legs. See bibl. 84, p. 102, no. 44, ill. p. 103.

MATERIALS: Primary: mahogany, mahogany veneers, light and dark wood inlays. Secondary: yellow pine, mahogany (side, front, and rear seat rails, three horizontal laminations)
PROVENANCE: Charles Carroll of Carrollton (1737–1832), Baltimore; by descent to Dorothea Harper Pennington Nelson
EXHIBITIONS: Bibl. 4, p. 95, no. 58, ill.; bibl. 82, p. 284, ill. p. 283 and p. 294, no. 129.
REFERENCES: Bibl. 87, pp. 177–178, ill. p. 178, fig. 4; "In the museums," *Antiques*, Jan. 1958, p. 84, ill.; bibl. 19, no. 429; bibl. 10, p. 223, no. 318, ill.; "Current and coming," *Antiques*, Oct. 1975, p. 596, ill.

24

24. SIDE CHAIR (ONE OF TWO) (1790–1810)

Baltimore
38⅜ × 20 × 20⅝ in. (97.5 × 50.8 × 52.4 cm.)
seat h.: 17 in. (43.2 cm.); seat d.: 17⅞ in. (45.4 cm.)
The Baltimore Museum of Art: Gift of Mrs. Henry V. Ward (BMA 1934.56.14)

Baltimore side chairs with heart-shaped or shield-shaped backs were produced in quantity in the late eighteenth and early nineteenth centuries, and along with oval-back chairs (see cat. no. 21) have survived in great numbers. They may have been the product of one large Baltimore cabinetmaking manufactory, or have been made in a number of different shops.[1] The variation on the theme of the heart back is usually found in the inlaid motif of the center splat. The most commonly employed decorations are three or four bellflower inlays of diminishing size, suspended by an inlaid loop and

25

25

NOTES:
1. For a full discussion of Baltimore's furniture manufactories and furniture warehouses of this period, see bibl. 84, pp. 74–76.
2. For an oval eagle inlay, see bibl. 4, p. 98, no. 61, ill.
3. Bibl. 4, p. 98, no. 61, ill.
MATERIALS: Primary: mahogany, light wood inlays. Secondary: tulip wood (side and front seat rails, diagonal braces)
PROVENANCE: Mrs. Henry V. Ward, Baltimore

joined by small circular pieces of inlay. More expensive oval eagle inlays are often employed in place of bellflowers, and in a similar side chair (see cat. no. 25) an inlaid shell design has been placed above the inlaid bellflower drop.[2] The seats of this particular model are almost always fully upholstered rather than being half-upholstered as is the norm for the oval-back chairs in Baltimore. The front legs can be molded with a bead as in this example or plain with spade feet (see cat. no. 25).[3] The mahogany rear seat rail has an applied flat shoe with a bead on the side edges. The front corners of the seat frame retain their original tulip wood diagonal braces. The Museum owns four other side chairs (BMA 1957.14a–d) from a different source close enough in their construction to suggest that they are part of the same set.

25 . SIDE CHAIR (ONE OF TWO) (1790–1810)

Maryland, probably Baltimore
38¾ × 21¼ × 18½ in. (98.5 × 54.9 × 47 cm.)
seat h.: 16⅞ in. (42.9 cm.); seat d.: 17¾ in. (45.1 cm.)
Collection of Dorothy McIlvain Scott, Baltimore: Promised Gift to The Baltimore Museum of Art

Side chairs with a modified heart-shaped back were produced in numbers in both Baltimore and Philadelphia during the Federal period. They are of a distinctive design and construction which, with oval and shield-back chairs, were especially popular in Baltimore. That these chairs have survived in quantity may be the direct result of volume production of "cabinetmaking manufactories" and the interaction among craftsmen in the cabinetmaking community.[1] Compared to the general Baltimore product, this side chair is exceptional in the inlaid decoration of its back: the central splat contains a

26

26

beautifully composed conch shell inlay; below this inlay, the characteristic Baltimore bellflower drop, with elongated petals, suspended from a small oval inlaid loop. On the two smaller side splats the bellflower motif is repeated, although in reduced size, with leaf inlays. On the interior the seat frame is strengthened at each corner by rather heavy diagonal braces of oak, notched into the seat rails. The stretchers are mortised to each other, and to the legs. The spade feet, somewhat atypical of Baltimore chairs of this period, are cut from the solid.[2] A card table of related design (cat. no. 99), purchased with the two side chairs, has the same Chase family provenance. The three pieces are probably part of a larger set of furniture purchased by Judge Samuel Chase when he moved from Annapolis to Baltimore after the Revolution.

NOTES:
1. Bibl. 84, pp. 70–77.
2. A matching side chair with the same original ownership is now in the Maryland Historical Society. See bibl. 84, pp. 105–106, no. 49, ill.

MATERIALS: Primary: mahogany, light and dark wood inlays. Secondary: tulip wood (seat rails), oak (seat braces)

PROVENANCE: Samuel Chase (1741–1811) of Annapolis and Baltimore; by descent to William Edward Steele, ca. 1880; David Stockwell, Inc., Wilmington, Delaware; Dorothy McIlvain Scott, Baltimore

EXHIBITIONS: Bibl. 11, p. 77, no. 61, ill.

26. SIDE CHAIR (ONE OF TWO) (1789–1803)

Providence, Rhode Island
Makers: attributed to John Carlile and Sons
39⅛ × 21 × 20 in. (99.4 × 53.4 × 50.8 cm.)
seat h.: 17 in. (43.2 cm.); seat d.: 18⅜ in. (46.7 cm.)
The Baltimore Museum of Art: Friends of the American Wing Fund (BMA 1983.6)

Found throughout New England, such side and arm chairs with a "kylix" splat have been connected to various cabinetmaking shops, either through documentation or attribution, including the shops of Benjamin Frothingham, Samuel McIntire, Goddard and Engs, and John Carlile and Sons. There is no doubt that this design was popular both with New England cabinetmakers and their clientele. The distinctive five-ribbed back splat, springing from a seven-part lunette fan at the base of the shield back and becoming at the top of the chair back an open ellipse filled with a carved kylix on an elongated pedestal, is the most repeated design motif in New England chairs. The kylix is consistently draped with carved swags of linked leaves hung from rosettes at the side and, from the top of the kylix, a fan-like anthemion carving extends into the crest rail. No exact prototype for these chair backs can be found in either Sheraton or Hepplewhite. The design for the kylix itself was probably derived from the works of Robert Adam. McIntire's sketch of such a chair back has in the past erroneously prompted many attributions to him.[1] Whether the design was of Rhode Island or Massachusetts origin cannot be determined, however, and McIntire was only one of many makers who adopted it.

This chair has been attributed to the cabinet-making shop of John Carlile and Sons of Providence, Rhode Island, first recorded in 1789. Carlile died in 1796 but his sons John Jr. and Samuel continued the business until at least 1803.[2] The Museum's chair and its mate are identical to two other chairs that carry the John Carlile and Sons label.[3] All four were purchased by two New England antique dealers, the two labeled chairs by one and the unlabeled, now in the Museum collection, by the other. The reappearance of these chairs has substantiated a long-held belief of many experts that chairs like these were made in Providence as well as Newport. The side seat rails are tenoned through the sides, and the side and medial stretchers are tenoned together, not the usual half dovetail which was the common New England practice. When acquired by the Museum, the two chairs had been refinished and reupholstered, the new brass nail pattern following clear evidence of the original.

NOTES:
1. Bibl. 42, ill., Supplement 102. The original drawing is in the collection of the Essex Institute in Salem, Massachusetts.
2. Joseph K. Ott, "Lesser-known Rhode Island cabinet-makers," *Antiques*, May 1982, p. 1156.
3. Bibl. 21, p. 28, no. 29, ill. p. 29; bibl. 69, p. 154, no. 68, ill. p. 155.

MATERIALS: Primary: mahogany. Secondary: black walnut, white oak (seat rails; rear rail has 3/8 in. mahogany facing), maple (open diagonal seat braces). Brass nails (not original)

PROVENANCE: Jerome Blum, Antiques, Lisbon-Jewett City, Connecticut

27

27. SIDE CHAIR (1790–1810)

Baltimore
36 × 20⅜ × 20¾ in. (91.5 × 51.8 × 52.7 cm.)
seat h.: 16¾ in. (42.6 cm.); seat d.: 17⅜ in. (44.1 cm.)
The Baltimore Museum of Art: Philip B. Perlman Bequest Fund (BMA 1964.9)

Chairs such as this one, with a balloon or racquet-shape splat very closely derived from a chair-back illustration in Plate 28 of Sheraton's 1802 *Drawing-Book*, were made in New York, Philadelphia, and Baltimore.[1] The chair is most closely related to a Philadelphia counterpart, but exhibits several pronounced Baltimore characteristics.[2] The chair seat is half upholstered rather than being fully upholstered, or of the slip-seat variety. Such half upholstery, with the remaining uncovered seat rail veneered, is found in many Baltimore side chairs of the period (see also cat. nos. 21 and 23).[3] The carved bellflowers or husks on the center splat are also of

27

28. SIDE CHAIR (1790–1820)

Boston area
35½ × 19⅞ × 15½ in. (90.2 × 50.5 × 39.4 cm.)
seat h.: 16⅝ in. (42.2 cm.); seat d.: 15⅜ in. (39.1 cm.)
Gift of Dorothy McIlvain Scott, Baltimore (BMA 1986.167)

This painted side chair, adapted from Plate 36, no. 1 of Thomas Sheraton's *Drawing-Book* (1791–1794), is one of a group of related chairs which share the same form, construction, and overall decorative scheme.[1] There are, however, slight variations in the ornamental motifs and in the back splat template dimensions of the group which suggest that the extant chairs represent at least two sets. Some of the chairs, like this example, reveal a somewhat more refined hand in the articulation of the splat elements when compared with others of the same general pattern. However, all share a similar decorative treatment. The splat is painted in a relatively sophisticated manner emphasizing a neoclassical bluish-green urn with swags flanked by marbleized colonnettes. This ornamentation appears to be entirely original. The chair's painted surface elsewhere (like others in the group) shows evidence of later overpainting and an alligatored asphaltic surface. Pigment analysis indicates that the original ground color was black with an ornamental blue stripe banding the center of the stiles and rails of the back, around the seat frame on both the top and outside rails, and down the front legs.[2] White striping and stylized rosettes in the corners had been covered by a chrome yellow banding. Similar vermilion and white floral tablets centered on the back and front seat rails are found on all the extant chairs of the group. While it is possible that they were executed by the same craftsman who painted the elegant splat, it cannot be precisely determined at what date these motifs were applied. The relatively loose handling of the flowers suggests that they may have been a later addition. Both types of ornamental painting were prevalent in New England during the late eighteenth and early nineteenth centuries but it is extremely difficult to identify specific decorators.[3] The back splat decoration shows an affinity to the type of painted ornament found on fireboards of the period while the more open floral tablets and simple rosettes suggest the type of motifs often seen on clock faces.

The Museum's chair is similar to a chair owned by Mr. and Mrs. Bertram K. Little which has been discussed in various publications as attributed to the Boston cabinetmaker John Seymour (ca. 1738–

the Baltimore variety (with elongated central petals) and in their manner of carving related to similar drops on a card table (cat. no. 100) and a chair (cat. no. 23). The half-veneered seat rails, curved at the sides and serpentine in the front, have a bead at the upholstery line and a double stripe of light wood stringing framing a dark wood stripe at the bottom. The leaf carving and narrow reeding of the right leg are found only on its front half and curiously enough do not extend all the way around the leg. However, since the leg is not a replacement, this seems to be how it came from the cabinetmaker's shop. There were originally diagonal braces in the front corners of the seat frame. The chair, according to previous private owners, came from Druid Hill, a house near Baltimore begun by Colonel Nicholas Rogers (1753–1822) in 1796 and finished in 1801, which in altered form now serves as offices for the Baltimore Zoological Society.

NOTES:
1. Bibl. 73.
2. Bibl. 47, p. 171, no. 151, ill. p. 172.
3. For an example with a related chair back, see bibl. 56, p. 153, no. 105, ill. p. 152.

MATERIALS: Primary: mahogany, mahogany veneers, light and dark wood inlays. Secondary: chestnut (rear seat rail), ash (side and front seat rails)

PROVENANCE: Rogers family of Druid Hill, Baltimore; J.W. Berry & Son, Antiques, Baltimore; BMA, by purchase, 1964

REFERENCES: Bibl. 28, p. 360, fig. 9; bibl. 35, p. 166, fig. VIII-21

28. SIDE CHAIR, (1790–1820). Boston area
Gift of Dorothy McIlvain Scott, Baltimore
(BMA 1986.167)

1818), based on a late nineteenth-century paper label with the inscription: Made by John Seymour for the Hon. Nathaniel Silsbee about 1790 when he built his house.[4] This label was discovered about 1905 when the chair seat was reupholstered, the original cane seat having been replaced sometime during the nineteenth century. (Credence has been given to the information on the label since it is unlikely that the name of John Seymour would have been of sufficient interest as early as 1905 for the attribution to be fabricated.) At the time the chair was acquired by the Littles, it had a direct line of descent in the family from its original owner, Nathaniel Silsbee, who in 1802 married Mary Crowninshield whose uncle was the wealthy merchant, Elias Hasket Derby of Salem, Massachusetts. While it is known that the Derby family favored the Seymours with extensive patronage well into the nineteenth century, there is no evidence to support an attribution to the Seymours.[5] If it and the related chairs were indeed by the Seymours, they would be unusual since most of their work displays finer craftsmanship; is executed in mahogany, satinwood, or maple; and is carved and inlaid for decorative effect rather than painted. Similar painted chairs known to have been owned in Salem include a set in the Essex Institute with related construction details and a similar design format.[6]

NOTES:
1. Bibl. 78, pp. 318–319, no. 215, ill.; bibl. 79, pp. 81–82, no. 55, ill.; bibl. 56, pp. 35–37, no. 36, ill. Other chairs are presently located at the Denver Art Museum; Bernard and S. Dean Levy, Inc., New York; The Metropolitan Museum of Art; the New-York Historical Society; Winterthur; and in other private collections.
2. Sample pigments examined by The Winterthur Museum and Garden, Analytical Laboratory, August 1986.
3. See Alice Knotts Bossert Cooney, "Ornamental Painting in Boston 1790–1830" (Master's thesis, The Winterthur Program, University of Delaware, 1978).
4. Bibl. 78, pp. 318–319, no. 215, ill.; bibl. 79, pp. 81–82, no. 55.
5. The celebrated commode made in 1809 by Thomas Seymour for Elizabeth Derby, for example, is in The Karolik Collection, Museum of Fine Arts, Boston.
6. Bibl. 79, p. 83.

MATERIALS: Painted birch. Natural cane (not original)

PROVENANCE: ex. coll. Boscobel Restoration, Inc., Garrison-on-Hudson, New York; Sotheby Parke-Bernet, New York, sale no. 3944, 22 Jan. 1977; Israel Sack, Inc.; Dorothy McIlvain Scott, Baltimore

REFERENCES: Bibl. 2, vol. 3, p. 619, no. 1403, ill.

29. ARMCHAIR (1800–1810)

Baltimore
Makers: John and Hugh Finlay
33¾ × 22¼ × 21 in. (85.8 × 56.5 × 53.4 cm.)
seat h.: 16 in. (40.7 cm.); seat d.: 14 in. (35.6 cm.)
The Baltimore Museum of Art: Gift of Lydia Howard de Roth and Nancy H. DeFord Venable, in Memory of their Mother, Lydia Howard DeFord; and Purchase Fund (BMA 1966.26.3)

Ten armchairs, two settees, and a marble top pier table compose this thirteen-piece suite of Baltimore painted furniture, long attributed to the brothers John (1777–1851) and Hugh (1781–1831) Finlay. A DeFord family memorandum written early in the twentieth century begins as follows: "List of names on the/furniture at Clermont,/made by Findlay [sic]."[1] By "the names on the furniture," the writer, probably Mrs. William DeFord of Baltimore (who resided at the letterhead address, 401 North Charles Street), meant her identification of the builder-owners and/or names of seventeen private houses and public buildings painted on the backs of the armchairs, settees, and on the skirt of the pier table. Clermont (or Claremont), the country estate of Mrs. DeFord's grandfather, John B. Morris (1785–1874), was located on the old Windsor Mill Road near Walbrook, and the furniture was apparently there when the memorandum was written.[2] Family tradition maintains that the set was orginally made for Morris about 1805.[3]

John Finlay, the first of the brothers to appear in the Baltimore City Directories, was listed as a painter on South Frederick Street in 1800; by 1803 Hugh Finlay had become his business partner. For the next three decades the city directories and newspaper advertisements record the Finlay brothers as "fancy furniture manufacturers," painters, and coachmakers, and by 1819 as owners of a "fancy furniture warehouse."[4] They frequently advertised in the *Federal Gazette and Baltimore Daily Advertiser*, offering a wide range of furniture "in all colors, gilt ornamented, and varnished in a style not equalled on the continent."[5] The ads also repeatedly stated that their various furniture forms could be decorated "with or without views adjacent to the city." Their shop often moved, but always within the cabinetmaking center of the city located in the area of Frederick, Baltimore, and Gay Streets. Research at the Museum of Early Southern Decorative Arts in Winston-Salem, North Carolina has revealed that for a short time in 1803 the Finlay brothers also had a painted furniture manufactory in Charleston, South Carolina.[6] Of the highest

29

29

quality, the Finlays' production surpassed that done in other American cabinetmaking centers of the early nineteenth century. Their superlative painted furniture is one of the important contributions made by Baltimore to American decorative arts of the period. Throughout those first four decades (encompassing a style change from the Federal to the classical archaeological style of the 1820's and 1830's), the Finlays were undoubtedly the chief producers of Baltimore painted furniture, and they trained in their shops journeymen and apprentices who imitated their product, perpetuating it long into the nineteenth century.

The Museum's thirteen-piece set of painted furniture by the Finlays has survived miraculously intact. Its painted surfaces are well preserved, and in style and decoration the furniture represents their finest product. Its decoration comprises a complete index of the design motifs of the Finlay shop.[7] The building shown on this armchair is

Rose Hill, which stood near Eutaw Place and Lanvale Street, built by Hugh McCurdy, ca. 1800. Homewood and Mount Clare are the only buildings depicted on the furniture that have survived. Homewood, ca. 1801–1803, built by Charles Carroll of Carrollton, stands today on the campus of The Johns Hopkins University. Mount Clare, ca. 1760, of which only the central section is original, was the home of Charles Carroll the Barrister, and is located in Carroll Park. The English-born landscape artist Francis Guy has been credited with painting the architectural views "adjacent to the city" on this and other furniture attributed to the Finlay shop.[8]

NOTES:
1. Now in the possession of The Baltimore Museum of Art. The stationery is watermarked with the date 1904.
2. Clermont, an estate of 150 acres on Gwynn's Run, was bordered by the Old Windsor Mill Road. The house, outbuildings, and property are clearly delineated on the

northwestern edge of Poppleton's 1823 *Plan of the City of Baltimore* as republished in 1852, the name of the property being spelled "Claremont." In 1871 sixty acres of Clermont were sold for the then suburban development of Walbrook. In the *Atlas of the City of Baltimore*, published in 1906 by G.W. Bromley and Co. of Philadelphia (Plate 26), the house at Clermont was shown in an overlay of proposed future streets; its location today is the northwest corner of Presstman and Poplar Grove Streets. According to Mrs. DeFord's memorandum, the family still owned the house in 1904.

3. Bibl. 18, pp. 76–77. Stiles Colwill suggests in his study of English-born landscape artist Francis Guy, 1760–1820 (who is believed to have painted the architectural scenes on the furniture), that since Morris did not arrive in Baltimore until 1806 and may not have had a large enough house for such a suite of furniture until his marriage in 1817, he may have purchased the set secondhand at auction. However, it is also possible that the set was owned first by his or his wife's parents, Thomas and Ann Adams Hollingsworth, or that the furniture could have descended in the Howard family of Baltimore and reached Clermont after Morris' death in 1874. One of his daughters married Frank Key Howard, the grandson of General John Eager Howard of Baltimore and the father of Lydia Howard DeFord.

4. For the listings of the Finlays in the Baltimore directories, see bibl. 27, p. 106 and bibl. 84, p. 281. The latter work also includes references to newspaper notices. One advertisement is illustrated in bibl. 27, p. 95. A discussion of the Finlays is found in bibl. 27, pp. 10–13 and pp. 20–27, and in bibl. 84, pp. 72 and 75.

5. *Federal Gazette and Baltimore Daily Advertiser*, 8 Nov. 1805.

6. Two newspaper advertisements appeared in 1803; in March one announcing that they manufacture at No. 24 Church St. a full range of painted furniture forms (*City Gazette and Daily Advertiser*, Charleston, South Carolina, 18 Mar. 1803). In their May advertisement the various forms are listed and the subscribers state they will be leaving Charleston in a few days (*City Gazette and Daily Advertiser*, Charleston, South Carolina, 6 May 1803).

7. The seventeen architectural views, many of them the only record of lost Baltimore buildings, were all reproduced and identified in bibl. 27, pp. 22–27. (The two houses illustrated on page 23 should have their captions reversed. The house identified as Rose Hill is actually Grace Hill and vice versa.) Seven of the architectural views are reproduced in bibl. 54, p. 238, pl. 226. The houses illustrated are Woodville, Mount Clare, Homewood, Willow Brook, Montebello, and Mount Deposit or Surrey.

8. The exhibition, *Francis Guy 1760–1820*, was held at the Maryland Historical Society 10 Apr.–15 Aug. 1981.

MATERIALS: Primary: maple (stiles, legs, crest rail, stay rail, side and front seat rails, splats). Secondary: ash (rear seat rail, arms, arm supports); painted black with gilt and polychrome decoration. Cane seats (not original)

PROVENANCE: John B. Morris (1785–1874), Baltimore; by descent to Lydia Howard DeFord; Lydia Howard de Roth and Nancy H. DeFord Venable

EXHIBITIONS: Bibl. 27, p. 20, no. 3, ill. and pp. 22–27; bibl. 18, pp. 76–83; bibl. 11, pp. 78–79, no. 62, ill.

REFERENCES: Bibl. 54, pp. 238–239 and 246; bibl. 35, p. 167, fig. VIII-24; bibl. 33, p. 133, fig. 218

30. SIDE CHAIR (1800–1810)

Baltimore
Makers: attributed to John and Hugh Finlay
33¼ × 19 × 19¼ in. (84.5 × 48.3 × 48.9 cm.)
seat h.: 16⅛ in. (41 cm.); seat d.: 15⅝ in. (39.7 cm.)
The Baltimore Museum of Art: The George C. Jenkins Fund, by exchange (BMA 1969.8.3)

The set of Baltimore painted furniture to which this chair belongs is the largest extant set known. The Museum owns a pier table (cat. no. 122), a card table (cat. no. 101), a window seat (cat. no. 40), and two more side chairs. The original complete set, made about 1800 for the Buchanan family, was composed of the pier table, a pair of card tables, two window seats, a settee, and ten side chairs.[1] The six pieces in the Museum's collection, including three of the surviving nine chairs, were acquired from the descendants of William Buchanan, a merchant from Carlisle, Pennsylvania, who came to Baltimore in 1759 to set up a shipping business. Because of the quality and similarity of design motifs, this set has, like cat. nos. 29, 39, and 121, been attributed to the shop of John and Hugh Finlay of Baltimore, although it is not entirely typical of their work. The stiles and crest rails of the chair backs of this set and of the armchairs discussed in the preceding entry are similar in design and decoration, as are the cane seats. However, the legs of these side chairs, with turnings at the top and joined by stretchers, are in the more common Sheraton fancy-chair style characteristic of other American cabinetmaking centers of the period. The caned seat is not directly worked into the front, side, and rear seat rails but is a separate screwed-on frame, easily removed to facilitate recaning. Bright yellow paint drips on the underside of the frames of all the surviving side chairs suggest that originally the caned seats were painted this color.[2] All the side chairs have the same painted polychrome and gilt decoration, except for the large painted panels centered in the crest rails which contain either agricultural, musical, or armorial trophies.

According to family tradition, Buchanan ordered the set before his death in 1804, perhaps to furnish one of two rowhouses he had built on North Gay Street for his three daughters.[3] It has been recorded that the painted furniture made for the home of the two unmarried daughters was the work of a "certain Robert Crawford."[4] No Robert Crawford is listed as a cabinetmaker in the Baltimore City Directories between 1800 and 1840.[5] To complicate further the question of attribution, furniture from

30

30

this same set sold to Winterthur by Mrs. Miles White, Jr., a prominent Baltimore collector, has been attributed in the past to Robert Fisher.[6] Fisher was indeed a local cabinetmaker, working at 35–37 South Gay Street from 1805–1810, and listed as a "chairmaker" as well as a maker of "fancy chairs."[7]

However, in the absence of documentation, it seems probable that this furniture was the product of the Finlay shop or of Finlay followers. Considered to be the second finest known set of Baltimore painted furniture, its decoration repeats much of the Finlay vocabulary; for example, the gilt saw-tooth-edged rectangular panels, oval gilt paterae, and polychrome trophies are all executed with the utmost technical skill.[8]

NOTES:
1. Three side chairs, the other card table and window seat, and the settee (which is an extension of the chair design) were sold to the Winterthur Museum in 1957 by Mrs. Miles White, Jr., who had acquired them early in this century from her Buchanan relatives. Bibl. 56, pp. 451–453, nos. 456–459. The Metropolitan Museum of Art acquired two Buchanan side chairs in an exchange with the Baltimore Museum which received two Baltimore painted chairs of a slightly later date, also attributed to the Finlays (see cat. no. 32). A ninth chair is privately owned by a Buchanan descendant in Pennsylvania. The tenth is said to have been lost in a fire in Virginia many years ago, according to Ulric O. Hutton, in conversation with WVE in 1969.
2. This was verified in 1984 when the Museum received another side chair (BMA 1984.115) whose original but broken seat was found to have painted yellow caning.
3. Bibl. 13, pp. 262 and 268–269. The site is now part of the War Memorial Plaza east of Baltimore's City Hall.
4. Crawford's name was said to have been inscribed on the side chair lost in a fire. Bibl. 13, p. 269.
5. Bibl. 27, pp. 96–129; bibl. 84, pp. 265–328.
6. Bibl. 55, vol. 1, p. 290; also bibl. 52, vol. 2, p. 311.
7. Bibl. 27, p. 106.
8. For a further discussion of characteristic furniture decoration by the Finlays and their shop, see cat. no. 29.

MATERIALS: Maple (legs, stiles, splat), tulip wood (seat rails), ash (stay rail), mahogany (removable seat frame); painted black with polychrome and gilt and bronze decoration. Cane seat (not original)

PROVENANCE: William Buchanan, Baltimore; and/or the Misses Sydney and Margaret Buchanan; by descent to Ulric O. Hutton, Brinklow

EXHIBITIONS: Bibl. 27, pp. 28–29, no. 6, ill.

31

31. SIDE CHAIR (1794–1799)

Baltimore
Maker: Jacob Cole
32½ × 18¼ × 18½ in. (82.6 × 46.4 × 47 cm.)
seat h.: 17⅜ in. (44.1 cm.); seat d.: 15¼ in. (38.8 cm.)
The Baltimore Museum of Art: Friends of the American
Wing Fund (BMA 1980.427)

So little is known about the Windsor chair industry in Baltimore that were it not for the J. Cole brand, this square-back chair would probably be ascribed to Philadelphia. In fact it has been suggested that chairs with the earlier H-stretchers rather than box stretchers and two bamboo turnings on the legs are of Pennsylvania origin.[1] In this example the seat is unusually thick, measuring nearly two and one-half inches, with an incised line at its back top edge in front of the posts and spindles and at the top edge of the seat on the sides and front. It has been stripped of its original green paint, remains of which can be seen on portions of the chair. The name J. Cole, branded at the front of the bottom of the shaped plank seat, presumably stands for Jacob Cole, a Windsor chairmaker in the Old Town section of Baltimore. He first advertised in a Baltimore newspaper in 1794 as a Windsor chairmaker at 73 Front Street. Cole's estate was disbursed upon his death in 1801. In 1799 a Godfrey and Jacob Cole were in business together as turners and chairmakers on York Street in Old Town.[2]

NOTES:
1. Bibl. 70, p. 132.
2. Cole's death date is found in the *American and Daily Advertiser*, Baltimore, 2 Oct. 1801. Godfrey may have been a brother of Jacob, as perhaps was George Cole, chairmaker and joiner at 1 High Street, Old Town, in 1804, chair and spinning wheel maker at 8 High Street in 1810. A Frederick Cole (perhaps still another brother, or son) was working as a chairmaker at the 8 High Street address in 1816. Bibl. 84, p. 274.

MATERIALS: Beech, maple, white pine (seat)
PROVENANCE: Jaime Galindo, Antiques, Baltimore; BMA, by purchase, 1980

31

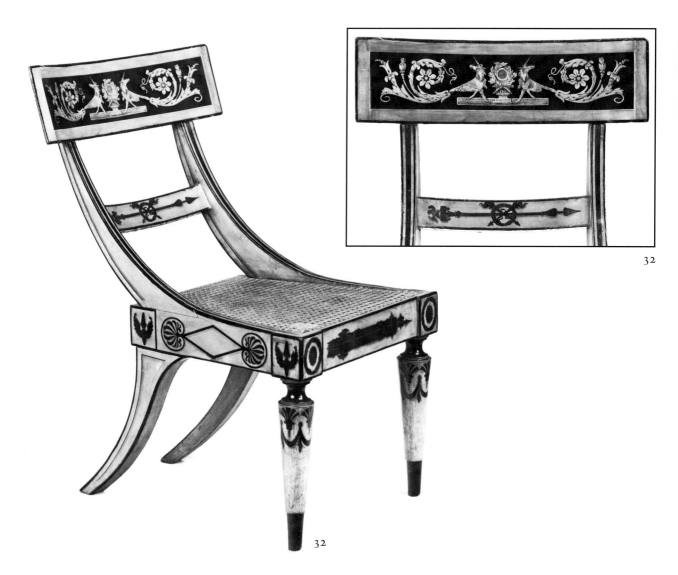

32

32

32. SIDE CHAIR (ONE OF TWO) (1820–1830)

Baltimore

33⅞ × 20⅜ × 24³⁄₁₆ in. (86.1 × 51.8 × 61.5 cm.)
seat h.: 16½ in. (41.9 cm.); seat d.: 16⅜ in. (41.6 cm.)
The Baltimore Museum of Art: The George C. Jenkins
and Decorative Arts Funds, by exchange with The
Metropolitan Museum of Art, New York (BMA 1972.46.2)

This side chair is one of eleven surviving chairs
that must have originally numbered a dozen. Seven
side chairs from the same set are in the Metropolitan Museum in New York, and two belong to a
descendant of the original owner.[1] Of Baltimore
painted furniture in the classical archaeological
style, these chairs are the most sophisticated in
design and decoration. The Greek klismos form is
shown in the raked seat back and rear legs while
the turned front legs are of Roman origin. The
polychrome and gilt decoration on the chair's back
is derived from an "ornament for a frieze or tablet"
illustrated in plate 56 of Thomas Sheraton's *The
Cabinet-Maker and Upholsterer's Drawing-Book*.[2]
This design which is repeated on all of the chairs
is used as part of the decoration of a set of Baltimore
painted furniture of the same period.[3] However,
the animal motif at the center of the design can
be, variously, sphinxes, griffins, unicorns, or swans.
The Museum's chairs incorporate the unicorn and
swan motifs. The other decoration is more purely
classical in origin: the eagle standard with a laurel
wreath and torches at its center on the stay rail of
the back; bound fasces on the front seat rail; and
the palmettes, anthemion, drapery, and winged
thunderbolts.

In 1809 the Baltimore shop of John and Hugh Finlay produced a set of painted furniture for The White House from drawings by the architect Benjamin H. Latrobe (1764–1820) which reveal designs for side chairs very much in the same classical archaeological style.[4]

NOTES:
1. The Metropolitan Museum of Art purchased nine of the chairs in 1965 from an antique dealer in Baltimore, and carefully restored and stabilized their painted surfaces. In 1972 two of the chairs were traded to the Baltimore Museum for two painted side chairs from the set of furniture made for the Buchanan family of Baltimore about 1800 (see cat. no. 30).
2. Bibl. 73.
3. Bibl. 27, pp. 75–76, no. 49, ill.; p. 80, no. 52, ill.; p. 81, no. 53, ill.
4. Bibl. 27, p. 12, ill.

MATERIALS: Maple and cherry painted yellow with polychrome and gilt stenciled and freehand decoration. Cane seat (not original)

PROVENANCE: Arunah S. Abell (1806–1888), Woodburne, Baltimore; by descent to Margaret Abell Fenwick; Norton Asner, Antiques, Baltimore; The Metropolitan Museum of Art; BMA, by purchase, 1972

EXHIBITIONS: Bibl. 59, no. 46, ill.; bibl. 11, p. 82, no. 65, ill.

REFERENCES: James Biddle, "Collecting American art for the Metropolitan: 1961–1966," *Antiques*, Apr. 1967, p. 483, ill.

33. SIDE CHAIR (1850–1870)

American
45⅞ × 20¼ × 22 in. (116.6 × 51.5 × 55.9 cm.)
seat h.: 14¼ in. (36.2 cm.); seat d.: 19½ in. (49.5 cm.)
The Baltimore Museum of Art: Gift of Dr. and Mrs. William H. Woody, in Memory of Mrs. Sydney Wetherall Matthews (BMA 1970.48.1)

The high back and strong verticality of this side chair bespeak the Gothic Revival style of the 1850's, but the chair's ornament and other elements of its design are of the Renaissance Revival style of the 1870's. The crest rail of the chair back, complete with flanking finials and almost three-dimensional carving at its center, is architectural in feeling—a reduced version of the arched pediment tops on wardrobes or headboards in the Renaissance Revival style. The exaggerated volutes at the top and bottom of each stile, the curvilinear bottom rail of the chair back, and the design of the turned front legs are part of the vocabulary of the American cabinetmaker working in this eclectic revival style. The needlepoint seat covering is original.

MATERIALS: Walnut

PROVENANCE: Sydney Wetherall Matthews, Baltimore; Dr. and Mrs. William H. Woody, 1970

EXHIBITIONS: Bibl. 3

33

34. EASY CHAIR (1760–1790)

Eastern Massachusetts
47 × 35 × 26⅛ in. (119.4 × 88.9 × 66.4 cm.)
seat h.: 13⅛ in. (33.4 cm.); seat d.: 22¼ in. (56.5 cm.)
The Baltimore Museum of Art: Gift of Mr. and Mrs.
W.T. Dixon Gibbs, Baltimore (BMA 1983.251)

The essential feature of the eighteenth-century Massachusetts easy chair form was what made it easy—its lavish, well-cushioned upholstery. Of the handful of cabriole-leg easy chairs retaining their eighteenth-century covering only one has nail-trimmed edges.[1] The recent discovery of that chair (descended in the family of Major Nathan Low of Ipswich, Massachusetts) permitted the accurate period reupholstering of the Museum's chair which, though it had lost its original upholstery, had unmistakably been covered and trimmed in the same manner as the Low chair—a continuous trail of nail holes, many with square brass shanks broken off in them, was found along the perimeters of the stripped frame. The brilliant brass nails used to trim the outside edges are in sharp contrast to the all-woven binding most commonly found on this kind of chair. Until the discovery of the Low chair,

34

original upholstery using brass nail trim was only known on easy chairs with straight molded legs.[2] Such chairs with horizontally scrolled arms and serpentine crest and wings used brass nails as the sole trimming to cover seams and define edges. Neither of these previously known methods of trimming—using all nails or all-woven binding—was deemed appropriate for the Museum's chair. What did seem correct was to integrate both kinds of trim, because the chair could not have been trimmed with nails in one critical area—the inside fore edge of the wings. There the inch-wide wooden stile would have been padded out to a depth of three inches and so provide no place to anchor brass nails, but there was no precedent for finishing a chair in this way until the Low chair was discovered.

The Low chair verified the theory that cabriole chairs were trimmed with both nails and binding, were meant to be well-padded, and that the use of nails as trim did not in any way alter the manner in which the wings were upholstered. Rather, it was the late eighteenth-century neoclassical fashion for lighter furniture that called for the removal of padding and the elimination of the three-inch-wide strip which boxed the wing fore edges. The upholstery of chairs such as this example does not represent a transitional phase between the rococo and neoclassical but is fully within the earlier tradition and simply represents a previously unknown manner of trimming. That no other easy chair but the Low family example has been found to document this mix of brass and woven trim is somewhat puzzling, for brass nails required less labor to install and were cheaper than binding.[3] On this chair the arched crest is set on top of the stiles, a construction feature adapted for serpentine crested chairs. Used by Boston craftsmen by 1760, the technique allowed for the shaping of a single board rather than carving ears on the stiles and shaping a crest to set between them.[4]

NOTES:

1. Easy chairs with original upholstery incorporating woven binding are in the collection of the Metropolitan Museum. Bibl. 39, pp. 122–124, no. 72, ill.; the Bayou Bend collection, bibl. 83, p. 50, no. 90, ill. p. 51; The Brooklyn Museum, Brock Jobe, "The Boston Furniture Industry, 1720–1740," in bibl. 85, p. 35, fig. 25; the collection of Colonel Daniel Putnam Association of Newport, Rhode Island; and the Wadsworth Atheneum. The latter two chairs were exhibited in "The Regulator's Art," 1983, at the Connecticut Historical Society. The nail-trimmed chair from the Low family was first published by Sotheby's, *Fine American Furniture, Folk Art and Oriental Carpets*, sale cat., 26 Oct. 1985, sale no. 5376, lot 76, ill.

34. EASY CHAIR, (1760–1790). Eastern Massachusetts
The Baltimore Museum of Art:
Gift of Mr. and Mrs. W. T. Dixon Gibbs, Baltimore (BMA 1983.251)

2. Bibl. 2, vol. 2, p. 381, no. 961, ill.
3. Bibl. 46, p. 365. In a list of costs for covering an easy chair in the accounts of Boston upholsterer Samuel Grant, the binding is more expensive than the nearly eight yards of upholstery fabric needed to cover the chair.
4. Bibl. 46, p. 364.

MATERIALS: Primary: mahogany. Secondary: maple (rear legs, frame), chestnut (rear stretcher), white pine (arm cones)

PROVENANCE: Mr. and Mrs. John Sears Gibbs, Jr., Baltimore; Mr. and Mrs. W.T. Dixon Gibbs

REFERENCES: Bibl. 55, vol. 1, pp. 239–240, no. 394, ill.

35

35. ARMCHAIR (1850–1870)

New York
Maker: attributed to the shop of John Henry Belter
44¾ × 26½ × 31¾ in. (113.7 × 67.3 × 80.7 cm.)
seat h.: 13¾ in. (34.9 cm.); seat d.: 23¼ in. (51.9 cm.); casters: 1½ in. (3.8 cm.)
The Baltimore Museum of Art: Gift of Abram Moses, in Memory of his Wife, Carrie Gutman Moses (BMA 1953.225.4)

See discussion in cat. no. 46.

MATERIALS: Rosewood (legs, stiles, arms, top crest ornament, facing on front seat rail, veneer on side seat rails and on front and back of laminant core), pine (kerf sawn and bent side seat rails), chestnut (inner seat frame)

PROVENANCE: Joel and Bertha Kayton Gutman, Baltimore; Carrie Gutman Moses (Mrs. Abram); Abram Moses

36. ARMCHAIR (1865–1875)

Possibly Baltimore
44¼ × 26⅝ × 31½ in. (112.4 × 67.7 × 80 cm.)
seat h.: 12¹¹⁄₁₆ in. (32.2 cm.); seat d.: 24 in. (61 cm.); casters 1½ in. (3.8 cm.)
The Baltimore Museum of Art: Gift from the Estate of Margaret Anna Abell (BMA 1977.42.2)

This Renaissance Revival-style upholstered armchair, and a matching sofa also in the Museum's collection, are the only known surviving pieces of what surely would have been a suite of furniture. Thought to have been in use in the 1870's at Guilford, the country house outside Baltimore of the Abell family, the chair and sofa (not illustrated), like cat. nos. 73 and 119, may have been owned first by Guilford's builder, William McDonald who sold the house and its contents to Arunah S. Abell in 1872.[1] Typical Renaissance Revival design elements are found in the carved cartouche at the center of the crest rail; the incised-line decoration on the stiles of the chair back and on the seat rails, in the shaping of the turned front legs, and especially in the carved heads, drapery, and tassels on the arm supports. The overall shape of the chair has been derived from French styles of Louis XV and Louis XVI. Such carved heads and draped torsos were used as arm supports in most of America's major cabinetmaking centers during the period.[2] The similar assemblage of design and decorative motifs points to a common but unknown design source.

   The sofa which is en suite with this armchair has the same decorative elements. Its back is in three sections; the center and larger section is a wider version of the chair back. The incised-line

36

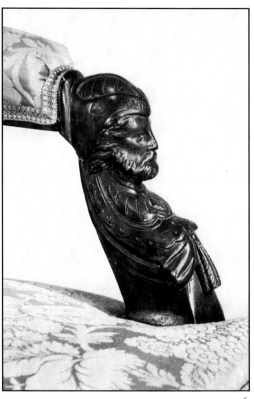

36

decoration on the seat rails shows traces of having been gilded originally. The sofa, unlike the matching armchair, has not been restored and retains much of its original green damask upholstery.

NOTES:
1. A more detailed discussion of the house and its nineteenth-century owners is found under cat. no. 119.
2. Carved female heads are characteristic of the work of the Newark, New Jersey firm of Jelliff and Co.; see bibl. 59, no. 174 and also Ulysses G. Dietz, *Century of Revivals: Nineteenth-Century American Furniture from the Collection of The Newark Museum* (an exhibition held Sept. 1982–July 1983), *The Newark Museum Quarterly*, Spring/Summer 1980 (published 1983), p. 45, no. 37, ill., and p. 47, no. 39, ill. Female heads of related design and with similarly carved drapery and tassels on the supports are found on numerous pieces of furniture produced by the Phoenix Furniture Company in Grand Rapids, Michigan, prior to 1878. See Kenneth L. Ames, "Grand Rapids Furniture at the Time of the Centennial," *Winterthur Portfolio 10*, The Henry Francis du Pont Winterthur Museum (Charlottesville: University Press of Virginia, 1975), p. 45, figs. 15 and 16.

MATERIALS: Mahogany (back, arms, legs), walnut (seat rails). Casters (not original)

PROVENANCE: Possibly William McDonald (1830–1864), Baltimore; Arunah S. Abell, by purchase, 1872; by descent to Margaret Anna Abell

37. DAYBED (COUCH) (1720–1740)

Pennsylvania, possibly Maryland
41½ × 22⅞ × 70⅜ in. (105.5 × 58.1 × 178.8 cm.)
seat h.: 16 in. (40.7 cm.); seat d.: 64 in. (162.6 cm.)
The Baltimore Museum of Art: Gift of Mr. and Mrs.
William M. Ellicott (BMA 1933.38.1)

"Couch" was the early eighteenth-century term for both a small sofa and what would today be called a daybed, with its connotations of use for resting rather than sleeping, not necessarily in a bedroom.[1] This fine example, with a provenance that substantiates its Pennsylvania attribution, was presented to the Museum in 1933 by a descendant of Andrew Ellicott, who came to Maryland from Bucks County, Pennsylvania in 1774. A high chest of drawers (cat. no. 51), sharing the family tradition of Ellicott's ownership, was probably ordered after he arrived in Maryland; the couch was presumably

37

37

brought with him from Pennsylvania. Its design is typical of seating furniture associated with Chester County.[2] Although the Ellicott family came from Bucks County, Bucks, Montgomery, and Chester Counties all shared a regional style strongly influenced by the traditions of their many German settlers. The heavy splats and arched crest rail of the back are Germanic rather than English in origin. Similar backs are found on chairs made in Chester and neighboring counties. On the inside edge of the two side stiles, lower rail, and arched crest rail, there is a continuous star-punch design, a decoration characteristic of this area but also employed elsewhere in later periods (see cat. nos. 95 and 131). The turned back supports, legs, and stretchers are, when compared to other known Pennsylvania couches of this period, exceptional in design and execution. The back of the couch, as in other examples, originally reclined, held in position perhaps by rope or a leather thong. The frame is entirely of walnut as is an inner upholstery frame, a mid-nineteenth-century addition. Originally a one-piece canvas bottom, or a canvas bottom laced to canvas strips attached to the frame, would have

supported the cushion. There is no evidence that the couch was ever caned; the seat frame, which is not original, is covered with modern upholsterer's webbing.

NOTES:
1. Bibl. 46, pp. 315–318.
2. Margaret Berwind Schiffer, *Furniture and Its Makers of Chester County, Pennsylvania*, rev. ed. (Exton, Pennsylvania: Schiffer Publishing, 1978), figs. 157 and 158.

MATERIALS: Walnut; walnut inner seat frame (not original)

PROVENANCE: Ellicott family of Bucks County, Pennsylvania, and Ellicott City; by descent to William M. Ellicott

REFERENCES: Bibl. 55, vol. 1, p. 284, no. 503, ill. p. 283

38. SETTEE (1775–1800)

Frederick
Maker: attributed to Anthony Poultney
35¼ × 79⅛ × 26¾ in. (89.6 × 201.1 × 68 cm.)
seat h.: 15½ in. (39.4 cm.); seat d.: 23¾ in. (60.3 cm.)
The Baltimore Museum of Art: The George C. Jenkins Fund, by exchange (BMA 1968.33A)

In most aspects this settee is unlike the familiar Windsor settees of Pennsylvania or New England.[1] Its pronounced rectilinear form and turned mem-

38

38

bers are difficult to relate to examples from any area. Present knowledge about the manufacture of Windsor chairs or settees anywhere in Maryland is scanty, but what few documented examples there are closely follow the regional characteristics of Pennsylvania and the other middle colonies. Except for its turned stretchers, which are indeed somewhat atypical, and the arms which terminate in carved knuckles, the settee would seem to be the product of a craftsman with architectural background rather than someone who was simply a chair and/or cabinetmaker. The back posts of two vase turnings of diminishing size and the vase-turned arm supports and front legs are like turned newel posts and balusters of stairways in post-Revolutionary eighteenth-century Maryland houses in Montgomery, Frederick, and Washington Counties. These rural dwellings are generally less architecturally advanced when compared to Baltimore Federal houses of the same period. The settee came from Falling Green, a house still standing near Olney, Montgomery County, built in the 1770's by a James Brooke. Roger B. Farquhar described this settee as standing in the hall at Falling Green, and as having been made for a Gerard Brooke around the end of the eighteenth century. Another Montgomery County house, Cherry Grove, built by a Richard Thomas and later purchased by Farquhar, is said to have been furnished with an identical settee. Both pieces are attributed to "the famous Quaker cabinet maker Anthony Poultney," who is said to have been born in 1752 and who died in 1805.[2]

The Cherry Grove settee now at Stratford Hall, while not identical to the Museum's example, is very similar in appearance.[3] Its front legs are heavier, more closely spaced, and use paired plain turned

stretchers, while the Museum's example has a longer expanse supported by four, not five, sets of legs and single stretchers. The maker may have learned from the Stratford example that he could afford to build less massively without compromising sturdiness. The Stratford settee retains the spool and flattened-ball turned feet which would also have been found on the Museum's settee before they were cut off at the spool. The Stratford Hall settee's seat is covered with a piece of leather attached with brass upholstery nails at the inner edge of the seat rails, apparently a reconstruction of the original upholstery. The Museum's settee may have been similarly covered, but its seat is now composed of two painted boards placed lengthwise and nailed into a rabbet cut on the inner edge of the side and rear seat rails. The front seat rail is similarly rabbeted but a narrow black strip has been used to fill it in. The whole is supported by three crosswise braces screwed into the underside of the rails. The center legs are round tenoned through the seat rabbet with through pins to secure them. Now stripped, the settee was originally painted green, then black.

NOTES:
1. Bibl. 70, p. 150, no. 184, ill.; p. 153, no. 189, ill.; p. 157, no. 197, ill.
2. Roger B. Farquhar, *Historic Montgomery County, Maryland* (Baltimore: Privately printed, 1952). Falling Green is discussed on p. 161, Cherry Grove on p. 121. The Cherry Grove settee was purchased by the Stratford Hall Foundation, Virginia, in 1940. Farquhar's 1935 letter to the Foundation mentions three other Poultney benches in the Sandy Spring area of Montgomery County: this one from Falling Green, a second owned by the Iddings family (present location unknown), but gives no information about the third. He gives Poultney's dates as 1752 to 1805; the death date can be verified in the *Frederick Town Herald* for 27 July 1805. Poultney's will (14 Sept. 1803, Frederick County Wills, Hall of Records, Annapolis) gives his wife's name, Susanna Plummer, but sheds no light on his occupation. More information on Poultney is found in volume 1 of J. Thomas Scharf's *History of Western Maryland* (2 vols., 1882; reprint, Baltimore: Regional Publishing Co., 1968). Forty-seven acres in Frederick County were resurveyed for Anthony Poultney in 1799, and about 1782 he had a flour mill at Monrovia about nine miles from Frederick, and he also operated a button factory. He and his family were members of the Monocacy Quaker Meeting.
3. An article in the *Baltimore Sun*, 24 Dec. 1905, includes a photograph of the Cherry Grove settee against the stairway in the entrance hall.

MATERIALS: Oak (seat rails, braces), maple (legs, stiles), ash (stretchers, arms, spindles, back rails)

PROVENANCE: Gerard Brooke, Cherry Grove, Montgomery County, ca. 1780; by descent to Edith Brooke Green and Mary Green; Stoll Kemp, Antiques, New Market, 1968; BMA, by purchase, 1968

REFERENCES: Bibl. 10, ill. frontispiece

39. SETTEE, (1800–1810). Baltimore
Makers: John and Hugh Finlay
The Baltimore Museum of Art: Gift of Lydia Howard deRoth and Nancy H. DeFord Venable,
in Memory of their Mother, Lydia Howard DeFord; and Purchase Fund (BMA 1966.26.12)

39. SETTEE (1800–1810)

Baltimore
Makers: John and Hugh Finlay
33⅝ × 51⅜ × 22 in. (85.4 × 130.5 × 55.9 cm.)
seat h.: 17 in. (43.2 cm.); seat d.: 19¼ in. (48.9 cm.)
The Baltimore Museum of Art: Gift of Lydia Howard deRoth and Nancy H. DeFord Venable, in Memory of their Mother, Lydia Howard DeFord; and Purchase Fund (BMA 1966.26.12)

This settee is one of two in a set of thirteen pieces of painted furniture. Depicted on the crest rail are the Walter Dorsey House; Montebello, ca. 1797, built by General Samuel Smith; and the Vineyard, ca. 1800, the country seat of William Gilmor, Sr.[1] For a discussion of the set as a whole see cat. no. 29. The pier table from this set is cat. no. 121. The settee's construction is similar to that of the arm-chairs in that the crest rail is screwed to the stiles from the rear; the upper arm is attached with screws to the outside of the rear stile, and the arm support is similarly held in place on the seat rail. It differs from the chairs in two respects: the use of through rather than hidden tenons for the rear of the side seat rails, and the joint of the two front interior legs into the seat rail. The usual tenon extends from the top of the leg into the mid-line of the rail while a broad, shallow dovetail is cut into the face of the rail allowing the blossom-painted paterae of the stile face to slide up into it, thus providing a doubly secure joint.

NOTES:
1. The Walter Dorsey House is thought to have been located in the present area of Lanvale Street and Fremont Avenue. Montebello, designed by William Birch (1755–1834) of Philadelphia (south of 33rd Street and east of the Alameda), was destroyed early in this century. A watercolor of the house and floor plan by Birch are in the Museum's collection. The Vineyard, near the inter-section of 29th Street and Greenmount Avenue, is memorialized by a Vineyard Lane in the vicinity.

MATERIALS: Maple (crest and stay rails, stiles, legs, seat cross braces), ash (seat rails, arms); painted black polychrome with gilt and bronze decoration
PROVENANCE: John B. Morris (1785–1874), Baltimore; by descent to Lydia Howard DeFord; Lydia Howard deRoth and Nancy H. DeFord Venable
EXHIBITIONS: Bibl. 4, p. 156, no. 98, ill.; bibl. 27, p. 20, no. 4, ill. and pp. 22–27; bibl. 18, pp. 76–83
REFERENCES: Bibl. 54, pp. 238–239 and 246; bibl. 75, p. 243, fig. 8; bibl. 22, p. 33, ill. pp. 32–33; *BMA Record*, Apr. 1972, ill.; bibl. 33, p. 132, figs. 217 and 217a

40. WINDOW SEAT (1800–1810)

Baltimore
Makers: attributed to John and Hugh Finlay
31½ × 49⅝ × 13⅞ in. (80 × 126.1 × 35.3 cm.)
seat h.: 18⅛ in. (46.1 cm.); seat d.: 13⅞ in. (35.3 cm.)
The Baltimore Museum of Art: Gift of Ulric O. Hutton (BMA 1972.19)

Two caned window seats, one owned by the Bal-timore Museum and the other at Winterthur, were obviously especially constructed to fit inside the deep window recesses of a masonry Baltimore town

40

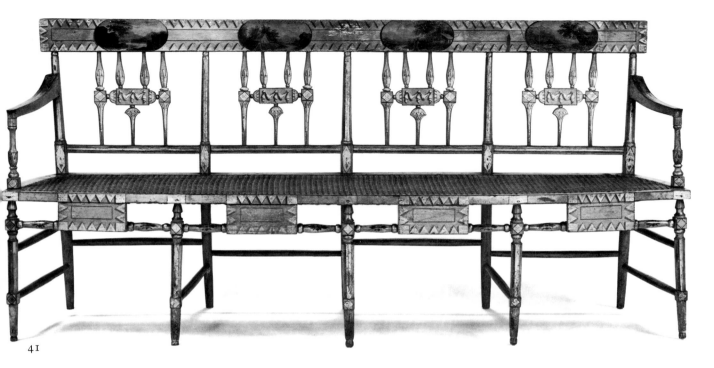

41

house of the early nineteenth century.[1] The seats were part of a larger set of painted furniture made for the Buchanan family of Baltimore that included a chair (cat. no. 30), card table (cat. no. 101), and pier table (cat. no. 122) also in the Museum's collection. The complete set of painted furniture could well have been used in one of the two brick town houses that are the subject of the architectural view depicted on the pier table's skirt. The top rails of both bench ends are also curved outward to fit around window framings. The decoration matches the other pieces in the set. On the center and at each end of the top rails, instead of an architectural view, there are armorial and musical trophies painted in gilt and polychrome glazes. These motifs are part of the Finlay vocabulary and appear, with the addition of agricultural implements, in the center painted panels of the crest rails in the surviving nine chairs of the set (see cat. no. 30). The present cane seat is not original, for the earliest caning was smaller and painted a bright yellow. The medial brace under the caned seat is turned and bent like a Windsor chair spindle. The painted surface has not been restored, but all of the feet have been restored to match the intact Winterthur example.

NOTES:
1. An advertisement placed by the Finlay Brothers in the *Federal Gazette and Baltimore Daily Advertiser* of 24 Oct. 1803 lists for sale, among many other articles of furniture, "window and recess seats."

MATERIALS: Maple (legs, stiles, medial brace), tulip wood (seat rails, arm/crest rails); painted black with polychrome and gilt and bronze decoration. Restored feet. Cane seat (not original)
PROVENANCE: William Buchanan, Baltimore; the Misses Sydney and Margaret Buchanan; by descent to Ulric O. Hutton, Brinklow
EXHIBITIONS: Bibl. 27, p. 30, no. 7, ill.

41. SETTEE (1814–1815)

Baltimore
Maker: Thomas Renshaw; Ornamenter: John Barnhart
35⅜ × 75⅞ × 23⅜ in. (89.9 × 192.8 × 59.4 cm.)
seat h.: 17¼ in. (43.8 cm.); seat d.: 20⅝ in. (52.4 cm.)
The Baltimore Museum of Art: Purchased as the gift of Robert G. Merrick, Mrs. D'Arcy Paul, J. Gilman D'Arcy Paul, Mrs. Alvin Thalheimer, and Mrs. Miles White, Jr. (BMA 1950.51)

This caned, four-back settee is to date the only known piece of Baltimore painted furniture marked with the names of both its maker and ornamenter. Printed in black letters across the stay rails of the two center backs is THoˢs RENSHAW Nᵒ 37. Sᵗ Gay Sᵗ Baltᵉ John Barnhart Ornamenter. Two matching side chairs are in the Museum's collection. Because Baltimore painted furniture was usually made en suite, the three pieces must have originally been part of a larger set. In the city directories Renshaw is listed at 37 South Gay Street for only 1814 and 1815.[1] Born in Harford County about 1780, he was working as a Windsor chair

maker in Georgetown, D.C. in 1801, and as a cabinetmaker in Baltimore by 1811 before moving to Chillicothe, Ohio in 1816.[2] Less is known about Barnhart, who is listed for 1822–1823, 1824, and 1827 in the Baltimore City Directories at York Avenue (Old Town) as a letterer and sign painter, and in 1829 as an "ornamental painter." This settee and its matching side chairs are interesting and important documents although they do not represent the highest quality of Baltimore painted furniture. The more sophisticated work by the brothers Finlay and their close followers (see cat. nos. 29, 39, and 121) represent the finest achievements, while the Renshaw-Barnhart settee is a more common example of painted furniture, based on the Sheraton fancy-chair traditions being produced elsewhere in early nineteenth-century America. A painted settee and an armchair belonging to the Maryland Historical Society,[3] four other side chairs owned by the Museum (BMA 1970.29a–d), and an armchair at Winterthur are among the numerous pieces of painted furniture probably produced during Renshaw and Barnhart's brief joint venture.[4]

Although John Barnhart is recorded as the settee's ornamenter, it is doubtful that he painted the four romantic landscape panels on the crest rail, whose finished quality contrasts sharply with the rather coarse sawtooth gilt decoration. Once the settee was completed and decorated, a landscape artist like Baltimore's Dutch-born Cornelius de Beet (ca. 1772–1840) would have been called in to add the final touches. De Beet's name appears in the city directories from 1810 to 1840 as variously fancy painter, painter, and ornamental painter.[5] He was as well an artist in the academic tradition; one of his still lifes is in the Museum's collection (BMA 1961.37).[6] He is also known to have worked for a while with John and Hugh Finlay "ornamenting Windsor chairs," and may well be responsible for

many landscape views on Baltimore painted furniture, whether made by the Finlays, Renshaw, or in other Baltimore shops.[7]

NOTES:
1. Bibl. 27, p. 121.
2. This and other information on Thomas Renshaw is found in bibl. 84, pp. 109–110 and 161.
3. Bibl. 84, p. 161, no. 122, ill. For more information on Barnhart, see pp. 109–110, no. 56.
4. Bibl. 56, p. 450, no. 454, ill.
5. Bibl. 27, p. 103.
6. Sona K. Johnston, *American Paintings, 1750–1900, from the Collection of The Baltimore Museum of Art* (The Baltimore Museum of Art, 1983), pp. 43–44, no. 25, ill. p. 44.
7. Bibl. 27, p. 12.

MATERIALS: Maple (arms, legs, stretchers), tulip wood (crest, tablets), walnut (seat and stay rails, seat cross braces); painted a putty color with polychrome and gilt and bronze decoration. Cane seat (not original)

PROVENANCE: Mrs. Rush Sturges; BMA, by purchase, 1950

EXHIBITIONS: Bibl. 27, pp. 42–43, no. 20, ill. p. 43

REFERENCES: Zilla Rider Lea, ed., *The Ornamented Chair: Its Development in America (1700–1890)*, Rutland, Vermont: Charles E. Tuttle Co., 1960, p. 153, figs. 19 and 20; Wendell D. Garrett, Paul F. Norton, Allan Gowans, and Joseph T. Butler, *The Arts in America: The Nineteenth Century*, New York: Charles Scribner's Sons, 1969, p. 296, pl. 222; "In the museums," *Antiques*, Oct. 1959, p. 352, ill.

42. SOFA (1795–1810)

Baltimore
39¼ × 81 × 32¾ in. (99.7 × 205.8 × 83.2 cm.)
seat h.: 15½ in. (39.4 cm.); seat d.: 29¾ in. (75.6 cm.)
The Baltimore Museum of Art: Gift of Harry R. Slack IV and W. Cameron Slack, in Honor of Elizabeth Blanchard Randall Slack (BMA 1969.49)

Plate 24 in both the 1788 and 1794 editions of Hepplewhite's *Cabinet-Maker and Upholsterer's Guide* was a key design source for such sofas. The flowing design with continuous arms and crest was a striking change from boxier Chippendale-

42

style sofas where sides and back met at right angles. When the Baltimore cabinetmaking firm of Bankson and Lawson advertised "Cabriole and plain sofas," it was the term cabriole which they would have used to indicate the elegant lines of this sofa.[1] Cabriole as an adjective referred to the curved back, arms, and arm supports, and the continuous curved upholstered back. Such sofas were produced everywhere in the Federal period, but as a particular product of late eighteenth-century Baltimore, they survive in some number, displaying in their design an overall uniformity. Within this design standard there are some variations, as in this example which is upholstered over the seat rail, while two other fine examples, one at the Maryland Historical Society[2] and the other at Winterthur,[3] have half-upholstered front seat rails. The Winterthur example with a simple curved rather than serpentine curved back has, like the sofa at the Maryland Historical Society, a mahogany crest rail, while the Museum's sofa is upholstered over the crest rail. Only the mahogany arm rests and curved supports are exposed. The oval shell inlays at the top of the two end front legs are very like the shell inlaid into the center splat of a Maryland side chair (cat. no. 25). This sofa, given to the Museum by descendants of Brian Philpot of Baltimore, is said

42

to have been used at Stamford, his summer house on Mantua Mill Road in Baltimore County, now the Green Spring Valley Hounds. It has been re-upholstered in green haircloth, following the original brass nail pattern. The brass cup casters are restorations.

NOTES:
1. The advertisement from the *Maryland Journal* of 17 June 1788 is reprinted in Alfred Coxe Prime, *The Arts and Crafts in Philadelphia, Maryland and South Carolina, 1786–1800* (Topsfield, Massachusetts: The Walpole Society; vol. 1, 1929; vol. 2, 1932), vol. 2, p. 167.
2. Bibl. 84, p. 160, no. 121, ill. pp. 160 and 34, pl. XII.
3. Bibl. 56, p. 301, no. 266, ill. p. 302.
MATERIALS: Primary: mahogany, light and dark wood inlays. Secondary: walnut (front rail), tulip wood. Brass nails and casters (not original)
PROVENANCE: Brian Philpot (1750–1812), Baltimore; by descent to Elizabeth Blanchard Randall Slack; Harry R. Slack IV and W. Cameron Slack
EXHIBITIONS: Bibl. 4, p. 148, no. 95, ill. p. 149
REFERENCES: Bibl. 55, vol. 1, p. 308, no. 548, ill. p. 310

43. SOFA (1790–1810)

Mid-Atlantic states
38⅞ × 62¾ × 28⅝ in. (98.8 × 159.4 × 72.7 cm.)
seat h.: 15½ in. (39.4 cm.); seat d.: 24½ in. (62.3 cm.)
The Baltimore Museum of Art: Anonymous Gift (BMA 1981.206)

This sofa is a rare example of the cabriole form in a diminutive size. A comparison with the preceding entry reveals that this shorter version accommodates a beautifully proportioned arched, rather than serpentine, crest which is not upholstered over but finished with a molded rail. However, in order to maintain the symmetry so desired in neoclassical design, this small sofa has the same number of legs, four at the front and back, as the full size form. Its simple lines are enlivened by inlay on the front stiles and legs. An oval patera of branch grain mahogany on the outside stiles and the herringbone mahogany panel on the faces of all four front legs are surrounded with plain dark and

43

43

light wood stringing. Above the original brass ferrules and casters the legs have two bands that incorporate similar stringing. Nail shanks embedded below the crest molding indicate that the original upholstery would have had brass upholstery nail trim. Several plates in Hepplewhite's *Cabinet-Maker and Upholsterer's Guide* show the popularity of such trim as well as a smooth low seat such as is seen in cat. no. 42.[1] Twentieth-century reupholstering incorporating springs has caused this sofa's seat to be unusually high.

NOTES:
1. Bibl. 40, pls. 15, 21, 22, 24, and 27.

MATERIALS: Mahogany (legs, stiles), tulip wood (seat braces), maple (crest rail)

PROVENANCE: Joseph Kindig, Jr., Antiques, York, Pennsylvania; Private Collection, Baltimore

44. COUCH (1815–1825)
Baltimore
Maker: possibly attributed to the shop of William Camp
30⅞ × 89 × 25½ in. (78.5 × 226.1 × 64.8 cm.)
seat h.: 13⁵⁄₁₆ in. (33.8 cm.); seat d.: 25½ in. (64.8 cm.)
The Baltimore Museum of Art: Gift of Senator George L. Radcliffe (BMA 1972.75.1)

This furniture form in the early nineteenth century was known variously as a Grecian couch, sopha [sic], squab, settee, or lounge. It is an adaptation of a Roman banqueting couch prototype as interpreted in English design books such as Thomas Sheraton's *The Cabinet Dictionary* (London, 1803, pl. 50), and later in New York and Philadelphia price books. This couch from the Museum's collection is most likely one of a bookend-like reverse pair. That element of decoration most characteristic of Baltimore Empire-style furniture is the broad reeding that extends in a continuous sweep from the scrolled arms across the front seat rail. There is a pair of couches in the Maryland Historical Society, one couch each at the Peale Museum in Baltimore and in the collection of Yale University, and another couch whose present whereabouts is unknown, all virtually identical to the example in the Museum's collection.[1] The two couches at the Maryland Historical Society and the one which cannot at present be located, all share the same family provenance as the Museum's example. The above mentioned six Baltimore Empire couches are similar to another pair in the collection of the Maryland Historical Society which are documented to the Baltimore cabinetmaker William Camp by the original bill of sale dated 1818 from Camp to Jacob I. Cohen of Baltimore.[2] This pair of couches, however, differs slightly from the others in having reeding on the saber legs rather than carved acanthus leaves and lacks the carved rosettes on the scrolled ends. In all other respects, including construction, design, and measurements, all eight couches appear to be essentially the same. The ornate brass mounts seen on the Museum's couch and those matching it are found in rare instances on other Baltimore furniture of this period.[3]

NOTES:
1. Bibl. 84, p. 165, no. 128, ill.; bibl. 47, pp. 236–237, no. 222, ill.; bibl. 55, vol. I, p. 328, no. 581, ill. p. 330.
2. Bibl. 84, p. 164, no. 127, ill.
3. Bibl. 27, p. 72, no. 46, ill.

MATERIALS: Mahogany (back, face of arms, seat rails, legs), tulip wood and white pine (slip-seat frame, seat braces), oak (interior seat rails and stiles)

PROVENANCE: John McKim, Jr., Baltimore; David Telfaire McKim; Emilie McKim Reed; Elizabeth G. McIlvaine; Senator and Mrs. George L. Radcliffe

REFERENCES: Bibl. 84, p. 165, no. 128, n. 3

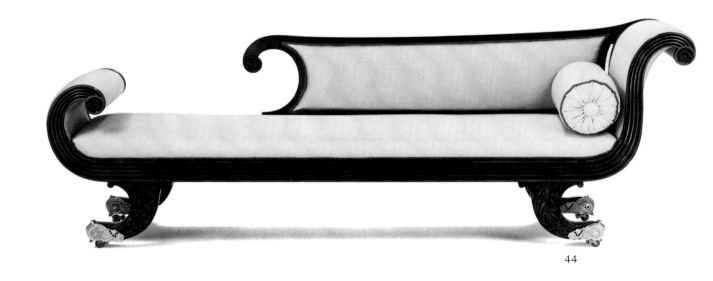

44

45

44

45

45. SOFA (1820–1840)

Mid-Atlantic states
32⅝ × 91½ × 27⅛ in. (82.9 × 232.5 × 68.9 cm.)
seat h.: 17 in. (43.2 cm.); seat d.: 24⅜ in. (61.9 cm.)
The Baltimore Museum of Art: Nelson and Juanita Greif
Gutman Collection, and Bequest of C. Edward Snyder,
by exchange (BMA 1976.46)

Although this sofa has no known Baltimore or Maryland provenance, it was purchased at auction in Baltimore County in 1976 and its secondary woods, tulip wood and yellow pine, indicate a mid-Atlantic origin. Examples of Baltimore and Philadelphia Empire-style furniture are often difficult to differentiate, and similar sofas could have also been made by Washington, D.C. and Georgetown cabinetmakers. The quality of the carving is unusual for the period; rather than being broad and flat, it is detailed and well modeled.[1] The design for the carved legs and paw feet could have been derived from designs of Thomas Hope or George Smith.[2] But the combination of motifs chosen for the carved decoration on the leg brackets is most distinctive: acanthus leaves and the head of an

eagle grasping in its beak two swags of ruffle-edged drapery. Detailed leaf carving also decorates the inset-paneled block where the arms meet the seat rail, the fronts of the Y-shaped scrolled arms, and the inset panels at each end of the crest rail.[3] When acquired by the Museum, the sofa was reupholstered in black haircloth. The bottom of the seat frame is not webbed but rather formed of two boards running lengthwise, supported by two medial braces. The rear face of the sofa back is similarly paneled with tulip wood but finished with an unpadded cover of haircloth.

NOTES:
1. For examples of other Baltimore Empire sofas of the same period and style, see bibl. 84, p. 167, no. 131, ill. and pp. 167–168, no. 132, ill.
2. Bibl. 43, pl. 41, no. 12 and bibl. 74, pl. 65.
3. For another sofa of possible Baltimore origin with similarly shaped arms, see bibl. 55, vol. 1, p. 336, no. 591, ill. p. 335.

MATERIALS: Primary: mahogany, mahogany veneers. Secondary: tulip wood and yellow pine (inner frame).
PROVENANCE: Richard Opfer, Auctioneer, Timonium, 1976; BMA, by purchase, 1976

46

46. SOFA (1850–1870)

New York
Maker: attributed to the shop of John Henry Belter
48¾ × 82¼ × 31½ in. (123.9 × 209 × 80 cm.)
seat h.: 11⅜ in. (28.9 cm.); seat d.: 26⅞ in. (68.3 cm.)
The Baltimore Museum of Art: Gift of Abram Moses,
in Memory of his Wife, Carrie Gutman Moses
(BMA 1953.225.1)

Elaborately carved and laminated furniture in the Rococo Revival style of the mid-nineteenth century has become almost synonymous with the name of John Henry Belter (1804–1863), a German immigrant craftsman who came to New York City and by 1844 was listed in city directories as a cabinetmaker with his own shop. Indeed, so widespread was the influence of the distinctive furniture style which Belter evolved that even in his own time, work in a similar vein by other cabinetmakers was known as "Belter furniture."[1] The pieces actually produced by Belter, however, are far superior in design and workmanship to contemporary imitations. Richness of detail and proficiency of technique distinguish his production. His virtuosity and command of technological innovation in furniture manufacture were noted by Dun and Company (predecessors of Dun and Bradstreet) who

recorded that Belter "Makes first rate work, too gd to be profit."[2]

While Belter's label states that he made "All Kinds of Fine Furniture," most surviving examples from his shop are parlor sets. His dining room, bedroom, and other furniture forms are rare.[3] New England and Philadelphia cabinetmakers also produced furniture in the Rococo Revival style but, by and large, their work is heavier and less refined than Belter's. Recent scholarship has attempted to define the characteristics of his furniture in an effort to distinguish it from the larger body of furniture in this style.[4] Belter made many sets of seating furniture using the same pattern but with slight variations in the carved motifs. Most of his furniture is laminated in very thin layers of veneer. Pierced and carved furniture in openwork "arabesques" incorporating naturalistic motifs such as acorns, grapes, flowers, and leaves within a sinuous framework reveals an ornamental concept of great inventiveness which Belter called "Arabasket." Belter received four patents protecting his innovative designs.[5] The most important was for a lamination process in spherical molds with successive layers of thin veneers applied at right angles to each other. Although Belter did produce some pieces of furniture which were not laminated, his most important work utilized this method of construction. Although threatened by patent infringements, his shop continued in business until 1867, four years after his death.

The Museum's pieces which include this sofa, a pair of meridiennes (cat. no. 47), and an armchair (cat. no. 35) are some of the finest examples extant attributed to Belter's shop. The laminated construction, and carved and pierced ornament all display the highest order of craftmanship. The armchair and meridiennes have seven-part laminations while the sofa has a five-part laminate. The several patterns represented here show an affinity in their carved motifs to other examples of Belter furniture in the Metropolitan Museum,[6] and in a private collection.[7] Since there are no known design books or catalogues from the Belter shop, the names of the designs are unknown. However, the forms and motifs are related to documented Belter furniture. The carved roses on the legs and the French feet are typical elements as are the grape clusters and the floral crest. The undulating skirts on the sofa and meridiennes (cat. no. 47) are richly decorated with a continuous line of floral ornament. The ruffled peanut-shaped shells, cabriole legs, and C-scrolls recall the eighteenth-century designs that inspired the Rococo Revival, while the exaggerated curves and realistic details reveal its nineteenth-century interpretation.[8] Variations in carved motifs and execution suggest that these pieces may have come from more than one set. The furniture was owned by Joel and Bertha Kayton Gutman who were married in 1852 and lived on Eutaw Place in Baltimore.

NOTES:
1. Ernst Hagen, "Personal Experiences of an Old Cabinet-maker, Brooklyn" (Oct. 1908), The Henry Francis du Pont Winterthur Museum, Joseph Downs Manuscript Collection, no. 75 x 80.37.
2. Bibl. 71, p. 36.
3. Bibl. 71, p. 35.
4. Bibl. 71, pp. 10–11, lists thirty-two conclusions concerning the characteristics of Belter furniture. See also Mary Ellen Martin, "German Influences on Mid-Nineteenth Century American Taste: The Cabinetmaker John Henry Belter as Case Study," Master's thesis presented at the Winterthur Museum 25th Annual Conference on German-American Culture, 1983.
5. David A. Hanks, *Innovative Furniture in America from 1800 to the Present* (New York: Horizon Press, 1981), pp. 52–55.
6. Bibl. 59, no. 125, ill.
7. Bibl. 71, p. 44, no. 8, ill.
8. Bibl. 71, pp. 24–36.

MATERIALS: Primary: rosewood (legs, stiles, arms, top crest ornament, facing on side and front seat rails), rosewood veneer (rear rail, front and back of five-layer laminant core of back). Secondary: ash (front and side seat rails), pine (rear seat rail), mahogany (medial seat brace)

PROVENANCE: Joel and Bertha Kayton Gutman, Baltimore; Carrie Gutman Moses (Mrs. Abram); Abram Moses

REFERENCES: Bibl. 63, p. 48

47. MERIDIENNE (1850–1870)

New York
Maker: attributed to the shop of John Henry Belter
34¾ × 37¼ × 27½ in. (88.3 × 94.7 × 69.9 cm.)
seat h.: 13 in. (33 cm.); seat d.: 21½ in. (54.6 cm.);
casters: 1¾ in. (4.4 cm.)
The Baltimore Museum of Art: Gift of Abram Moses, in Memory of his Wife, Carrie Gutman Moses (BMA 1953.225.2)

See discussion under cat. no. 46. Meridienne is a French term for a short couch or daybed having one arm and a partial back panel curving downward from the higher to the lower end.

MATERIALS: Primary: rosewood (legs, stiles, arm, facing side and front seat rails), rosewood veneer (rear rail, front and back of seven-layer laminant core of back). Secondary: ash (seat rails)

PROVENANCE: Joel and Bertha Kayton Gutman, Baltimore; Carrie Gutman Moses (Mrs. Abram); Abram Moses

REFERENCES: Bibl. 35, p. 216, fig. X-13

47

48

48. SOFA (1848)

New York
Maker: attributed to Burns and Trainque
Designer: attributed to Alexander Jackson Davis
47 × 78¼ × 26½ in. (119.4 × 198.8 × 67.3 cm.)
seat h.: 15½ in. (39.4 cm.); seat d.: 23½ in. (59.7 cm.)
The Baltimore Museum of Art: Decorative Arts Fund
(BMA 1985.16)

In 1845 the American architect Alexander Jackson Davis (1803–1892) designed a Gothic Revival house called Belmead for Phillip St. George Cocke of Powhatan County, Virginia.[1] The huge structure, which still stands on the James River about forty miles above Richmond, was finished by 1848, when the owner purchased this settee as part of a ten-piece parlor suite. As an architect and designer of interiors, Davis is known, from surviving drawings and sketches in his hand, to have designed furniture in the Gothic style.[2] In the case of the design for the Belmead parlour suite, the extent of his involvement is not precisely known. However, in May 1848 Davis and Cocke met in New York with the cabinetmaker William Burns (1805?–1867), and since Davis charged Cocke for his time it suggests that he consulted on the furniture designs.[3] Although the overall shape and leg turnings of the two settees and eight chairs of the original suite have been called atypical of Davis' designs,[4] "the pierced trefoil brackets under the seat rails, spiraling leafage in the crestings, and other foliate details are reminiscent of Davis' usage."[5] William Burns came to New York from Scotland in 1833. From 1842–1856 he was in partnership with Peter Trainque, with his brother Thomas Burns from 1857–1859, and in business alone from then until 1866. Andrew Jackson Downing praised the firm of Burns and Trainque, whose large shop on Broadway employed as many as eighteen workers, as the makers of the most "correct Gothic furniture" in America.[6] English design sources for the sofa, particularly for the Gothic leg braces, can be found in Ackermann's *Repository of the Arts* (London, 1817). But the most influential source would seem to be Richard Bridgens, who illustrated an upholstered Gothic chair that is very much like the settees and chairs from Belmead.[7] All share wide flattened Tudor-arch shaped crest rails on their backs with carved foliate corbels at the sides;

turned and ringed legs; pendants beneath the lower back rail; and raised moldings at the top and bottom of the seat rails. It has been suggested that Davis wished to parallel in this set of parlor furniture some of the exterior architectural elements on the façade of Belmead.[8]

The settee has been repaired, refinished, and reupholstered. There is a veneer restoration of seven inches on the front and back of the left end of the crest rail. The original frame is intact. The vertical braces of the back have been restored to their original location as have the two inside medial seat braces. The front casters have been replaced.

NOTES:
1. See Roger Hale Newton, *Town and Davis: Architects* (New York: Columbia University Press, 1942), pp. 270–272 for a discussion of Belmead.
2. Bibl. 23, pp. 1014–1027; fig. 1, p. 1014; fig. 2, p. 1016; figs. 12 and 13, p. 1025; fig. 14, p. 1026; and fig. 16, p. 1027.
3. *Day Book*, vol. 1, Alexander Jackson Davis Papers, New York Public Library, New York, p. 361.
4. The other settee is in the Museum of Fine Arts, Boston; other chairs from the set are at present in the New York State Museum at Albany, The High Museum of Art in Atlanta, The Metropolitan Museum of Art, The St. Louis Art Museum, the Virginia Museum of Fine Arts, and the Indianapolis Museum of Art. For a discussion and illustration of a chair from the set, see John L. Scherer, *New York Furniture at the New York State Museum* (Old Town Alexandria, Virginia: Highland House Publishers, 1984), p. 132, no. 130, ill. p. 133.
5. Bibl. 23, p. 1021.
6. Andrew Jackson Downing, *The Architecture of Country Houses* (New York: D. Appleton and Co., 1850), p. 440.
7. Richard Bridgens, *Furniture with Candelabra and Interior Decorations Designed by R. Bridgens* (London: 1838).
8. Lynn E. Springer, *American Furniture, The St. Louis Art Museum Bulletin*, Summer 1980, p. 33.

MATERIALS: Primary: rosewood, rosewood veneers. Secondary: ash (front and side seat rails), chestnut (rear seat rail). Front casters (not original)

PROVENANCE: Philip St. George Cocke, Belmead, Powhatan County, Virginia; John Bowdoin Cocke; Lucy Hamilton Cocke Elliott; John Page Elliott, Charlottesville, Virginia; Ramon Osuna, Washington, D.C.; David A. Hanks, New York; Peter Hill, Inc., East Lempster, New Hampshire; BMA, by purchase, 1985

REFERENCES: Bibl. 23, p. 1021

48

Case Furniture

49. HIGH CHEST (1733–1739)

Boston
Japanner: Robert Davis
68 1/16 × 43 3/4 × 24 1/2 in. (172.9 × 111.2 × 62.3 cm.)
The Baltimore Museum of Art: Purchased as the gift of
Mr. and Mrs. Francis C. Taliaferro, in Memory of Mr.
and Mrs. Austin McLanahan (BMA 1970.37.4)

Robert Davis (working ca. 1733–d. 1739) is one of
only two Boston japanners whose work decorating
high chests is documented. William Randle (working 1715–1733), his father-in-law and one-time
partner, is the other; his work is known through
a William and Mary-style chest descended in the
family of John and Abigail Adams.[1] Since Randle's
initials also appear next to Davis' signature on this
high chest, he probably had some part in its decoration. One theory suggests that Robert Davis
received his training in London as no record of his
birth can be located in Boston. A Robert Davis was
bound as an apprentice on January 7, 1710, to the
London Painter-Stainers Company, and if this is
the same Robert Davis he may have emigrated to
this country after 1717, following the usual seven-
year apprenticeship. The first verified date for
Davis' presence in Boston is his 1735 marriage to
Elizabeth Randle; however, the dual inscription on
this chest may indicate that Davis was working
with William Randle before 1735, since by 1733
Randle had become an innkeeper. At the time of
his death in 1739, Davis had an apprentice, Stephen
Whiting, who traded in japanned goods until 1773.[2]

William Randle can be associated with at least
two cabinetmakers: Nathaniel Holmes (working
1725–1740) who paid Randle to decorate a high
chest and dressing table in 1734, and John Scottow
(ca. 1701–1790) for whom he decorated a dressing
table, signing both his own and Scottow's name
on the back.[3] Although Davis probably continued
to decorate cases for the same makers as his former
partner Randle, no documentation exists.[4]

The Museum's high chest is most closely allied
to one in the Museum of Fine Arts, Boston.[5] Both
have an intricately molded flat pediment contain-

49

ing a shallow drawer fronted by the deeply coved
section. Below the cornice drawer are ten more
drawers. The shallow center drawer of the Boston
example's base section has a shaped apron arching
higher underneath it, while the Museum chest's
center drawer is the same height as its flanking
drawers, as are the arches in the apron. The blocked
area of the center drawer is decorated with an
inverted shell creating an umbrella-like design
unique in japanned furniture. The legs of both
chests are very upright cabrioles with knee brackets
formed by cutting a "C" on the inside of the knee
itself and adding a small lobe which is glued to
the case. The flat pad feet overhang the thick
cylindrical disks on all sides. The front legs are
angled following the point created by the junction

of the case sides and front, the rear legs point to the side, and on this piece the foot has a medial ridge. The variations in the japanned decoration of the two chests make clear the point that similarity of cases is not a reliable indicator of who the japanner was. Designs for japanned decoration were drawn from published sources known to all in the craft.[6] In his interpretation of these designs, Davis exhibited a fluent, lightly drawn style but employed fairly simplistic elements that are not skillfully related to each other. In his work there is a fanciful disregard for proportion and little integration with the flat background elements.

The surface of the Museum's chest is heavily crazed and a nineteenth-century coat of black paint once obscured all but the raised figures. Conservation treatment has revealed that originally there had been little decoration between the raised gilded areas.[7] Davis' style as established by this piece can be found on seven other high chests.[8] The case itself is in good condition, although the skirt originally had two pendants. The divider between the bottom and fourth drawer of the chest's top section, the one bearing Davis' signature and Randle's initials, was inverted in the eighteenth or early nineteenth century as the result of the drawer side wearing a deep channel. The lack of a lock mortise in the original underside of the divider indicates that the lock in the bottom drawer was installed when the inversion was done. The lock is similar, if not identical, to the earlier hardware. The chest has a history of ownership in the Harkness family of the North Shore of Massachusetts and Portland, Maine.

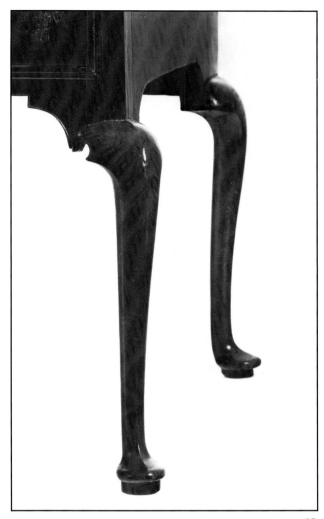

49

NOTES:
1. Richard H. Randall, Jr., "William Randall, Boston japanner," *Antiques*, May 1974, p. 1127.
2. Bibl. 68, p. 1090, n. 3 and n. 11.
3. Bibl. 68, p. 1088. The Scottow dressing table, now stripped of its decoration, was advertised in *Antiques*, Feb. 1984, p. 312.
4. Davis is known to have japanned a clock case for William Claggett, a Newport clockmaker. A complete discussion of William Claggett and the Davis-signed japanned tall case clock is found in Robert P. Emlen, "A masterful William Claggett clock," *Antiques*, Sept. 1980, pp. 502–507.
5. Bibl. 66, pp. 66–68, no. 52, ill.
6. Dean A. Fales, "Boston Japanned Furniture," in bibl. 85, p. 57, n. 9.
7. The 1971 conservation report of Thorp Brothers, Inc., is in the Museum's Registration files.
8. Seven chests attributed to Robert Davis and/or Stephen Whiting are discussed at length in bibl. 46, p. 199. Davis' signature found on the Claggett tall clock mentioned above is of little help in identifying his style because of extensive overpainting in the late nineteenth century.

MATERIALS: Primary: maple (drawer fronts, stiles, legs, base apron, moldings). Secondary: white pine; painted black with gesso, gold leaf, and gilt decoration. Three replaced bails

PROVENANCE: Harkness family of Marblehead, Massachusetts; by descent to John Harkness, Hamilton, Massachusetts; Roland Hammond, Antiques, North Andover, Massachusetts; BMA, by purchase, 1970

REFERENCES: William Voss Elder III, "Japanned High Chest Restored Successfully," *BMA Record*, Nov. 1972, cover and p. 2, ill.; Ruth Davidson, "Museum accessions," *Antiques*, June 1973, p. 1070, ill.; bibl. 68, pp. 1082–1091, pl. I, p. 1089; Dean A. Fales, "Boston Japanned Furniture," in bibl. 85, pp. 49–75, fig. 35, p. 52; Dean A. Fales, "American Painted Furniture, 1660–1880," *Antiques*, Mar. 1972, p. 514, ill.; bibl. 46, pp. 197–201, no. 36, ill.

50

Annapolis
96⅜ × 44½ × 24¾ in. (244.9 × 113.1 × 62.9 cm.)
case h.: 91⅛ in. (231.5 cm.)
The Baltimore Museum of Art: Gift of a Group of Friends
in Memory of Howard Sill (BMA 1929.13.1)

When Howard Sill, one of Maryland's earliest collectors, acquired this high chest of drawers in the opening years of this century, he probably thought that it was Philadelphia in origin.[1] It was not until the landmark exhibition of *Baltimore Furniture*, held in 1947 at The Baltimore Museum of Art, that Chippendale-style furniture produced in Maryland before and shortly after the Revolution was definitively identified.[2] This beautifully proportioned piece found by Sill near Chestertown on Maryland's Eastern Shore, is perhaps the perfect "textbook" example of the Maryland Chippendale style in this particular form. Chippendale furniture, produced in eighteenth-century Baltimore or Annapolis and influenced by the more cosmopolitan style of nearby Philadelphia, is usually less elaborate than its Philadelphia counterpart but nonetheless exhibits in its design, construction, and decoration certain broad regional characteristics.[3]

The Museum's high chest combines most of these characteristics. Its tall attenuated form differs from the usually broader and squatter Philadelphia examples. Rather than fluted corner columns the front corners of the top and bottom sections are chamfered and fluted and terminate in a lamb's tongue. The broken scroll pediment of the top is also higher than those commonly found on Philadelphia high chests. Additional Maryland characteristics are the carved shell pendant from the scalloped skirt of the base, as well as the extended acanthus-leaf carvings on the knees of each cabriole leg. The pendant shell and the shell on the center top drawer are closely related and, although not duplicates, were certainly carved by the same hand.[4] Leaf, tendril, and floral carvings flank the carved shell on the top drawer. The four-petaled flower is a design element peculiar to carving on other Maryland pieces with Annapolis provenances.[5]

From about 1765 to 1780 there had been an intense period of building in Annapolis. The exceptional late Georgian town houses that still dominate the Annapolis cityscape all date from about 1765 to 1780. They are the work of such builder-architects as William Buckland, William Noke, and Joseph Horatio Anderson. As a consequence of this building boom, an exceptional group

Fig. 50a. Carved shell from center of architrave, Abbey or Ringgold House.

50

50

of craftsmen, among them carvers who could turn their talents to carved decoration on furniture, were at this time in Annapolis. However, furniture production was still limited when compared with Philadelphia and other more populous Northern cabinetmaking centers. (The population of Annapolis on the eve of the Revolution numbered less than 1,500 persons.) Identifiable pieces of Annapolis Chippendale furniture, discounting the transitional work of John Shaw, still number fewer than a dozen.[6]

The applied openwork shell motif above the center top drawer is related to similarly carved shell decoration on two interior architraves of a room from the Abbey or Ringgold House in Chestertown, now installed in The Baltimore Museum of Art (fig. 50a).[7] The carved blossoms on the scroll ends of the pediment of this high chest are original but the three finials, as well as the plinths for the two side finials, are restorations. The front board of the pediment is tenoned into the front stiles and supported from behind by two vertical braces. There are full dustboards between the drawers of the top case. The tongue and groove backboards of this top section are horizontally applied, and nailed into the rabbeted edges of the case sides. The top boards of the base run front to back and are also tongue and groove. The back of the lower case is of one board tenoned into the rear stiles. Each of the rather squared ball-and-claw feet has an unusual notching on the back of its ankle above the rear claw.[8] Most of the brass hardware is original.

NOTES:
1. Howard Sill (1867–1927), Baltimore architect, antiquarian, collector, and co-author, with J. Hall Pleasants of *Maryland Silversmiths, 1715–1830* (Baltimore: Lord Baltimore Press, 1930).
2. See bibl. 4.
3. In bibl. 9, Luke Beckerdite points out that many of these Maryland characteristics can either singly or in combined form be found in some dressing tables and high chests of drawers made in Philadelphia.
4. A dressing table in the Bayou Bend Collection, Houston, has an almost identically carved pendant shell. The scalloping of its front and side skirts is the same as that found on the Museum's high chest. Were it not for the

fact that the high chest has chamfered corners in both sections and the dressing table quarter-round columns, the two pieces could have been made to match. Bibl. 83, p. 61, no. 120, ill.

5. For other examples, see bibl. 4, p. 175, no. 112, ill. and p. 180, no. 117, ill.; bibl. 29, p. 33, no. 17, ill. and p. 36, no. 20, ill.

6. Bibl. 30.

7. The Abbey or Ringgold House originally dates from about 1743; however, before the Revolution Thomas Ringgold, Sr. installed a fashionable late Georgian interior in the house. When the woodwork was taken down in 1932, the cipher WB and the date 1771 were found on the reverse side of one of the panels. Long thought to be the initials of the Annapolis architect William Buckland (1734–1774), Luke Beckerdite in his article "William Buckland Reconsidered: Architectural Carving in Chesapeake Maryland, 1771–1774" (*Journal of Early Southern Decorative Arts*, Nov. 1982, pp. 72–76) questioned the Buckland attribution. The letters WB are now thought to be the initials of an unknown craftsman, perhaps a carpenter-joiner. Beckerdite's subsequent research strongly suggests Hercules Courtenay (1744?–1784) of Philadelphia as the probable carver of the elaborate architraves over the doorways and the overmantel woodwork.

8. The dressing table at Bayou Bend displays the same notching on its ball-and-claw feet.

MATERIALS: Primary: mahogany. Secondary: yellow pine, tulip wood, sweet gum. Brass hardware (some not original)

PROVENANCE: Howard Sill, Baltimore; Mary Frances DuVal Sill (Mrs. Howard); BMA, by purchase, 1929

EXHIBITIONS: Bibl. 4, p. 186, no. 124, ill. p. 187; bibl. 29, p. 82, no. 58, ill. pp. 82–83; bibl. 12, p. 117, no. 101, ill.; bibl. 11, p. 68, no. 52, ill.

REFERENCES: Bibl. 55, vol. 1, p. 378, no. 662, ill. p. 377; "In the museums," *Antiques*, Oct. 1959, p. 352, ill.; bibl. 28, p. 358, pl. I, p. 356

51

51. HIGH CHEST (1760–1780)

Maryland, possibly Baltimore
89⅜ × 43 × 24¾ in. (227.1 × 109.3 × 62.9 cm.)
The Baltimore Museum of Art: Gift of Charles Ellis Ellicott, Jr. and Family (BMA 1968.10)

When this high chest of drawers was presented to the Museum in 1968 by Charles Ellis Ellicott, Jr. and family, it was stated that the piece had been in his family "for at least 160 years, having been owned by Thomas Ellicott (1777–1859) at or shortly after his marriage in 1806."[1] Thomas Ellicott was the son of Andrew Ellicott who came to Maryland with his brother from Bucks County, Pennsylvania in 1774 and built mills on the Patapsco River above Elkridge Landing at what would come to be known as Ellicott City. Also in the collection is a William and Mary daybed of Pennsylvania origin (cat. no. 37) that the Ellicott family could have brought from Pennsylvania to Maryland. While this high chest could have been produced in Pennsylvania on the eve of their departure, it is more likely that it is of Maryland, probably Baltimore, manufacture. The Ellicott brothers, with successful business ventures in Baltimore, would have chosen a local source for such an important piece of furniture. The known dressing tables and high chests in private and public collections thought to be of Maryland (Baltimore or Annapolis) rather than Philadelphia origin have shared design characteristics rather than closely related carved decoration. (These characteristics have been outlined in the previous entry.) Those present in this piece are its tall rather attenuated form, high double-scroll pediment, fluted and chamfered front corners in both top and bottom sections, pendant shell suspended from the scalloped skirt of the base, and deep acanthus-leaf carving on the knees of the cabriole legs. The seven-lobed shell on the top center drawer is more three-dimensional than the flatly carved five-lobed pendant shell.[2] Identical pinprick stippled decoration is found at the base of each shell and as a background edge around the top shell. The leaf carving flanking the shell of the top drawer is partially restored.

The upper scrolled pediment is roofed with spaced covering boards nailed to the faceboard and to a correspondingly shaped backboard. The boards and intervening spaces were covered many years ago with a black waterproof canvas-like material. The dustboards between each drawer of the top section stop three inches short of the backboards. These horizontal backboards are tongued and grooved and nailed into rabbets on the rear edges of the side boards. There are no dustboards in the base section. Here the single backboard is tenoned into the stiles and secured with pins. Three of the brass pulls and plates are replicas of the original hardware. The original hardware on the right and left small bottom drawers in the base was cut for a key and moved up to align with newly installed drawer locks, probably in the late nineteenth century. The original post holes were neatly filled but are still easily discerned. When this high chest was acquired by the Museum, the rosettes on the scrolls of the pediment and the finials had been long missing. Those now adorning the piece are modern replacements based on designs of the period.

NOTES:
1. Letter of 9 Apr. 1968 in the Museum's files.
2. There is in a private collection a dressing table with an almost identically carved shell. The acanthus-leaf carvings on the knees of its cabriole legs are also closely related to those on this high chest of drawers (see bibl. 29, p. 71, no. 49, ill. pp. 70–71).

MATERIALS: Primary: mahogany. Secondary: tulip wood. Brass hardware (three not original)
PROVENANCE: Ellicott family of Ellicott City; by descent to Charles Ellis Ellicott, Jr., Baltimore
EXHIBITIONS: Bibl. 29, p. 84, no. 59, ill. pp. 84–85
REFERENCES: Bibl. 55, vol. 1, p. 372, no. 659, ill. p. 373

52. HIGH CHEST (1750–1785)

Maryland or Philadelphia
93¾ × 43¼ × 24 in. (238.2 × 109.9 × 61 cm.)
case h.: 89⅞ in. (228.4 cm.)
Collection of Dorothy McIlvain Scott, Baltimore: Promised Gift to The Baltimore Museum of Art

Lacking a known provenance and in design and construction not distinctly of Philadelphia origin, this high chest of drawers has been attributed to Maryland or Philadelphia. With the exception of its high bonnet top and attenuated shape, the other shared characteristics of Maryland high chests of drawers (i.e., those made in Baltimore or Annapolis in the Chippendale style as defined in cat. nos. 50 and 51) are not in evidence. The rather naive scalloped design of the base section contrasts with the competently carved shells and flanking leafy tendrils on the bottom and top center drawers. The same leaf carving with the addition of a floral rosette and medallion is found at the top of the upper case under the scroll pediment. Nail holes reveal that there was other carved ornament, now missing in the pediment. The applied carved floral rosettes on the scroll ends and the finials are original.

The back of the upper case is made up of three vertical lapped boards and set in a rabbet in the sides of the case. The top of the upper case is dovetailed into the sides. The scroll pediment has a conforming backboard and is strengthened from behind by three braces with chamfered edges. The drawers of the top section are divided by full dustboards. The backboard of the base section is composed of two horizontally placed boards tenoned into the rear stiles. While the dustboards of the top section are yellow pine, those of the base are mahogany.

52

MATERIALS: Primary: mahogany. Secondary: yellow pine (top section dustboards, backboards, drawers), tulip wood (stops for top center drawer only), mahogany (bottom section dustboards). Brass hardware (not original)

PROVENANCE: David Stockwell, Inc., Wilmington, Delaware, 1973; Dorothy McIlvain Scott, Baltimore

53. HIGH CHEST (1760–1780)

Boston area
95⅛ × 41¼ × 22⅛ in. (241.7 × 104.8 × 562 cm.)
case h.: 87⅛ in. (221.4 cm.)
Collection of Dorothy McIlvain Scott, Baltimore: Promised Gift to The Baltimore Museum of Art

This pedimented high chest displays the design vocabulary characteristic of New England interpretations of the form: a five-tier upper case, a four-drawer lower case, and a flat-arched skirt with pendant drops.[1] The relatively plain façade, spare lines, and controlled proportions also are typically New England, and it also has the two shell drawers usually found on other regional examples. On this piece, however, the drawers are richly carved and given further emphasis by the lack of carved decoration elsewhere. The abbreviated lobate shells above scrolled and floral ornament within a punch-

52

53

work reserve are the work of an unidentified carver. Similar intricately carved shells have been found on a number of pieces of furniture associated with the Boston area, although the majority of these appear to be by a different hand.[2] It has been suggested that the carved shells on the Museum's high chest relate to those found on furniture from the shop of the cabinetmaker Benjamin Frothingham (1734–1809) of Charlestown, Massachusetts.[3] A comparison of the shells on Frothingham pieces as well as an analysis of their stylistic and construction details reveals insufficient evidence to support this attribution, however. Unusual features of the high chest include the slightly notched knee brackets and the dimensions of the rear legs and ball-and-claw feet which are shorter and smaller in circumference than the two front legs. Whether these legs are replacements is difficult to determine since the case shows no signs of manipulation.

NOTES:
1. Bibl. 46, p. 208.
2. Richard H. Randall, Jr., "Benjamin Frothingham," in bibl. 85, p. 241.
3. For additional information about Frothingham, see Dexter Edwin Spalding, "Benjⁿ Frothingham of Charlestown, Cabinetmaker and Soldier," *Antiques*, Dec. 1928, pp. 536–537; Mabel Munson Swan, "Major Benjamin Frothingham, cabinetmaker," *Antiques*, Nov. 1952, pp. 392–395; bibl. 85, pp. 223–249.

MATERIALS: Primary: mahogany. Secondary: white pine
PROVENANCE: David Stockwell, Inc., Wilmington, Delaware, 1971; Dorothy McIlvain Scott, Baltimore
REFERENCES: *Antiques*, May 1966, p. 615

53

54

54. CHEST-ON-CHEST (1770–1790)

Norwich, Connecticut area
95⅞ × 46 × 23⅜ in. (243.6 × 116.9 × 59.4 cm.)
case h.: 86¼ in. (219.2 cm.)
Collection of Dorothy McIlvain Scott, Baltimore: Promised
Gift to The Baltimore Museum of Art

This large chest-on-chest now believed to have been made in Norwich about 1780 is one of the finest examples of surviving late eighteenth-century Connecticut furniture. Certain design elements such as the blocked drawer fronts of both the top and bottom sections, the fluted pilasters and carved Corinthian capitals at each side of the drawers of the top section, the scroll pediment, a top center drawer with fan carving, corkscrew flame finials mounted on plinths, the beautifully carved shells on the top drawer front of the bottom section, as well as the cabriole ball-and-claw feet are all derived from Massachusetts and Rhode Island furniture of the period. The piece combines a Boston-type pediment with a Newport-type front for example. Yet its diverse features are put together in such a way as to make the piece both successful in design and of distinctly Connecticut origin. The lower section is essentially a typical Connecticut form: a chest of three block-and-shell drawers on cabriole legs with scrolled skirt. Two other similar examples of this type of chest-on-chest are known. In the late nineteenth century H. Eugene Bolles (1838–1910), one of America's pioneer collectors, had acquired this piece from a Jonathan George Washington Trumbull of Norwich, Connecticut. His father, and possible first owner of the piece, was David Trumbull (1751–1822) of Lebanon, Connecticut. This chest-on-chest is one of four pieces of furniture, related in design and believed to have been made in Norwich, that have descended in the Trumbull family.[1]

The four related pieces of furniture made by a still unidentified cabinetmaker consist of this chest-on-chest, a four-drawer blocked chest of drawers, a marble-topped serving table, and a candle stand.[2] The same wave-and-scroll motif of the table's skirt is repeated in the front skirts of the chest-on-chest and the chest of drawers. The webbed ball-and-claw feet of the four pieces are closely related in design and similarly carved. In the manner of their carving the Corinthian capitals of the quarter columns on the chest of drawers are very like the capitals on the pilasters of the chest-on-chest's top section as well as the carved capital of the fluted pillar on the candle stand.[3] The backboard of the chest-on-chest's top section is one very wide board

54

54

54

dovetailed to the side with a separate single board backing the pediment. One board also forms the backing for the base section, but in this instance its side edges are chamfered and it is slotted into the sides. The top of the lower case section is dovetailed to the sides. The four cabriole legs are square-tenoned into the base. Overall the chest is in outstanding condition, even retaining its original finials and hardware, with the possible exception of the small pulls on the carved drawer front.

NOTES:
1. Bibl. 58, p. 48.
2. Bibl. 50, pp. 524–529; p. 525, figs. 2 and 3; p. 526, fig. 4; p. 527, fig. 5.
3. For information on the Trumbull family, see Robert F. Trent, "Legacy of a Provincial Elite: New London County Joined Chairs, 1720–1790," *The Connecticut Historical Society Bulletin*, Fall 1985, pp. 16–17.

MATERIALS: Primary: cherry. Secondary: white pine (case top, back, and bottom, drawer rails, drawer bodies). Small pulls may be restorations.

PROVENANCE: Trumbull family of Norwich, Connecticut; David Trumbull (1751–1822), Lebanon, Connecticut; Jonathan George Washington Trumbull (1789–1853) married Jane Eliza Lathrop (1795–1843) of Norwich, daughter of Daniel Lathrop (1769–1825); H. Eugene Bolles (1838–1910), Boston; The Metropolitan Museum of Art, New York, 1909–1948; Miss Ima Hogg, Bayou Bend Collection, Houston,

1948–1965; Israel Sack, Inc., New York; Dorothy McIlvain Scott, Baltimore, 1980

EXHIBITIONS: John T. Kirk, Wadsworth Atheneum, *Connecticut Furniture, Seventeenth and Eighteenth Centuries*, 1967, p. 62, no. 104, ill.; bibl. 58, p. 48, no. 48, ill.

REFERENCES: Bibl. 52, 1926, pp. 117–119, fig. 116; Wallace Nutting, *Furniture Treasury*, 3 vols., Framingham, Massachusetts: Old America Co., vol. 1, 1928, no. 323, ill.; bibl. 55, vol. 1, p. 356, no. 624, ill. p. 355; bibl. 2, vol. 5, p. 1121, no. P2270, ill.; *Antiques*, Mar. 1966, inside front cover; bibl. 50, pp. 524–529, fig. 4, p. 526; John T. Kirk, *Early American Furniture*, New York: Alfred A. Knopf, 1970, pp. 107 and 110, no. 89, ill. p. 107

55

55. CHEST-ON-CHEST (1785–1800)

Newburyport, Massachusetts area
86½ × 44½ × 21¾ in. (219.8 × 113.1 × 55.3 cm.)
case h.: 82¾ in. (210.3 cm.)
The Baltimore Museum of Art: Friends of the American
Wing Fund (BMA 1984.48)

In design this bonnet-top, oxbow-front chest-on-chest is closely related to documented examples made in Newburyport, Massachusetts. The Newburyport Public Library owns a number of pieces of furniture made by local cabinetmaker Abner Toppan (1764–1836) for the Bannister family in 1795, of which two, a mahogany desk-and-bookcase and a chest-on-chest, are like the Museum's piece.[1] The base sections of all three have an oxbow-shaped top drawer above three serpentine drawers. On each chest the molded swan's neck scrolls of the pediment end in applied pinwheels. In addition, the Museum's chest-on-chest and the Newburyport Library desk-and-bookcase both have a carved pinwheel below the central plinth. The ogee bracket feet, the pilasters, and capitals of the top sections, and the carved urn-and-flame finials of all three pieces are also similar. The Library's pieces (firmly documented as the work of Abner Toppan in 1795) as well as a desk made by Toppan for William Little in 1795, are in the Chippendale style and illustrate the fact that furniture in this style was made in Newburyport after the Revolution and even into the nineteenth century.[2] While this chest seems to be associated with Toppan's work, some variant construction features indicate that it is probably not a product of his shop. Most important among these is the lack of the giant dovetail used to attach the front base molding to the case bottom.

55

Here the upper strip of base molding is glued and nailed on top of the bottom board. A desk-and-bookcase (cat. no. 78) with many of the same design elements of this chest-on-chest is attributed to Toppan because it shares the construction features with the Newburyport Library pieces which this chest lacks. There are indications that sometime in the past this chest may have been painted white; the present finish is recent. The original brasses have had some small repairs. The initials SRB are painted in gray letters eight inches high on the backboards of the upper case.

NOTES:
1. Bibl. 80, pp. 224–225, figs. 6, 7, and 10.
2. Dexter Edwin Spalding, "Abner Toppan, Cabinet-maker," *Antiques*, June 1929, p. 493, fig. 1.

MATERIALS: Primary: mahogany. Secondary: white pine. Ring pull (not original)

PROVENANCE: Sotheby's, New York, 1983; C.L. Prickett, Inc., Yardley, Pennsylvania; BMA, by purchase, 1984

REFERENCES: *Important American Furniture, Folk Art and Related Decorative Arts*, sale cat., Sotheby's, New York, 21 and 22 Oct. 1983, sale no. 5094, lot 308, ill.; *Antiques*, Jan. 1984, p. 31

56. CHEST-ON-CHEST (1760–1780)

Philadelphia
97¾ × 47 × 24 in. (248.4 × 119.4 × 61 cm.)
case h.: 91 1/16 in. (231.4 cm.)
Private Collection, Baltimore: Promised Gift to The Baltimore Museum of Art

In design this Philadelphia chest-on-chest follows the usual format employed by that city's cabinet-makers working in the pre-Revolutionary Chippendale style. The bottom of the two superimposed case pieces is mounted on ogee bracket feet; the front corners of both these pieces have inset fluted quarter columns; there are three top drawers, the center of which is carved with a shell and flanking leafy sprigs; the scrolls of the pediment terminate in carved floral rosettes; an elaborately carved cartouche is mounted on a plinth between the scrolls; carved urns with flame finials are found on the front corners of the top. In this example there is some variation from the norm in the use of two half-width drawers rather than one full-width drawer at the top of the base section. The intaglio carving of the shell centered with a rosette in relief is related to the carved drawer on a dressing table in the collection of The Metropolitan Museum of Art.[1] In both cases leaves extend from the

56

56

sides of the rosette, overlaying the lower third of the shell itself. While the carving of the shells is closely related, that of the flanking tendrils is not. The upper and lower cases of this chest have full dustboards. The rabbeted horizontal backboards of both sections are nailed into rabbets cut into the side boards. The urn-and-flame finials appear to be original as do the pediment rosettes, although the exact age of the cartouche cannot be determined. The drawer fronts have suffered from many changes of hardware, particularly on the upper case.

NOTES:
1. Bibl. 39, pp. 251–252, no. 163, ill. pp. 251 and 350.
MATERIALS: Primary: mahogany. Secondary: tulip wood (dustboards, drawer bottoms), yellow pine (top, bottom, and back of case, drawer sides). Brass hardware (not original)
PROVENANCE: Joseph Kindig, Jr., Antiques, York, Pennsylvania; Private Collection, Baltimore

57. CHEST-ON-CHEST (1770–1780)

Philadelphia
90½ × 46¾ × 24¼ in. (230 × 118.8 × 61.6 cm.)
case h.: 86½ in. (219.8 cm.)
Collection of Dorothy McIlvain Scott, Baltimore: Promised Gift to The Baltimore Museum of Art

The drawer arrangement established in the Queen Anne period for Philadelphia or Pennsylvania chest-on-chests is perpetuated in this example in the Chippendale style, made ca. 1770–1780. The common format consisted of three small top drawers of equal width over two half-width drawers over three full-width drawers of graduated size, top to bottom, in the upper case, and three more full-width graduated drawers in the lower case. Here, to this basic chest-on-chest design, have been added a carved fret below the cornice, a carved latticework and scrolled pediment, and the central pediment ornament which is a carved and pierced basket of flowers. The result is the transformation of a straightforward chest-on-chest into an imposing and aesthetically pleasing piece of furniture. Such chest-on-chests, considered among the major productions of the Philadelphia cabinetmaker working in the Chippendale style, are represented in most major museum collections of American furniture.[1] Attributions are most often made to the cabinet-making shops of Thomas Affleck (1740–1795) with James Reynolds (ca. 1736–1794) as the possible carver. However, there is to date only one documented example, now owned by Colonial Williamsburg, of a Philadelphia chest-on-chest of this type known to have been made by Affleck.[2] Research on Reynolds' work has determined that the carved elements on the Museum example are indeed by his hand.[3] The pediment scrolls are enriched with rococo leaf carvings. The ends of the inner high-reaching, reverse-curve carved leaves were apparently broken off many years ago and any uneven ends neatly sawed off. Almost identically carved leaf motifs are found on a Philadelphia secretary-bookcase and an orrery owned by the University of Pennsylvania.[4] The carved frieze below the secretary-bookcase's cornice is also identical to that on the Museum's chest-on-chest.[5] However, without documentary evidence this chest-on-chest cannot be with assurance attributed to Thomas Affleck. So many Philadelphia cabinetmakers produced this furniture form in the last quarter of the eighteenth century, and skilled carvers like Reynolds were employed by more than one shop.

57

57

The back of the upper case is of three horizontal tongue and groove boards. Only two are used in the lower case, nailed in a rabbet to the sides and to the bottom board. Original full dustboards have been cut down to three-quarters size in the upper case. The solid mahogany faces of the drawer dividers are fitted in a groove cut in the case sides, not visible from the front. The lower case has full dustboards; the back is of two horizontal tongue and groove boards attached like those of the top section. The ogee bracket feet are original. The pierced latticework is attached to the pediment scrolls by screws and glue. The thin facing of the plinth supporting the carved basket and flowers may not be original. (Possibly the original was an applied carved half-round plinth like those found on many of the related pieces.)[6] Before the piece was sold at auction in 1982, brasses which matched those on another chest-on-chest owned by the E.W. Smiths (bibl. 44, pl. 140) were reproduced. Repairs were made to the central area of the carved basket and flowers.[7]

NOTES:
1. See bibl. 62, pp. 95–97, no. 76, ill. p. 96; bibl. 39, pp. 226–228, no. 147, ill.
2. Recent scholarship has determined that while Thomas Affleck was certainly the cabinetmaker responsible for the Williamsburg chest-on-chest, the elaborate carving of its scrolled pediment is not by James Reynolds, but by another, still unknown, master carver. Bibl. 44, pl. 123.

3. For a discussion of Reynolds, see Luke Beckerdite, "Philadelphia carving shops Part I: James Reynolds," *Antiques*, May 1984, pp. 1120–1133. Subsequent research has led to Beckerdite's conclusion that Reynolds was the carver of the BMA chest-on-chest.
4. Bibl. 44, pls. 95 and 126.
5. This same frieze design is found on two other pieces of furniture partially illustrated in bibl. 44, pls. 120 and 146.
6. Bibl. 39, pp. 226–228, no. 147, ill.; bibl. 83, p. 67, no. 131, ill.
7. A photograph of this chest-on-chest shows it with incorrect later hardware and the carved basket and flowers in fragmentary condition. Bibl. 44, pl. 148.

MATERIALS: Primary: mahogany, mahogany veneers. Secondary: tulip wood (drawer sides and backs, dustboards), yellow pine (back and bottom boards, tops of upper and lower cases, drawer dividers, pediment backboard, drawer bottoms). Brass handles (not original)

PROVENANCE: Wharton family of Philadelphia; Mr. and Mrs. Edward Wanton Smith, 1935; C.G. Sloan & Co., Inc., Washington, D.C., 1982; Dorothy McIlvain Scott, Baltimore

REFERENCES: Bibl. 44, pl. 148

58

58. DRESSING TABLE (1715–1730)

New England
29¾ × 34⅞ × 20⅞ in. (75.6 × 88.6 × 53 cm.)
The Baltimore Museum of Art: Purchased as the gift of Mr. and Mrs. Francis C. Taliaferro, in Memory of Mr. and Mrs. Austin McLanahan (BMA 1974.36)

William-and-Mary style dressing tables were made in numbers in the Boston area about 1720–1740, and more Massachusetts pieces survive than from other early eighteenth-century cabinetmaking centers such as New York or Philadelphia. The Mas-

sachusetts dressing tables share many characteristics—rich veneered tops, cases, and drawer fronts; ogee arches and scalloping on the front and side skirts further defined by an applied beading; trumpet or vase-shaped conically turned legs ending in ball feet with disk bases; the legs round-tenoned through the stretchers and feet; the four legs connected by crossed, angled double-serpentine stretchers with a finial as a tenon at the crossing; and two turned drops at the arched opening at the front skirt center. The dressing table in the Museum collection is quite similar in design to a dressing table now owned by the Society for the Preservation of New England Antiquities,[1] and also to a table in a private collection.[2] (The former table differs from the Museum example in that it has two rather than one tier of drawers.) Here the top is formed of two panels of mirror-image veneer, the whole framed by two herringbone borders with an intervening border of the same veneer as the central panel. There is an applied thumbnail molding on the front and side edges of the top which overhangs the case on all four sides and a double bead molding around the sides and bottoms of the drawer openings. Each drawer front is veneered with a herringbone veneer border. The case front is also veneered; however, the sides are of solid walnut. The drops and finial on the base stretcher appear to be original, but the drawer pulls are replacements.

NOTES:
1. Bibl. 46, pp. 180–183, no. 29, ill. p. 181.
2. Helen Comstock, "American furniture in the collection of Mr. and Mrs. Edward H. Tevriz," *Antiques*, Feb. 1966, p. 261, ill.

MATERIALS: Primary: walnut, walnut veneers. Secondary: white pine. Brass pulls (not original)

PROVENANCE: H.R. Sandor, Inc., New Hope, Pennsylvania; BMA, by purchase, 1974

59. DRESSING TABLE (1730–1770)

Philadelphia or Burlington, New Jersey area
28⅜ × 34⅛ × 20⅜ in. (72.1 × 86.7 × 51.8 cm.)
Collection of Dorothy McIlvain Scott, Baltimore: Promised Gift to The Baltimore Museum of Art

Notable for its pristine condition, this dressing table has a rich patina and a pleasingly unified form. While the overhanging top with molded edge and notched corners is common to many Philadelphia area dressing tables, the drawer arrangement varies from standard Philadelphia practice. Instead of one long drawer over three small drawers,

59

NOTES:
1. Bibl. 62, p. 25, no. 21.
2. Louis B. Wright, George B. Tatum, John W. McCoubrey, and Robert C. Smith, *The Arts in America: The Colonial Period* (New York: Charles Scribner's Sons, 1966), p. 266, pl. 189.

MATERIALS: Primary: black walnut. Secondary: tulip wood (drawer sides and backs), white pine (medial braces, inner framing members, drawer bottoms and runners). Brass handles (two not original)

PROVENANCE: Possibly Alexander and Anna Fox Chalmers, Philadelphia; Mary Chalmers and George Tallman, 22 Oct. 1766 (or 1765?); George Tallman II; George Tallman III; Catherine Tallman, Philadelphia and Washington, D.C.; Anna Hunt Tallman Hopkins, Washington, D.C.; Elizabeth Beall Hopkins Luttrell; Saidee Luttrell Cousins; Albert H. Cousins, Jr., Baltimore; Dorothy McIlvain Scott

60

here the two upper drawers are positioned over three small drawers, of which the center one is somewhat longer and shallower to accommodate the triple-arched shape of the central skirt. This design element is particularly successful in using the out-turned cusps as transitions to the flat-topped side arches. Some of the table's features—the squared cabriole legs with sharply pointed knees conforming to the angle of the case, the tight Spanish foot with crisp ankle moldings and knuckles, and the flat-topped arches on the skirt—reflect the influence of Boston cabinetmaking practices which filtered down to the Philadelphia area through trade between the cities, or the work of Boston-trained joiners.[1] It is known that Boston chairs with Spanish feet were imported to Philadelphia as early as 1742.[2]

While a number of related Delaware Valley dressing tables with Spanish feet are known, it is probable that this example belongs to the Philadelphia-Burlington school of cabinetry. An inscription on the back of the top right drawer, Mary Chalmers married to George Tallman/October 22, 1766, suggests that the table was acquired at the time of their marriage. It descended through six generations of Tallman family before purchase by the present owner (see also cat. no. 56). The legs, their cuffs, and squared Spanish feet are cut from one piece of wood. The stiles of the legs extend partially into the case and are secured by glue blocks.

60. DRESSING TABLE (1740–1780)

Massachusetts, probably Essex County
31½ × 33¾ × 21¾ in. (80 × 85.8 × 55.3 cm.)
Collection of Dorothy McIlvain Scott, Baltimore: Promised Gift to The Baltimore Museum of Art

The organization of this dressing table, with one full-width drawer placed over three deeper, narrower ones, and an overhanging top with notched corners supported by graceful cabriole legs ending in raised pad feet, is characteristic of Massachusetts dressing tables of the period and common until the time of the Revolution. The carved ten-lobe shell on the lower center drawer is flatter and less articulated than those on similar Newport dressing tables. Such carved shells on Massachusetts dressing tables are usually placed above a central concavity in the skirt. The front skirts are usually, as in this example, composed of ogee curves flanking a small ogee cutout, or shaped with three flat-headed ogee arches.[1] The vertical bottom drawer partitions have shoulder dovetails to join skirt and divider under the large top drawer. The divider is also shoulder dovetailed into the stiles, and the drawer rails are tenoned into the backboards. The center bottom drawer was once fitted with a pull handle above the shell, as the post holes have been filled. The present brasses are old but not original.

NOTES:
1. Bibl. 39, pp. 246–247, no. 160, ill. pp. 246 and 353.
MATERIALS: Primary: mahogany. Secondary: white pine. Brass hardware (not original)
PROVENANCE: David Stockwell, Inc., Wilmington, Delaware; Dorothy McIlvain Scott, Baltimore

61

61. DRESSING TABLE (1760–1780)

Maryland or Philadelphia
29 × 35¾ × 21 in. (73.7 × 90.8 × 53.4 cm.)
The Baltimore Museum of Art: Bequest of Philip B. Perlman (BMA 1960.41.3)

When this dressing table was first exhibited at The Baltimore Museum of Art in 1947, it was considered an example of Maryland Chippendale furniture which, whether made in Annapolis or Baltimore, was obviously influenced by the Philadelphia Chippendale style.[1] Two of Baltimore's most important pre-Revolutionary cabinetmakers, Robert Moore and Gerrard Hopkins, had been trained in Philadelphia, and first worked there. Hopkins is also thought to have worked for Moore in Philadelphia before removing to Maryland.[2] Comparable ties between Philadelphia and Annapolis have not as yet been established.

A more positive identification of a number of pieces as Baltimore rather than Philadelphia has been made possible through the labeled Gerrard Hopkins chest of drawers (see fig. 15a).[3] Either Maryland or Philadelphia has been given as the possible place of manufacture for the dressing table here. A very similar dressing table in the Winterthur collection, first published in 1952 as from Philadelphia, is now thought to be of Maryland or Philadelphia origin.[4] The pronounced scalloping of the base and three bottom drawers of equal width are characteristic of dressing tables and high chests of drawers with Maryland attributions.[5]

The right outside face of the table's center drawer carries several pencil inscriptions. The name Timothy Hanson in flowing script is legible as well as the date 1760, which appears more than once.[6] The table's Chippendale elements such as ball-and-claw feet and quarter columns combined with earlier design elements like simple shells on the drawers, skirt, and knees, and uncarved knee brackets, are more appropriate to furniture made in Maryland than in Philadelphia. The dressing table has dustboards under the three drawers of the lower tier. The quarter columns are each made in three pieces: a fluted quarter-round shaft between a turned capital and base, each of which also includes a small fluted columnar section. Only the lock escutcheon is original.

NOTES:
1. Bibl. 4.
2. Bibl. 84, p. 46.
3. Bibl. 28, pp. 354–361, ill. p. 358, figs. 4 and 5. For a complete discussion of Hopkins and related pieces, see cat. no. 15.
4. For other examples see bibl. 4, p. 183, no. 120, ill. and p. 184, no. 121, ill.
5. Bibl. 25, no. 329; later discussed by R. Peter Mooz, "Style in Country Art," pp. 235–264, especially pp. 251–255, fig. 8, as published in Quimby edition, *Winterthur Conference Report*, 1969 (Charlottesville: University Press of Virginia, 1969).
6. Hanson was a well-known family name in late eighteenth-century Maryland. They lived in Southern Maryland as well as in Anne Arundel and what became Howard County.
MATERIALS: Primary: mahogany. Secondary: yellow pine, tulip wood, cedar. Steel drawer lock, brass hardware (not original)

EXHIBITIONS: Bibl. 4, p. 185, no. 122, ill.; BMA, "Philip B. Perlman Bequest," 3 Sept.–1 Oct. 1961; bibl. 29, p. 74, no. 51, ill.
REFERENCES: Bibl. 1, p. 405; bibl. 5, p. 10, no. 3, ill. p. 7
PROVENANCE: Philip B. Perlman, Baltimore

62

62. DRESSING TABLE (1760–1780)

Philadelphia
29¼ × 35⅞ × 19⅞ in. (74.3 × 91.2 × 50.5 cm.)
Private Collection, Baltimore: Promised Gift to The Baltimore Museum of Art

This well-proportioned dressing table exhibits obvious Philadelphia characteristics in its design and decoration, one long top drawer above three lower drawers, the larger center drawer with carved and applied decoration being the standard format employed by Philadelphia cabinetmakers in the pre-Revolutionary period. The front skirt is scalloped and the side skirts have similar low arched cutouts. In more fully developed examples of the Chippendale period, the knees and brackets may, like the center bottom drawer, be embellished with leaf carvings. In this example the typical Philadelphia five-lobed shell, a holdover from the earlier Queen Anne period, is carved on the front knees. The tightly carved shell on the center bottom drawer has a stippled background. The brass pull is centered in a pinwheel-like carved blossom, and the delicate leaf carving placed below this pinwheel is an unusual and refined touch. The flanking carved tendrils that intersect to form reverse curves at the ends are a design motif found repeatedly on

Philadelphia furniture of this period, and should not be considered the work of a single cabinetmaker or shop.[1] Open but not full splits in the bottom of the top drawer were probably covered in the eighteenth century with strips of blue and white checked linen material. The original top is of two pieces of walnut. The brasses are of the period and their posts have been placed in the post holes of the originals. In the past the drawers had been fitted with larger pulls. The locks are original.

62

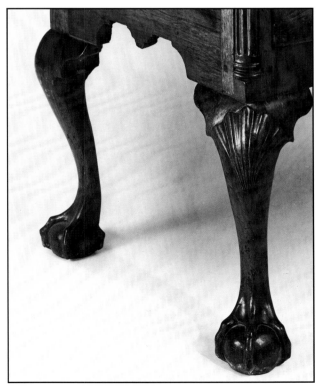

62

63. DRESSING TABLE, (1750–1785). Philadelphia area
Collection of Dorothy McIlvain Scott, Baltimore:
Promised Gift to The Baltimore Museum of Art

NOTES:
1. For other examples see bibl. 39, pp. 251–252, no. 163, ill. p. 251; pp. 253–255, no. 165, ill.; and pp. 255–257, no. 166, ill. p. 256; bibl. 83, p. 60, no. 117, ill. and p. 61, no. 118, ill.
MATERIALS: Primary: walnut. Secondary: tulip wood (drawer construction), yellow pine (drawer rails). Brass hardware (not original)
PROVENANCE: Joseph Kindig, Jr., Antiques, York, Pennsylvania; Private Collection, Baltimore
REFERENCES: Bibl. 77, p. 629, ill.

63. DRESSING TABLE (1750–1785)

Philadelphia area
32⅛ × 35¾ × 21³⁄₁₆ in. (81.6 × 90.8 × 53.8 cm.)
Collection of Dorothy McIlvain Scott, Baltimore: Promised Gift to The Baltimore Museum of Art

A comparison of the base of a high chest of drawers in The Metropolitan Museum of Art and this dressing table shows only slight differences in the skillful carvings on the knees, knee brackets, and the shell and its surrounding foliage.[1] The shaping of the front and side skirts is the same. The drawer fronts, with the exception of the carved center drawers, are faced with highly figured mahogany veneers on both the high chest and dressing table and the bottom shell drawer on both is carved from the solid. In addition the hardware on both pieces is original and identical. Related construction details include the use on both pieces, of vertical drawer partitions slotted into the two horizontal backboards; the front top rails are single-pegged, the side boards triple-pegged to the stiles. They differ in that the dressing table uses single pegs to secure the front skirt and the high chest, with a deeper skirt, is doubled-pegged.

The high chest of drawers at the Metropolitan has a well established provenance: it was first owned by Joseph Moulder of Philadelphia who died in 1799. An inventory of his estate lists both a high chest of drawers and "1 Mahogany dressing table" which may be the piece under discussion. However, ownership of the high chest from Joseph Moulder until its acquisition by the Metropolitan is well chronicled while that of the dressing table is not.[2]

NOTES:
1. The 1985 publication of Morrison H. Heckscher's, *American Furniture in The Metropolitan Museum of Art* (bibl. 39), includes an important Philadelphia high chest of drawers that he suggests is the matching piece to this dressing table, pp. 253–255, no. 165, ill. pp. 254, 347, 349, and 350. His references are the numerous advertisements in *Antiques* magazine for its sale beginning in 1949 and ending in January of 1974, a few

months before it was acquired by the donor. Heckscher also points out the relationship between these two matching pieces and the famous Van Pelt high chest of drawers at Winterthur and a high chest of drawers in the Karolik Collection at the Museum of Fine Arts, Boston. The Winterthur chest is illustrated in bibl. 25, no. 195, and the Museum of Fine Arts chest appears in bibl. 42, pp. 58–59, no. 33.
2. Bibl. 39, p. 253.

63

63

MATERIALS: Primary: mahogany, mahogany veneers. Secondary: yellow pine, tulip wood, white cedar
PROVENANCE: David Stockwell, Inc., Wilmington, Delaware, 1949; Dorothy McIlvain Scott, Baltimore
REFERENCES: *Antiques*, Feb. 1949, p. 106; *Antiques*, Oct. 1971, p. 465; *Antiques*, Jan. 1974, p. 1

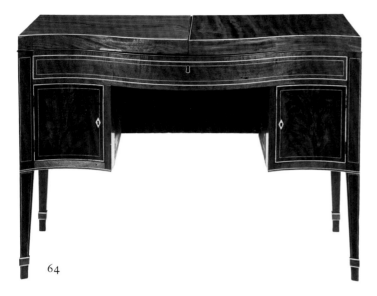

64

64. DRESSING TABLE (1790–1810)

Baltimore
28⅞ × 39⅜ × 20⅜ in. (73.4 × 100.1 × 51.8 cm.)
top open: 78¹/₁₆ in. (198.4 cm.)
The Baltimore Museum of Art: Friends of the American Wing Fund (BMA 1981.115)

This dressing table form is rare in American Federal furniture although there are many English prototypes which have in this century been called "Beau Brummels."[1] It shares a Buchanan family provenance with four pieces of painted furniture belonging to the Museum (see cat. nos. 30, 40, 101, 122).[2] The serpentine front under the two-sectioned hinged top has a false drawer front simulated by the use of line inlays and further suggested by a brass bound center keyhole which actually serves to lock the lids. When opened up, the two side-hinged tops are supported only by their abutment with the case sides, an impractical arrangement always subject to breakage. For some reason the grain of the mahogany boards of these two lids was installed in opposite directions. The left interior is beautifully fitted at the front with four lidded compartments, one silver-foil lined for the storage of powders. To the rear are two removable wooden trays, one fitted to hold combs. In the right interior

are four compartments and a hinged and ratcheted writing board. At the center there was originally a hinged and ratcheted mirror which has been entirely restored. There is additional storage space under the mirror and writing board. Below the elaborately fitted top are two storage compartments with curved line inlaid doors on each side of the kneehole, without drawers or shelves.

When acquired by the Museum in 1981, the dressing table underwent complete restoration with replacement of the missing mirror unit, and repairs to the cuffs on each leg, veneer, and inlay.

NOTES:
1. From the English dandy, George Bryan Brummel (1778–1840).
2. For a complete discussion of the Buchanan family of Baltimore, see cat. no. 30.

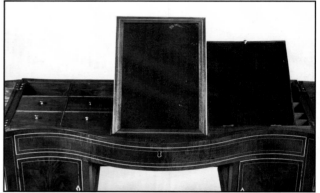

64

MATERIALS: Primary: mahogany, mahogany veneers, light wood stringing. Secondary: tulip wood, ash (front rail of upper case)
PROVENANCE: William Buchanan, Baltimore; and/or the Misses Sydney and Margaret Buchanan; by descent to Ulric O. Hutton, Brinklow; Rose G. Hutton; BMA, by purchase, 1981

65. DRESSING TABLE (1800–1815)

Coastal Northern New England
36 × 35⅞ × 17⅝ in. (91.5 × 91.2 × 44.8 cm.)
Collection of Dorothy McIlvain Scott, Baltimore: Promised Gift to The Baltimore Museum of Art

This dressing table was formerly attributed to the shop of John and Thomas Seymour, father and son cabinetmakers who worked in Boston in the first decades of the nineteenth century.[1] However, recent research on American furniture suggests a more general attribution to the New England school, rather than a specific shop. Undoubtedly, the Seymours exercised a strong influence from their prominent position in the region's largest city, but inlays and furniture designs once thought exclusive to their shop are now known to have been used by other cabinetmakers in the area.[2] In fact, the Seymours are thought to have sold their inlays to other local furniture makers.[3] A period inscription on the inside bottom of the table's large drawer, Mary [. . .] Gerrish Kittery, suggests that the table may have been made north of Boston. Kittery, Maine, is across the Piscataqua River from Portsmouth, New Hampshire, where such cabinetmakers as Langley Boardman, Jonathan Judkins, and William Senter were producing fine Federal-style furniture.[4]

The tops of the table and the drawered compartment which conforms to the shape of the case below are of solid mahogany. The mirror veneers of the drawer fronts and the panel's side aprons are of branch birch framed by an inlay. The table's side skirts under the veneer are composed of three pieces of horizontally laminated wood. The white pine backboard is tenoned into the stiles of the rear legs. It has been suggested that the turned and reeded legs were cut down, and that the slightly flared feet below the ring cuffs were the beginning

65

of the long bulbous feet found on certain pieces of Salem furniture.[5] However, both the height and proportions of the dressing table would seem to contradict this theory.

NOTES:
1. Bibl. 78, p. 282, no. 180, ill.
2. See bibl. 34, pp. 138–139 and bibl. 67, pp. 105–106.
3. Bibl. 67, p. 106.
4. New Hampshire Historical Society, *Plain & Elegant, Rich & Common: Documented New Hampshire Furniture, 1750–1850* (Concord: New Hampshire Historical Society, 1979), pp. 22–29, nos. 1–4, ill. and pp. 32–41, nos. 6–10, ill.
5. Bibl. 78, p. 282.

MATERIALS: Primary: mahogany, birch veneers, light and dark wood inlays. Secondary: white pine

PROVENANCE: Probably the Gerrish family of Kittery, Maine; Collection of Charles K. Davis, Fairfield, Connecticut; David Stockwell, Inc., Wilmington, Delaware; Dorothy McIlvain Scott, Baltimore

REFERENCES: Bibl. 78, p. 282, no. 180, ill.; "Antiques in Domestic Settings: The Home of Mr. and Mrs. Charles K. Davis," *Antiques*, Jan. 1941, p. 20, fig. 6

65

66

on Boston blockfront furniture. The shaped pendant drop with conforming block behind it is original. The top has an overhanging molded front and sides conforming to the straight sides and blocked facade of the case. The sides are dovetailed to the top. Facing strips are glued to the front edges of the sides and are beaded along the drawers; the drawer dividers also have a beaded edge around each drawer. The back is composed of three horizontal tongue and groove boards nailed into a rabbet. The original straight bracket feet have recessed rear bracing and flanking glue blocks.

NOTES:
1. Margaretta M. Lovell, "Boston Blockfront Furniture," in bibl. 85, pp. 77–136.
2. Bibl. 46, p. 140.

MATERIALS: Primary: mahogany. Secondary: white pine (drawer sides, backs, and bottoms, inner frame), chestnut (back). Brass escutcheons (one not original)

PROVENANCE: David Stockwell, Inc., Wilmington, Delaware; Dorothy McIlvain Scott, Baltimore

66. CHEST OF DRAWERS (1750–1780)

Boston area
30 × 35¼ × 20¾ in. (76.2 × 89.6 × 52.7 cm.)
Collection of Dorothy McIlvain Scott, Baltimore: Promised Gift to The Baltimore Museum of Art

Often called a "swelled" front in the eighteenth century, the blocked facade on case pieces of furniture became a distinct regional preference in New England, particularly in the cabinetmaking centers of Newport and Boston which each developed its own interpretation of the design. In Boston two types of blocking can be discerned on surviving pieces of furniture: the rounded front appears to have been popular for smaller case pieces, such as this four-drawer chest with straight bracket feet, while the squared or flattened front, although also found on four-drawer chests, was the preferred form for larger case pieces.[1] The rounded façade on this chest is similar to that found on a group of chests, notable for their fine dovetailing, which also share related elements such as base moldings, support blocking, drawer configuration, and foot construction.[2] While it has been proposed that the similarities in construction of this group of blockfront pieces may indicate the shop of Benjamin Frothingham (1734–1809), the celebrated Charlestown cabinetmaker, there do not appear to be enough shared details to link this chest of drawers to the so-called Frothingham group. It remains, however, a fine example of Boston-area cabinetwork. A distinctive construction feature is the giant dovetail in the center of the base, often found

67

67. CHEST OF DRAWERS (1775–1800)

Danvers-Salem, Massachusetts area
34⅛ × 38⅞ × 22 in. (86.7 × 98.8 × 55.9 cm.)
Collection of Dorothy McIlvain Scott, Baltimore: Promised Gift to The Baltimore Museum of Art

This chest of drawers is virtually identical to a chest with serpentine front once owned by a mem-

67

NOTES:
1. Bibl. 46, pp. 161–164, no. 22, ill.
2. Bibl. 46, p. 164.
3. Chests by Ebenezer Martin are illustrated in bibl. 66, p. 52, no. 41 and *Antiques*, May 1984, inside front cover. An unattributed chest is found in Barry A. Greenlaw, *New England Furniture at Williamsburg* (Williamsburg, Virginia: The Colonial Williamsburg Foundation, 1974), p. 85, no. 74, ill. p. 84.

MATERIALS: Primary: mahogany. Secondary: white pine. Brass hardware (bottom drawer not original)

PROVENANCE: David Stockwell, Wilmington, Delaware, 1976; Dorothy McIlvain Scott, Baltimore

68

ber of the Dale family of Danvers, Massachusetts, near Salem.[1] Both share similar design features such as the carved pendant scallop shell, sharply pointed knees, elongated scalloped knee brackets, and bold ball-and-claw feet, elements associated with the Salem area. Similar pieces known to have been made in Salem, however, often demonstrate a more sophisticated execution, suggesting that the two chests and a related group of case pieces with like elements may have been produced by a shop outside Salem that perpetuated the regional mode. Documentation of the ownership of one of this group of case pieces, a desk, to the Danvers area confirms the probability that the pieces were produced in the area.[2] Other chests without the pendant shell but similar in overall form, by cabinetmakers such as Ebenezer Martin of Marblehead, attest to the popularity of this type on the North Shore; a number of similar unattributed chests are extant.[3] This exceptional chest of drawers is distinguished not only by its graceful serpentine shape but also by the particularly adroit selection and use of figured mahogany for the drawer fronts. The swirled patterns of the wood create movement and pattern in an interesting counterpoint to the serpentine façade. In addition, the sharply pointed knees and tightly drawn back ankles, as well as the strong and fully developed claws which grasp the almost round ball firmly, all contribute to a sprightliness which lightens the form. The fine proportions and the well-integrated parts add to the success of the design.

68. CHEST OF DRAWERS (1780–1790)

Maryland or Pennsylvania
36 × 41¾ × 24⅛ in. (91.6 × 106.1 × 61.3 cm.)
Private Collection, Baltimore: Promised Gift to The Baltimore Museum of Art

Except for its original circular brass handles and applied beading on the drawer edges, this chest of drawers is in the Chippendale style. The molded edge of the top and bottom of the case, the canted corners, and the heavy ogee bracket feet are all found on chests of drawers made in the 1760's and 1770's. However, the manner of drawer front construction reinforces the image given by the neoclassical brasses. Like curved aprons of Federal card tables, each of the drawer fronts is made up of horizontally laminated pieces of wood, in this instance of four members of equal width, and the lamination then covered with choice mahogany veneer. Such construction was a standard feature of Federal-period Baltimore serpentine-front chests of drawers. The sides and top are of solid mahogany, and there are no dustboards. The drawer dividers, with mahogany fronts and tulip wood backing, are about one-third of the case's depth. Two horizontal yellow pine boards are set into a rabbet on the rear case edges.

MATERIALS: Primary: mahogany, mahogany veneers. Secondary: tulip wood (drawer sides, backs, and bottoms), yellow pine (back, drawer rails, blocking)

PROVENANCE: Joseph Kindig, Jr., Antiques, York, Pennsylvania; Private Collection, Baltimore

69

69. CHEST OF DRAWERS (1790–1810)

Maryland
38¼ × 41⅛ × 21½ in. (97.2 × 104.5 × 54.6 cm.)
The Baltimore Museum of Art: Gift of Mrs. Francis White, from the Collection of Mrs. Miles White, Jr. (BMA 1973.76.226)

This chest of drawers is of a very pronounced serpentine form, the ends of the curved drawers and case being on the same plane as their centers. Another unusual construction feature is the forty-five degree angle of the front corners of the top, case, and feet. The broad light wood inlaid band, framed with thin black stringing around the top

edge, also forms an edge on the top. It is repeated at the base above the serpentine-shaped front and side aprons. The inlaid ellipses on each drawer front are of a dark stringing set between inlays of light stringing. The drawer fronts are of mahogany veneered faces on three horizontally laminated pieces of tulip wood. The drawer dividers and rails are fitted in channels cut in the case sides.

MATERIALS: Primary: mahogany, mahogany veneers, light and dark wood inlays. Secondary: tulip wood. Brass hardware (not original)

PROVENANCE: Birckhead family of Baltimore; Mrs. Miles White, Jr.; Francis White; Nancy Brewster White (Mrs. Francis)

REFERENCES: Bibl. 55, vol. 1, p. 406, no. 729, ill. p. 407

70. CHEST 1794

Pennsylvania
Maker: John Selzer
22¹³⁄₁₆ × 52 × 22⅝ in. (58 × 132.1 × 57.5 cm.)
The Baltimore Museum of Art: Friends of the American Wing Fund (BMA 1971.3)

The right and left painted front panels on this Pennsylvania chest bear the signature of John Selzer (1774–1845), a house carpenter-joiner, and the date 1794.[1] The dated signatures which appear on the vases of the two outermost front panels were apparently scratched onto the painted surface when it was still wet. Both Selzer and his father Christian Selzer (1749–1831) lived in the Jonestown area (then Dauphin, but now Lebanon County) of southeastern Pennsylvania. John obviously learned both joinery and decorative painting from his father, for chests by Christian Selzer are very similar. Both men consistently signed their work of which much has survived.[2] It is presumed that the Selzers made the chests they decorated; the heaviness of the construction and the single unit moldings are all indicative of house joinery training. The three arched-top floral panels have dark painted frames and are surrounded by a mottled, fancifully grain-painted red ground. Three original painted rectilinear panels on the lid's top are so worn as to be barely visible. In the construction of the chest the dovetailing is visible at the corners. At the top left inside there is a till with a molded front edge on its lid similar to the edge of the projecting molding of the till's bottom board. The inner side board of the till slides up to reveal a secret compartment below the till floor. The interior strap hinges have shaped ends; the lock's works are exposed. The pierced and shaped escutcheon is original.

70

NOTES:
1. Beatrice B. Garvan, *The Pennsylvania German Collection* (Philadelphia: Philadelphia Museum of Art, 1982), p. 368.
2. Other examples of chests by the Selzers are found in bibl. 33, pp. 256–257, no. 446, ill.; bibl. 66, pp. 22–23, no. 18, ill.; and Monroe H. Fabian, *The Pennsylvania-German Decorated Chest* (New York: Universe Books, 1978), p. 140, no. 105, ill. and p. 141, no. 107, ill.

MATERIALS: Primary: yellow pine. Secondary: tulip wood; painted with polychrome decoration
PROVENANCE: Cynthia Fehr, Antiques, New Market; BMA, by purchase, 1970
EXHIBITIONS: Bibl. 3; bibl. 12, p. 118, no. 102, ill.
REFERENCES: Bibl. 35, p. 194, ill. p. 195, fig. IX-17

70

71. LINEN PRESS (1797)

Annapolis
Maker: John Shaw
92 × 51½ × 25 in. (233.8 × 130.9 × 63.5 cm.)
The Baltimore Museum of Art: Friends of the American Wing Fund (BMA 1975.76)

Also known as a wardrobe in late eighteenth-century design books and used for the storage of clothing and linen, this example is similar to Plates 85 and 88 of Hepplewhite's *Guide* which show designs for a "Wardrobe" having rectangular panels with incurved corners and inlaid ovals on the doors as well as straight bracket feet.[1]

Like much of the furniture of John Shaw (1745–1829), the linen press is conservative in its overall design scheme and somewhat transitional, owing debts to both the Chippendale and Federal styles. Shaw, who emigrated from Scotland to Annapolis during the early 1760's, enjoyed much success in the cabinetmaking trade. After early intermittent partnerships with a fellow Scot, Archibald Chisolm, Shaw was well established by the early 1790's. He had a large shop employing a number of journeymen and apprentices where a distinctive furniture idiom was developed. His workmen often added their initials and the date to Shaw's printed paper label which was affixed to furniture produced

71

71

there. On this press the initials on the label pasted on the inside back of the third slide in the upper section may be either J A or I H flanking the date 1797. Unfortunately, the specific journeyman or apprentice responsible for the press cannot be identified.[2] Two other linen presses bearing Shaw's label are known, both of which have flat tops.[3] This example is distinguished by the addition of a scrolled pediment with a pierced fretwork of interlaced C-scrolls above the dentilled cornice. The scrolled ends are further emphasized by inlaid stars. The pediment design is characteristic of the Shaw shop, and appears on two other desk-and-bookcase forms, each bearing a Shaw label.[4] The inlaid urn or kylix on the top central panel is identical to inlaid panels found on the billiard table made for the Lloyd family of Annapolis and Wye House, Talbot County.[5] This inlay was probably imported.

The upper section is fitted on the interior with five sliding shelves, essentially drawers, with low-cut fronts. The top section has a four-paneled back while the lower case is backed with tongue and groove boards. Very thin mahogany drawer dividers are laminated to the three-quarter depth dust-boards, which are the same thickness as the dividers and fit in grooves cut in the case sides. The hardware is original. At the time of its acquisition by the Museum, the piece was refinished.

NOTES:
1. Bibl. 40.
2. For a more complete discussion of John Shaw and his work, see bibl. 30.
3. Bibl. 30, pp. 104–108, nos. 34 and 35, ill.
4. Bibl. 30, pp. 118–121, no. 40, ill. and pp. 138–140, no. 49, ill.
5. Bibl. 30, pp. 147–150, no. 52, ill.

MATERIALS: Primary: mahogany, mahogany veneers, light, dark, and stained wood inlays. Secondary: tulip wood, yellow pine

PROVENANCE: Dr. George Brown, Annapolis and Baltimore; Robert Brown; Grace Brown Albert; Mary Buchanan Albert Myers; Alex Cooper Auctioneers, Baltimore, 1975; BMA, by purchase, 1975

EXHIBITIONS: Bibl. 30, pp. 115–118, no. 39, ill.

REFERENCES: Bibl. 6, p. 373, ill. p. 365, pl. II

72. WARDROBE (1830–1840)

Baltimore
Maker: John Needles
89 × 49½ × 26 in. (226.1 × 125.8 × 66.1 cm.)
The Baltimore Museum of Art: Gift of Mrs. John O.
Needles (BMA 1961.45)

"I well remember the beautiful bird's eye maple doors, two tall ones between the parlors and four others opening into the long hall," wrote Mary Needles, about the house her cabinetmaker father built in Baltimore in 1836 and for which he undoubtedly provided the interior finish work.[1] John Needles (1786–1878), a Quaker, was born in Talbot County, on Maryland's Eastern Shore. His cabinetmaker father, Edward, died when John was twelve years old and he was apprenticed to James Neal, an Easton cabinetmaker.[2] Needles came to Baltimore in 1808 and by 1810 began his own business. He worked as a cabinetmaker for the

72

72

next forty-three years, finally retiring in 1853 to become an itinerant minister.

This wardrobe, which descended through Needles' family until given to The Baltimore Museum of Art, is a striking example of his fondness for maple cabinetwork.[3] It combines three types of figured veneers: bird's-eye, tiger or striped, and a variety of striped maple aptly called waterfall; the latter is found on the cornice. A secretary-bookcase with the stenciled mark of John Needles (cat. no. 81) uses bird's-eye maple veneers to provide contrast with rosewood. Reversing this pattern, Needles here uses dark woods to contrast with a principally light wood case. The stop-fluted pilasters are of walnut and the capitals, feet, and thin molding strips are of mahogany. The carved leaf capitals topped with Ionic scrolls are found on a number of pieces by or firmly attributed to John Needles, including the secretary-bookcase mentioned above, which has a similar removable cornice with low inset arch over double doors.[4] From its history we know this wardrobe was used by the maker's own family which is perhaps why the top board is a reused piece of poplar. Its first set of dovetail cuts were plugged, and veneers on the cornice sides were pieced out in a makeshift fashion.[5]

NOTES:
1. This excerpt from Mary Needles' memoirs is quoted in bibl. 57, p. 294.
2. Edward Needles Wright, ed., "John Needles (1786–1878): An Autobiography," *Journal of Quaker History*, Spring 1969, pp. 5, 6, 9, and 11.
3. The wardrobe shares a history with a dropleaf table, cat. no. 94. That table is the only piece of the several given by John Oliver Needles which is primarily veneered with figured walnut. All are of uniform, notably solid construction.
4. Similar capitals can be found on a pier table owned by the Maryland Historical Society illustrated in bibl. 84, pp. 192–193, no. 169, and a chest in the John O. Needles gift to the Museum (BMA 1953.226.5) as illustrated in bibl. 57, p. 295.
5. Conservation of this piece by William Tillman in 1985 provided confirmation that these were not later repairs but original materials.

MATERIALS: Primary: maple, maple veneers, mahogany, walnut. Secondary: tulip wood, yellow pine, chestnut. Lower interior fitted with three open faced clothes drawers.

PROVENANCE: John Needles, Baltimore; by descent to Mrs. John O. Needles

73. CABINET (1850–1870)

Probably New York
54⅜ × 58⅜ × 17¾ in. (138.2 × 148.3 × 45.1 cm.)
The Baltimore Museum of Art: Gift from the Estate of Margaret Anna Abell (BMA 1977.42.5)

This cabinet in the Renaissance Revival style has the same provenance as an upholstered armchair, cat. no. 36, and the Louis XV Revival-style etagere described in cat. no. 119. All three pieces of furniture came from Guilford, a Baltimore country house in the Italianate style built by a William McDonald of New York about 1852. In 1872 the house with its contents was sold to Arunah S. Abell (1806–1888). The cabinet is typical of its period in combining eclectic elements of European design from the sixteenth to the eighteenth centuries. Renaissance and mannerist details are found in the shaping of the pilasters on the front and sides. The elaborate inlays on the door and flanking panels are Louis XVI in origin, as is the gilt ormolu applied molding at the base of the top. Louis XV and XVI styles revived in the Second Empire were

73

73

readily adopted by American cabinetmakers. Since other furniture bought by McDonald for Guilford, such as the Alexander Roux etagere (cat. no. 119), came from New York, it is believed this Renaissance Revival cabinet was also made in that city. It resembles, especially in the shaping of its feet, a cabinet in the Lockwood-Matthews Mansion Museum, Norwalk, Connecticut, which is attributed to the New York cabinetmaking firm of Leon Marcotte (working 1848–1854).[1] Cabinets of related design were also made in New York by Roux and by the Herter Brothers. That the form was not restricted to that city is seen by a labeled example made by the Baltimore firm of Thomas Godey now in the High Museum, Atlanta.[2] In its basic form this Baltimore example resembles New York counterparts but employs different elements of decoration.

NOTES:
1. Bibl. 22, p. 21, ill. pp. 20–21. For other related examples, see bibl. 32, pp. 418–419, ill.
2. Bibl. 37, p. 31, ill.

MATERIALS: Primary: rosewood, bird's-eye maple, burl walnut, and mahogany veneers; dyed wood inlays; gilt and ebonized molding. Secondary: tulip wood (core of laminated or veneered surfaces, backboards, feet). Gilt brass mounts, gilt incised lines

PROVENANCE: Possibly William McDonald (1830–1864), Baltimore; Arunah S. Abell, by purchase, 1872; by descent to Margaret Anna Abell

REFERENCES: Sarah B. Sherrill, "Current and coming," *Antiques*, Feb. 1979, p. 240, ill.

Desks

74. DESK (1765–1780)

Eastern Massachusetts
43¾ × 43¼ × 24 in. (111.2 × 109.9 × 61 cm.)
The Baltimore Museum of Art: Bequest of Philip B.
Perlman (BMA 1960.41.2)

With its blocked drawer fronts and short cabriole legs and feet, this desk is a typical solid example of the many produced in the Boston-Salem area from about 1765 to as late as the 1780's. The desk is in exceptionally fine condition from its original hardware to its intact base and leg blocking and elaborate knee brackets. The interior, despite the blocked and shell-carved side drawers of the top tier, the similarly treated central compartment door, and the block-fronted intermediate drawers, is somewhat plainer than many other surviving examples. The pigeonholes appear never to have had valances, nor are there document drawers with the usual decorative engaged columns flanking the central compartment. The thumbnail-molded edges of the lower inside drawers are at variance with the plain fronted bead-surrounded base drawers which are the norm for these desks. The top edges of the interior drawer sides are molded with a single bead. The front base molding has a giant dovetail attachment to the case bottom and support strip below it. The prospect door retains its original lock but the left side of the door face has been patched and the escutcheon and key mortise removed. The sharp-kneed cabriole legs with ball-and-claw feet have the sharply raked inner claw characteristic of eastern Massachusetts cabinet-making of the period.

MATERIALS: Primary: mahogany. Secondary: white pine (drawer bodies, back and bottom boards, drawer dividers behind mahogany facing). Central door brass knob (not original)

PROVENANCE: Philip B. Perlman, Baltimore

EXHIBITIONS: BMA, "The Philip B. Perlman Bequest," 3 Sept.– 1 Oct. 1961; bibl. 12, p. 99, no. 70, ill.

REFERENCES: Bibl. 1, p. 405, ill. p. 418; bibl. 5, p. 10, no. 2, ill. p. 5

74

75. DESK (1760–1780)

Southern New England
43⅛ × 40⅜ × 20 in. (109.6 × 102.6 × 50.8 cm.)
The Baltimore Museum of Art: Gift of Mrs. Clark McIlwaine; Bequest of Philip B. Perlman; and Bequest of C. Edward Snyder, by exchange (BMA 1972.22)

It is most unusual to see the bombé form made outside of urban eastern Massachusetts. Certain naive aspects of this desk's design, and more particularly the materials used and methods by which it was constructed, suggest a rural origin in an area influenced by Boston fashions and where tulip wood and yellow and white pine would have been used as secondary woods, probably western Massachusetts or southern Connecticut.[1] The bombé case piece was an expensive and highly fashionable furnishing in its time. Mahogany is the only primary wood found in all other extant examples.[2] Black walnut, used in this piece, was no longer in favor at the end of the eighteenth century, particularly for stylish furniture. Another retardataire feature is found in the base where simple repeated ogee arches recall the skirts of Queen Anne high chests. Similarly patterned arches are found on a group of tea tables and chests from the Connecticut River Valley with overhanging tops and vigorously shaped chest bases.[3] The thumbnail-molded drawer edges are another sign that the cabinetmaker was not completely conversant with the urban form in which plain drawer faces were set into a case with a decorative edge bead applied to the drawer surround. Both the straight bracket-footed base and the line of the drawers ignore the curve created by the bulging case sides. The maker of this desk certainly had the ability to produce an ogee base, but he did not grasp what more sophisticated cabinetmakers realized—the need to accent the curved lines which made bombé furniture different and fashionable. The earliest examples of bombé pieces have in common rectangular drawers, as seen on this desk, but curved sides soon evolved. In the most complexly constructed examples, the curved vertical drawer face edge was carried through into the drawer body. More often, though the curves were a sham, the shaped drawer face was applied to a straight sided drawer. The maker of this desk may have been familiar only with the earliest rectangular-faced drawer examples. The desk's interior with its blocked drawers is related to urban examples, but the pigeonholes are carved with a distinctive blossom design of alternating pointed and long, looped petals on a stippled ground. Also unusual is the way the prospect door opens by dropping forward from interior bottom hinges.[4] Another construction element uncommon to urban Massachusetts examples is the shouldered dovetails of the drawer dividers and desk board: the

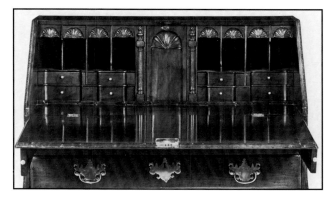

75

desk board and top board dividers are actually cut through the outside edge of the case sides. The typical lap-jointed backboards of urban case work are altered here by the use of tongue and groove joined edges.

NOTES:
1. Gilbert T. Vincent, "The Bombé Furniture of Boston," in bibl. 85, p. 137. Also bibl. 46, p. 151.
2. Bibl. 85, p. 196.
3. *The Great River: Art & Society of the Connecticut Valley, 1635–1820*, exhibition cat. (Hartford, Connecticut: Wadsworth Atheneum, 1985), pp. 222–225, nos. 102–104, ill.
4. More standard doors either pivot on side hinges or are unattached to the case and use steel pins protruding from the bottom edge to insert into holes in the desk board.

MATERIALS: Primary: black walnut. Secondary: white pine, tulip wood (backboards), pine (drawers), yellow pine (divider facing). Drawer brasses and escutcheons (not original)
PROVENANCE: John Walton, Antiques, New York, 1972; BMA, by purchase, 1972

76. CYLINDER DESK (1800–1810)

Annapolis or Baltimore
44½ × 42¾ × 21 in. (113.1 × 108.6 × 53.4 cm.)
The Baltimore Museum of Art: Friends of the American Wing Fund (BMA 1986.12)

Desks with cylinder fronts had become popular in England in the second half of the eighteenth century, although the form had been employed in France and elsewhere on the continent at a much earlier date. The actual mechanism and method of construction of a curved top, revolving back into the case to become invisible when the desk is open, are illustrated in Sheraton.[1] Sheraton's instructions for the construction of a cylinder front include a mechanism which raises the front as the writing slide is pulled forward. This desk is less sophisticated and separates those functions into two manual operations. The cylinder itself is con-

75

76

structed of caul-curved boards which are veneered on the face with mahogany and backed with glued linen. The case itself is solidly constructed using full dustboards and the unusual feature of a full-width board as a brace between the rear feet. It is shaped with a flat-topped arch and employed in place of the two individual diagonally-cut boards which are standard for case pieces of this period. This example, made in Annapolis or Baltimore about 1800, belongs to a relatively small group of American Federal period desks with cylinder closing, and to an even smaller group thought to have been made in Maryland.[2]

The most closely related example, in The Art Institute of Chicago, is identical in design and its dimensions vary only by one-half inch. Although there are differences in details of decoration and the brasses, the two desks are almost certainly from the same shop.[3]

The two pictorial inlays on the Museum's desk, an eagle and the oval patera, are found on many pieces of Federal-period furniture produced in Maryland. The eagle with a shield body and star banner, holding an olive branch in one claw and an arrow in the other, is found on a chest of drawers in the Winterthur collection, on the slant front of a desk from a Baltimore collection, and, in a smaller version, on the stile of a card table bearing the label of Annapolis cabinetmaker John Shaw.[4]

NOTES:
1. Bibl. 73, pp. 97–100 and pl. 47.
2. These include two in the Winterthur collection illustrated in bibl. 56, pp. 236–237, no. 194 and pp. 238–239, no. 197, and two published in bibl. 4, p. 114, no. 73, ill. p. 115 and p. 122, no. 77, ill. p. 123, the latter owned by The Metropolitan Museum of Art (34.135).
3. Illustrated in an advertisement in *Antiques*, Oct. 1981, inside front cover.
4. The Winterthur chest is illustrated in bibl. 56, pp. 184–185, no. 141, with a detail on p. 39, fig. 125; the desk once owned by Edgar G. Miller, Jr. is published in bibl. 55, vol. 1, p. 440, no. 805, ill. p. 441; and a card table is pp. 111–112, no. 37, ill. in bibl. 30. In this same text the blossom patera is found on pp. 88–90, no. 24; pp. 96–97, no. 27; pp. 118–121, no. 40; and pp. 150–151, no. 53. A cylinder-front desk in the Winterthur collection has the same inlay, bibl. 56, p. 236, no. 194, ill. p. 237.

MATERIALS: Primary: mahogany (case sides, top, drawer dividers, interior drawers, large drawer fronts). Secondary: tulip wood (large drawer sides and bottoms, dust and back boards). Drawer brasses and escutcheons (not original)

PROVENANCE: Joseph Kindig, Jr., Antiques, York, Pennsylvania, 1947; Estate of Robert Atkinson, Chestertown; GKS Bush, Inc., Antiques, Washington, D.C., 1985; BMA, by purchase, 1986

EXHIBITIONS: Bibl. 4, p. 106, no. 69, ill. p. 107

REFERENCES: *Antiques*, Jan. 1986, p. 25

76

77. TAMBOUR DESK (1800–1810)

Boston
Maker: attributed to the shop of John and Thomas Seymour
47 × 37½ × 19⅜ in. (119.4 × 95.3 × 49.2 cm.)
The Baltimore Museum of Art: Purchased as the gift of Mr. and Mrs. Kenneth S. Battye, Baltimore (BMA 1971.1.1)

This desk shares the same early ownership as a tambour desk-and-bookcase in the Winterthur Museum.[1] The first owner of both desks was Ebenezer Parsons (1745/6–1819), son of the Reverend Moses Parsons of Byfield in Newbury, Massachusetts, and a successful Boston merchant. After his marriage

77. TAMBOUR DESK, (1800–1810). Boston
Attributed to the shop of John and Thomas Seymour
The Baltimore Museum of Art: Purchased as the gift
of Mr. and Mrs. Kenneth S. Battye, Baltimore (BMA 1971.1.1)

Newbury house. The small variations between the two Parsons' desks may be the result of one being purchased slightly later than the other, though one or both may have been bought ready-made, not on commission.

The most obvious difference between the Museum's piece and its mate at Winterthur is the addition of a bookcase section; otherwise the two desks are identical in size and decorative plan. Only upon close examination of each element of the decoration do small variations appear. The greatest disparity, if measured by size of elements, is perhaps the most subtle: the base section drawers of the Museum desk are veneered with two mirrored flitches of mahogany which form an ellipse centered on the vase-shaped ivory escutcheons. The long drawers of Winterthur's desk have four mahogany flitches forming paired swags centered on the two oval brass drawer pulls. The inlays which define the ends of the facade of both desks form a light and dark striped column. Both desks share the same columnar pattern flanking the tambour and at its center. They differ on the front

Fig. 77a. Lady's Tambour Desk and Bookcase. Attributed to the shop of John and Thomas Seymour, Boston, 1800–1810. Mahogany, walnut, and white pine; 75¼ × 37½ × 19 in. (191.2 × 95.3 × 48.3 cm.). The Henry Francis du Pont Winterthur Museum (57.570).

in 1767, he occupied a substantial house on Summer Street, and in 1801 built a large house in Newbury.[2] No doubt Parsons originally furnished his pre-Revolutionary Boston residence with furniture in the prevailing Chippendale-influenced style. This elegant tambour desk may have been an element in some fashionable redecorating around the turn of the century. Alternatively, it is possible that Parsons bought the new desk in 1801 for his

77

77

stiles where the Museum's desk has a striped inlay cut in half-inch pieces stacked in an alternating pattern and the other desk has stripes arranged in an elongated rectangle with a single center strip. A third decorative variation involves the inlay along the edge of the tambour section top board and on the hinged edge of the writing surface of both desks. The inlays are complements of each other, the same design but colored in an opposing fashion. The pattern, sometimes called the split pyramid, is on this example composed of a light wood strip with well-spaced dark semicircles. Splitting the center of the curve-sided pyramid formed between the half-circles is a dark vertical line.[3]

Both of the Parsons' desks are related to a number of tambour-topped desks published as the work of John and Thomas Seymour (working in Boston, 1794–1816), but whose attribution is not solid.[4] However, two labeled Seymour desks share some features with these Parsons' desks, including the split pyramid inlay, the same bellflower with dots inlaid on the tapered legs within an arch-topped string inlay surround, the column inlay on the tambour, and the striped inlay arranged in elongated rectangles on the stiles.[5] Here the brasses are

original and unlike the replacement pulls on the Winterthur piece. The tambour section interiors are painted light blue; the color was revealed on the Museum's desk when a later pink wash was removed in 1963.[6]

NOTES:
1. Bibl. 56, pp. 231–233, no. 186, ill. p. 230. The history of the Baltimore Museum's desk is recorded in a letter from Winthrop Sargent to David Stockwell now in the Museum's Registration files.
2. For information on Ebenezer Parsons, see *Newbury Vital Records to 1849, Vol. 1, Births* (Salem, Massachusetts: Essex Institute, 1891), p. 378; *The Boston Directory* (1789; reprint, Boston: Sampson Murdock Co. 1916), p. 33; Twenty-second Report of the Record Commissioners, U.S. Direct Tax of 1798, U.S. Census of 1790 for city of Boston (Boston: Rockwell and Churchill Printers, 1890), p. 380; and John J. Currier, *"Ould Newbury": Historical and Biographical Sketches* (Boston: Damrell and Upham, 1896), p. 328.
3. Bibl. 78, p. 107, no. 49, ill. p. 106.
4. Related desks whose attributions are not based on documentation by label, bill, or provenance are illustrated in bibl. 78, pp. 68–69, no. 19; pp. 82–85, no. 30; and pp. 108–109, no. 50.
5. Bibl. 78, pp. 48–51, no. 4, ill. and p. 55, no. 10, ill. p. 54.
6. See bill of sale, Museum's Registration files.

MATERIALS: Primary: mahogany, mahogany veneer, satinwood, other light and dark wood inlays. Secondary: white pine. Ivory inlays. Baize writing surface (not original)

PROVENANCE: Ebenezer Parsons, Boston and Newbury, Massachusetts; Gorham Parsons; Gorham Parsons Sargent; Sarah Sargent Worcester; Samuel Howard Worcester; Elizabeth Ann Scott Worcester; Lily Elizabeth Howard Worcester; Winthrop Sargent; BMA, by purchase, 1971

EXHIBITIONS: Bibl. 12, p. 105, no. 81, ill.

REFERENCES: *Antiques*, Apr. 1963, pp. 357 and 411; bibl. 79, p. 8, no. 2, ill.; Ruth A. Davidson, "Museum accessions," *Antiques*, Dec. 1973, p. 990

78. DESK-AND-BOOKCASE (1785–1800)

Newburyport, Massachusetts area
Maker: possibly the shop of Abner Toppan
100⅜ × 45½ × 25 in. (255.1 × 115.6 × 63.5 cm.)
case h.: 92⅛ in. (234.1 cm.)
Collection of Dorothy McIlvain Scott, Baltimore: Promised Gift to The Baltimore Museum of Art

While the desk-and-bookcase with broken-scroll pediment, paneled bookcase doors with ogee surround, and a blocked base is often found in eighteenth-century Boston furniture, this example is probably the product of a Newburyport area cabinetmaker.[1] In form and ornament it is similar to one in the Society for the Preservation of New England Antiquities which has been attributed to the shop of Abner Toppan (1764–1836)[2] and to another Toppan desk-and-bookcase owned by the

78

Newburyport Public Library and documented by a bill of sale.[3] It is even more closely allied, however, to a desk-and-bookcase in The Metropolitan Museum of Art which has also been tentatively ascribed to the Toppan shop.[4] Although these three related pieces have desk sections with serpentine fronts instead of a blocked front like the Museum's example, they all share other distinctive features suggesting the Newburyport origin. The bracket feet and the pinwheel rosettes in the scroll pediments and beneath the central finial, for example, appear to be by the same hand. While the carved pinwheel motif appears on a signed Jacob Sanderson desk-and-bookcase made in Salem[5] and on a desk-and-bookcase attributed to Abraham Watson also of Salem,[6] those pinwheels appear cramped by comparison and neither piece has applied pinwheels at the ends of the broken-scroll pediment. The use of carved ornament together with the richly figured veneers within the scalloped surround of the paneled doors and the sculptured quality of the blocked base combine to produce a

78

78

gether. There are shaped rear bracket braces with blocks behind and glue blocks around the front and sides of the bottom. There is also an interior bottom board. The baseboard is flush with the base molding and a giant dovetail joins the front base molding to the case bottom as on the three pieces discussed above. The elegant carved and gilded dove-with-branch appears to be original as do the flanking corkscrew finials.

NOTES:
1. Bibl. 34, pp. 238–239, no. 477, ill.
2. Bibl. 46, pp. 250–253, no. 52, ill.
3. Bibl. 80, p. 224, fig. 6.
4. Bibl. 39, pp. 275–276, no. 180, ill.
5. *Antiques*, Dec. 1957, inside front cover.
6. Dean A. Fales, Jr., *Essex County Furniture: Documented Treasures from Local Collections, 1660–1860* (Salem, Massachusetts: Essex Institute, 1965), no. 44, ill.
7. Jane C. Giffen, "The Moffatt-Ladd House at Portsmouth, New Hampshire: Part 2," *Connoisseur*, Nov. 1970, p. 203, fig. 13.

MATERIALS: Primary: mahogany. Secondary: white pine
PROVENANCE: David Stockwell, Inc., Wilmington, Delaware, 1975; Dorothy McIlvain Scott, Baltimore

particularly striking exterior. Similar desk-and-bookcases have been associated with coastal New Hampshire,[7] although differing in details from Newburyport examples. The bookcase section of this desk-and-bookcase has a back composed of three vertical lap-jointed boards. There is a support block behind the central plinth. The interior of the bookcase has round-headed valances pitched slightly backward. The compartment dividers have half-round applied moldings. The bookcase sides are dovetailed into the bottom and the front board is nailed to the bottom board. The Metropolitan Museum of Art's example and the Museum's desk both share markedly similar shallow stepped interiors with a plain bottom tier of drawers; recessed blocked drawers capped by carved shells above, alternating with serpentine drawers under triple cubbyholes; similar pilasters flanking the prospect door, which opens on pegs that fit into holes set in the base of the compartment. The interior drawers have fronts and backs dovetailed into the sides and bottoms pinned in a rabbet. The bottom of each exterior drawer sits in a groove in the front and sides and the top edge is cut with an inner bead. There is also a bead cut on the case around each drawer. Facing strips cover the front edge of the case sides. The back and bottom of the desk section are of two horizontal boards rabbeted to-

79. SECRETARY-BOOKCASE (1790–1810)

Charleston
101¾ × 49¹³⁄₁₆ × 24⁷⁄₁₆ in. (258.5 × 126.6 × 62.1 cm.)
case h.: 97¼ in. (247.1 cm.)
The Baltimore Museum of Art: Purchased as the gift of a Group of Friends of the Museum (BMA 1946.141)

Only in recent years has this secretary-bookcase been correctly ascribed to Charleston, South Carolina rather than Baltimore.[1] E. Milby Burton's studies of Charleston furniture and subsequent work at the Museum of Early Southern Decorative Arts have now established the characteristics of Charleston cabinetmaking which include the stringing and bellflower pattern on the veneered frieze of the cornice and pediment and plinth; the fretwork of the cornice; and the proportion of the widely spaced scrolls.[2] All these are repeated in a wardrobe now attributed to Charleston whose decorative elements are so like those on the Museum's example as to suggest that the two pieces of furniture came from the same cabinetmaking shop.[3] The inlaid blunt bellflowers on the center plinth of the scroll pediment and those on the legs with thin black line or "scratched" decoration are most characteristic of Charleston.[4] The drawer of the lower section folds down to afford a writing surface, and the interior is fitted with drawers, pigeonholes, and a central compartment with door.

NOTES:
1. When owned by collector Louis Guerineau Myers and exhibited in the Girl Scouts Loan Exhibition of 1929, it was called Baltimore, and in a 1947 exhibition of Baltimore and Maryland furniture, this attribution was unfortunately repeated. Bibl. 51, no. 707, ill.; bibl. 4, p. 118, no. 75, ill. p. 119.
2. Bibl. 14.
3. Bibl. 14, figs. 15 and 44.
4. Bibl. 14, p. 63.

MATERIALS: Primary: mahogany (sides, doors, stiles, legs, front of base top, drawer fronts, sides of secretary drawer, desk board), mahogany veneer (cornice, door fronts, secretary drawer face, panels on stiles and legs). Secondary: cedar (small drawers), yellow pine

PROVENANCE: L. Richmond, Freehold, New Jersey; Mrs. J. Amory Haskell; Robert E. Lee Memorial Foundation, Stratford Hall, Virginia; BMA, by purchase, 1946

EXHIBITIONS: Bibl. 51, no. 707, ill.; bibl. 4, p. 118, no. 75, ill. p. 119; bibl. 12, p. 122, no. 109, ill. p. 123

REFERENCES: Bibl. 14, fig. 67; *The Americana Collection of the Late Mrs. J. Amory Haskell*, Part 6, sale cat., sale no. 634, 13–16 Feb. 1945, Parke-Bernet Galleries, Inc., New York, p. 294, no. 1668, ill. p. 295

79

79

80

80. SECRETARY-BOOKCASE (1790–1810)

Baltimore
104½ × 51¼ × 21 in. (265.5 × 130.2 × 53.4 cm.)
The Baltimore Museum of Art: Bequest of C. Edward Snyder, by exchange (BMA 1970.33)

The use of the finest mahogany and mahogany veneers and oval bands of satinwood inlay characterize Baltimore furniture of the classical style. However, it is the use of églomisé glass panels that with high-style painted furniture is a unique contribution of Baltimore to furniture of the Federal period.

In this secretary-bookcase of three pieces, reverse painting on glass is used as a decorative element in the fenestration of the bookcase section and in the interior of the desk. In the upper third of the bookcase's glass doors are églomisé panels of musical trophies painted in gilt on a blue ground. Inside the hinged desk section, inset in the pivoting door to the central storage compartment and framed by line-inlaid satinwood veneer, is an oval églomisé panel. The subject matter is a standing halberdier, seemingly derived from an imported print by Salvator Rosa. A drawing attributed to Rosa and sold at Sotheby's in the same year that this piece of furniture was acquired by the Museum is the line for line inspiration for the figure painted in reverse on the oval glass panel.[1] Flanking the central compartment are two vertical letter drawers faced with églomisé panels of stylized gilt vases and arabesque designs on the same blue ground. The remainder of the desk's interior is composed of six upper and four lower pigeonholes which have arched tops. A blind or secret drawer, with these simulated arch tops in line inlay, is found above the central compartment and the flanking letter drawers. Below the pigeonholes at each side are stepped-out drawers. This exact same interior arrangement is found in another Baltimore secretary-bookcase sold by Parke-Bernet in 1970 and now in a private collection in Georgia.[2] This secretary-

80

bookcase also had églomisé panels, in this instance triangular, on the door to the central compartment and on the vertical letter drawers. It is of interest also to note that while it lacks églomisé decoration, the fenestration pattern of the two glass doors was identical to that of the secretary-bookcase owned by the Museum, and the dimensions of both pieces are very similar. The interiors and writing lids of both secretary-bookcases are flanked by oval inlaid doors opening to large storage compartments. The bases of the two pieces are however entirely different.

In the example owned by the Museum, these two large compartments are fitted for ledgers with removable mahogany dividers held in slots. In fact they are separately constructed mahogany boxes with ledger dividers that are removable. The secondary wood of the small interior drawers and two vertical letter drawers is cedar. The top section has two paneled backboards set vertically and rabbeted into the side boards of the case. The cornice and frieze are constructed as a separate unit and are removable. The secondary wood of the larger drawers of the lower case is tulip wood. The baize covering of the writing surface is a replacement. Its tooled leather border may be original.

NOTES:
1. Sotheby & Co., *Important Old Master Drawings*, sale cat., London, 26 Nov. 1970, p. 70, no. 42, ill.
2. Parke-Bernet Galleries, Inc., *Important XVIII Century American Furniture & Decorations*, sale cat., New York, sale no. 3106, 31 Oct. 1970, p. 50, no. 184, ill. p. 51.

MATERIALS: Primary: mahogany, mahogany veneers, satinwood, light and dark wood inlays. Secondary: cedar. Exterior brass pulls (not original). Eglomisé panels. Baize (not original)

PROVENANCE: Edyth Johns Cotten, Cylburn, Baltimore; sold at public auction, Galton Orsburn Co., Inc., 28–29 Sept. 1942; sold at public auction, Alex Cooper & Sons, 17 Mar. 1970; Israel Sack, Inc., New York; BMA, by purchase, 1970

EXHIBITIONS: Bibl. 12, p. 119, no. 104, ill.

REFERENCES: Bibl. 31, p. 71, no. 410, ill.; bibl. 28, p. 357, pl. II; Robert Morton, *Southern Antiques & Folk Art*, Birmingham, Alabama: Oxmoor House, 1976, p. 51; bibl. 35, p. 166, fig. VIII-22

81. SECRETARY-BOOKCASE (1830–1840)

Baltimore
Maker: John Needles
101½ × 52⅛ × 27⅛ in. (257.9 × 132.4 × 68.9 cm.)
The Baltimore Museum of Art: Gift of Mr. and Mrs. John Engalitcheff, Jr., and Gift of Robert and Jane Meyerhoff, by exchange (BMA 1977.36)

John Needles (1786–1878), Baltimore's long-lived cabinetmaker, marked the inside bottom of the large top drawer of the lower case of this secretary-

81

bookcase with a black ink stencil reading John Needles/Cabinet Maker/54 Hanover St./BALT°.[1] It was owned first by his daughter Mary of Sandy Spring, and was possibly a present from Needles at the time of her marriage.[2] In its basic form (in this case three separate units: base section, bookcase, and cornice section), the secretary-bookcase is ultimately based on French Restoration-style furniture of about 1815–1830, which Boston, New York, and Philadelphia cabinetmakers were also imitating at the time.[3] Here the flattened inset arch in the architrave of the cornice, the pilasters at the sides of the bookcase section, the shortened freestanding columnar supports of the base section, and especially the four bulbous melon-reeded feet topped with leaf carvings are design elements freely borrowed by Needles and other American cabinetmakers from the slightly earlier French style. Their use combined with other elements typify the Baltimore origin of this secretary-bookcase. Bird's-eye and burl maple veneers with mahogany were highly favored by both Baltimore and Philadelphia cabinetmakers in the first two decades of the nineteenth century. Here mahogany is interestingly combined with rosewood and mahogany veneers. The composite capitals of the veneered maple pilasters are finished with Ionic scrolls which are characteristic of Baltimore and are repeated in the round on the similarly veneered columns of the base section. They are like the capitals on a Baltimore pier table (cat. no. 123), while other examples of the form can be found on a writing table and bookcase, and three pier tables at the Maryland Historical Society.[4]

No exact design source for the fenestration of the glass doors is known but a very similar pattern was used in New York.[5] Also obscure is the possible design source for the rosewood decoration consisting of applied conical segments centering on a boss on the base section doors. Precedents for both the recessed Gothic-arched panel and quatrefoil inlays, the latter on both the bottom section and on the cornice architrave, are found in examples of Baltimore furniture made earlier in the nineteenth century (see cat. no. 117). The bottom center drawer of the lower case is a writing drawer fitted with a hinged and ratcheted writing surface.[6]

The sides of the base section are rosewood veneered with inset panels of paired select pieces of branch rosewood veneer. The cornice section can be removed from the bookcase like that on a wardrobe (cat. no. 72) by the same maker, and the bookcase shelves are adjustable. The drawer fronts (veneered with rosewood), sides, and back are mahogany, with bottoms of tulip wood. All the doors are mahogany veneered with rosewood and burl maple. The wooden knobs are recent replacements for glass knobs not original to the piece.

NOTES:
1. The stencil is framed in a wreath/garland oval. For a more thorough discussion of Needles, see cat. no. 94, and bibl. 84, pp. 87–88, 208–209, and 306.
2. This is suggested by Ms. Gregory Weidman, Curator of Furniture at the Maryland Historical Society, who is planning an exhibition of Needles' work and has done much research on him.
3. For related examples from Philadelphia, see bibl. 76, "Part IV: Some case pieces," Jan. 1974, pp. 180–193.
4. Bibl. 84, p. 142, no. 102, ill. and pp. 192–193, nos. 168 and 169, ill.
5. For a New York example, possibly by the firm of Joseph Meeks & Sons, New York, see bibl. 32, p. 273, ill.
6. Another secretary-bookcase with the same arrangement of bottom drawers, with a partial label inscribed Baltimore and probably by John Needles, is illustrated in George Van Derveer Gallenkamp and Richard P. Wunder, "Living with antiques: Brookside, in Orwell, Vermont," *Antiques*, June 1979, p. 1283, pl. V.

MATERIALS: Primary: mahogany, rosewood and burl maple veneers. Secondary: maple, white pine, tulip wood. Base section key cylinders marked PATENT. Baize writing surface (not original)

PROVENANCE: Mary Needles Roberts, Sandy Spring, 1837; by descent to Thomas A. and Jean T. Ladson, Cloverly, Sandy Spring; BMA, by purchase, 1977

REFERENCES: Bibl. 35, p. 128, fig. VI-40

81

Clocks

82. TALL CASE CLOCK (1755–1765)

Easton
Clockmaker: Joseph Bruff
100½ × 21 × 11 in. (255.4 × 53.4 × 28 cm.)
case h.: 94½ in. (240.1 cm.)
The Baltimore Museum of Art: Friends of the American
Wing Fund (BMA 1977.84)

Joseph Bruff (ca. 1730–1785) was the third gener-
ation of that family to work as a silversmith in
Talbot County.[1] His grandfather Thomas had prac-
ticed the trade there before his death in 1702, as
had his father Thomas Jr. who died in 1772.[2] This
Quaker family seems to have settled in Easton
near the courthouse in the early eighteenth century
perhaps attracted by the Third Haven Quaker
Meeting House, a few miles away. There were
many "Publick Houses at the Court House,"[3] one
of which might have been maintained by Joseph
Bruff who is known to have kept a tavern on
Washington Street.[4] In the *Pennsylvania Gazette*
of January 1767 he advertised as follows:

Goldsmith at Talbot Court House having procured a/
Hand from Glascow that has regularly bred a Watch/
finisher . . . that he undertakes to make and repair/
either repeating or plain Clocks and Watches. He
also/carries on the Goldsmiths and Jewellers Business
as/usual.[5]

The tall case clock may have been the joint product
of Joseph Bruff and the unnamed Scottish watchmaker, for it certainly dates from the late 1760's
or early 1770's. Beautifully engraved in script on
the applied roundel in the arch above the brass
dial is the name Joseph Bruff; below the name
TALBOT COURT in block letters is placed above
House in script. The quality of the engraving on
the dial as well as the ornate cast brass corner
spandrels attest to Bruff's skills as a silversmith.[6]
Exactly why the Bruff family first chose and remained in a relatively rural area of Maryland is
unknown.

It has been suggested that the design of the
clock's spandrels was derived from the work of

82

another Quaker clockmaker, Isaac Thomas, working in Chester County, Pennsylvania.[7] Thomas, in turn, is said to have copied his pattern from work by the English silversmith/clockmaker Thomas Wagstaff. Wagstaff, also a Quaker, is known to have had Philadelphia (and possibly Maryland) connections.[8] For Bruff the more direct influence would have been any of the Wagstaff tall case clocks to be found in plantation houses on Maryland's Eastern Shore, some of which he may have repaired in his shop. The present clock works are not original, but are nonetheless eighteenth-century American and have been attached to the dial for many years.

The case is more Queen Anne than Chippendale in style. When acquired by the Museum, that part of the bonnet above the plinth supports had been long removed. Its restoration and that of the finials were based on designs of other American and English examples for there was no known Bruff clock or other Maryland example to use as a prototype. The fretwork pattern repeats that carved below. Clocks of this date are extremely rare in the history of Maryland cabinetmaking. The shaping of the top of the case door and application of a corresponding ogee bolection molding around the edges of the case door and on the front of the base are other Queen Anne features. The bonnet moldings are of solid mahogany while larger moldings at the top and bottom of the waist have a yellow pine core. The clock case may have been made for Bruff by a local craftsman or brought to Talbot Court House from elsewhere.

NOTES:
1. Bibl. 36, pp. 49 and 244.
2. The first courthouse in Talbot County was not erected until 1710–1712 at a place then known as Pitt's Bridge on one of the small arms of the Tred Avon River. This location is now on North Washington Street in Easton. As a village grew around the courthouse and the nearby Third Haven Quaker Meeting House (erected 1682–1684), it first came to be known as Talbot Court House, then Talbot Town, and finally in 1788, by the present name of Easton, bibl. 61, p. 131.
3. Bibl. 61, p. 131.
4. Bibl. 36, p. 49.
5. Bibl. 36, p. 49.
6. A coffee pot by Bruff in the Museum's collection attests to his skill as a silversmith; it may be the most important extant piece of Maryland pre-Revolutionary silver. Jennifer F. Goldsborough, *Eighteenth and Nineteenth Century Maryland Silver in the Collection of The Baltimore Museum of Art* (The Baltimore Museum of Art, 1975), p. 34, no. 4, ill. and bibl. 36, p. 97, no. 60, ill.
7. Bibl. 36, p. 98.

82

8. G.H. Baillie, C. Clutton, and C.A. Ilbert. *Britten's Old Clocks and Watches and Their Makers*, 7th ed. (New York: Bonanza Books, 1956), p. 491. WVE has seen and knows of numerous Wagstaff tall case clocks that were in use in eighteenth-century Maryland, particularly on the Eastern Shore.

MATERIALS: Primary: walnut, mahogany. Secondary: yellow pine, tulip wood. Brass escutcheon (not original), finials (not original); eight-day movement with recoil escapement
PROVENANCE: Fogle Auctioneers, Frederick, 1977; BMA, by purchase, 10 Dec. 1977
EXHIBITIONS: Bibl. 36, p. 49, fig. 2 and p. 98, no. 61, ill.

83. TALL CASE CLOCK (1765–1775)

Philadelphia
Clockmaker: Edward Duffield
103 × 22 × 11¾ in. (261.7 × 55.9 × 29.9 cm.)
The Baltimore Museum of Art: Bequest of Philip B. Perlman (BMA 1960.41.19)

Edward Duffield (1720–1801) of Philadelphia made the works of this eight-day tall case clock. Duffield who advertised his services as a clockmaker from 1756–1775, in 1762 succeeded Thomas Stretch as keeper of the State House clock in Philadelphia.[1]

83

The silvered brass face, with an enameled phases-of-the-moon dial, here is inscribed E. Duffield Philadelphia in an arc above the date recorder. Duffield was one of Philadelphia's major clock-makers before the Revolution and his excellently constructed clock mechanisms are usually found in exceptional cases. The cases vary in style and design, indicating that Duffield enjoyed the services of a number of local cabinetmakers.

The most striking features of this clock are the gracefully slender proportions of its elongated case, the masterfully carved flame finials, the rosettes on the broken-scroll pediment, and the openwork cartouche surmounting the central plinth. The cartouche, of an asymmetrical design, combines C-scrolls, foliage, tendrils, and two flower blossoms. All of the carved elements are original. The bonnet itself, in contrast to the carvings at the top, is relatively plain in design. The colonnettes on either side of the dial are in the plain Doric style, not fluted as are the rear colonnettes. However, the quarter columns with turned capitals and bases found at the corners of the case and the base are fluted. The applied panel on the front of the clock base is an unusual construction feature, whose ogee-shaped top is repeated in the top of the door to the case. Although the case has been badly refinished, the use of exceptionally fine quality grained mahogany is still evident. On the clock's interior are a number of records of repairs, a few of which are on paper labels, but most simply are written on the inside back of the case.[2]

83

NOTES:
1. Bibl. 60, p. 183.
2. Pasted on the saddleboard of the works is the paper repair label of William Gibbons,/Clockmaker,/5 South 40th Street. Philadelphia. Inscribed on the top of the label is the name Dr. Newbold, probably an early owner. Of the eight inscriptions found on the inside of the case, the following are interesting as well as legible: J. Voorhees/cleaned/September/1830., Jas J. Lears cleaned June 16/83., C.F. Stephenson/Nov. 13th 1891.

MATERIALS: Primary: mahogany. Secondary: yellow pine, tulip wood, sweet gum (backboard). Eight-day movement with recoil escapement

PROVENANCE: Philip B. Perlman, Baltimore

EXHIBITIONS: Bibl. 12, p. 113, no. 93, ill.

REFERENCES: Bibl. 5, p. 9, no. 1, ill. pp. 6 and 8

84. TALL CASE CLOCK (1771–1780)

Baltimore, Fells Point
Clockmaker: John Belsner
98 × 22⅞ × 11⅞ in. (249 × 58.1 × 30.2 cm.)
case h.: 94¾ in. (240.8 cm.)
The Baltimore Museum of Art: Purchased as the gift of Mr. and Mrs. Francis C. Taliaferro (BMA 1967.3.2)

John Belsner who worked as a clockmaker in Baltimore ca. 1771–1785, in November of 1772

84

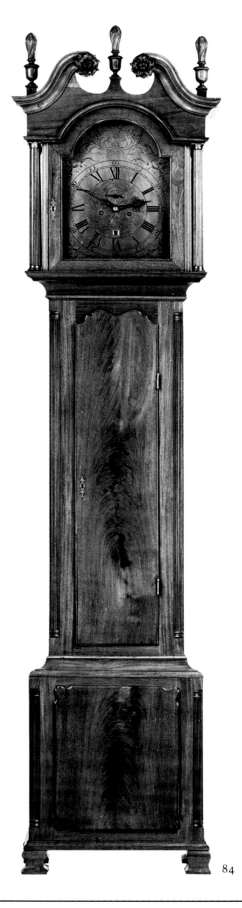

84

purchased with a Henry Brindle a lot in Fells Point.[1] In the deed and lease both men are referred to as "Clockmakers of Baltimore."[2] Their names do not appear in Baltimore records after the Revolution, for Belsner moved to Ephrata, Pennsylvania and died there in 1785 according to Ephrata Cloister archives in which he is listed as a brother.[3] One clock marked with his name and that of Ephrata is known.[4] It has been suggested that Belsner may have been trained and worked in Ephrata before coming to Baltimore.[5] At the present time the tall case clock is Belsner's only known Baltimore work. That the clock's mechanism displays German rather than English clockmaking characteristics has been attributed to Belsner's work or training in Ephrata. The brass dial, probably silvered originally, is engraved in two differing scripts, J. Belsner/Fells Point. The spandrels of the clock face, its arched top, and inner circle are all skillfully engraved with floral, leaf, and scroll designs, many of which are rococo in design. The dial circles, and Roman and arabic numbers are also incised on the brass plate.

The most pleasing aspect of the clock is its fine proportions. It is somewhat reduced in size compared to other tall case clocks of the period, particularly those made in Philadelphia. The case itself, however, is very much in the finest traditions of Philadelphia cabinetmaking. The raised panel with serpentine notched corners on the base, the ogee and scallop shaping of the top of the door to the case, as well as the treatment of the open scroll pediment are repeated on many Philadelphia clocks. These cabinetmaking designs could have easily reached late eighteenth-century Baltimore through such Philadelphia-trained cabinetmakers as Gerrard Hopkins (see cat. no. 15) or Robert Moore. A clock made by the clockmaker David Evans of Baltimore has a case, though of larger size, which is almost identical to the Museum's Belsner clock.[6] The three finials and the feet are restorations. The brass escutcheons and locks replace the original fittings but the brass capitals and bases of the fluted full colonnettes flanking the dial and of the rear half-round colonnettes are original. This tall case clock, like a high chest of drawers (cat. no. 50), was once owned by Howard Sill, one of Baltimore's earliest collectors and an authority on Maryland silver.

NOTES:
1. Bibl. 36, p. 83.
2. This to date is the only known reference to Brindle as a clockmaker and no works known to be his survive. Baltimore County Deeds, 1772, AL#F, f.280, Hall of Records, Annapolis.

3. Bibl. 88, p. 13.
4. Bibl. 88, p. 73, ill. p. 28.
5. Bibl. 36, p. 83.
6. Bibl. 11, p. 71, no. 55, ill.

MATERIALS: Primary: mahogany, mahogany laminate. Secondary: tulip wood, yellow pine; finials and feet (not original). Brass escutcheons (not original); eight-day movement with recoil escapement

PROVENANCE: Howard Sill (1867–1927), Baltimore; Mary Frances DuVal Sill (Mrs. Howard); Milton Finch; Pattison & Co., sale 26 Jan. 1967; BMA, by purchase, 1967

EXHIBITIONS: Bibl. 29, pp. 96–97, no. 67, ill.

REFERENCES: BMA News, nos. 1 & 2, 1968, ill. p. 39; Elizabeth Stillinger, The Antiques Guide to Decorative Arts in America, 1600–1875, New York: E.P. Dutton and Co., 1972, p. 279; bibl. 24, p. 39, ill. p. 38, fig. 58; bibl. 36, p. 83, no. 30, ill.

85. TALL CASE CLOCK (1780–1790)

Hagerstown
Clockmaker: George Woltz
92 × 22⅝ × 11¾ in. (233.8 × 57.5 × 29.9 cm.)
The Baltimore Museum of Art: Middendorf Foundation Fund (BMA 1972.16)

The maker of this tall case clock, John George Adam Woltz (1744–1811) of Hagerstown, was both a watch and clockmaker, and possibly also worked as a silversmith and cabinetmaker. Woltz's grandfather Frederick Reinhardt Woltz (1696–1782) came to America in 1731 from Switzerland, settling first in the German section of Pennsylvania. George Woltz, born in York, Pennsylvania, was the first child of Frederick's eldest son Peter. After apprenticing in Carlisle, Woltz moved to Hagerstown where he spent the rest of his life.[1] When exhibited with other Maryland tall case clocks as representative examples of the allied trade of clock and watchmaking in a 1984 exhibition, the Woltz clock was said to possess the "only one truly unusual striking system."[2] This "J-hook system" is a hybrid that evolved from English and German clockmaking traditions, and its rare use was confined to central Maryland and parts of Pennsylvania. Other construction features of the clock mechanism have led experts to believe that at one time Woltz worked with the York clockmaker Peter Schütz, a Swiss-born immigrant.[3] A center roundel on the engraved arch-topped brass dial bears the name George Woltz/ Hagers Town/No. 45. The engraved birds, leaves, vines, tulips, and other flowers above and in the dial and spandrels are in the decorative traditions of the Pennsylvania Germans, as are the carved rosettes on the scrolls of the pediment. The walnut

85

85

85

case is of extremely solid construction typical of furniture produced by Pennsylvania German cabinetmakers. The rails of the waist tenon through the stiles and are secured with double pins. Other clocks made by Woltz are housed in much more sophisticated cases of the Philadelphia style; however, even these examples have the same slightly swelling colonnettes on the hood found here.[4] The feet have been cut down about two inches, and it has never had finials. Bonaventure is written on the back of the pendulum in indelible ink.

NOTES:
1. Bibl. 64, pp. 124–126.
2. Bibl. 36. The Woltz clock, no. 346, p. 229, is also discussed on pp. 50–51, fig. 3 and p. 55. This catalogue contains a detailed discussion of the "J-Hook" system by Edward F. LaFond, Jr. entitled "Some Comment on Repeating Striking Systems Found on Maryland Clocks," pp. 60–63.
3. Bibl. 36, p. 62.
4. Bibl. 64, p. 124, figs. 1 and 2.

MATERIALS: Primary: walnut. Secondary: yellow pine. Brass escutcheon (not original); eight-day movement with anchor recoil escapement

PROVENANCE: Max Blum, Antiques, Philadelphia; Dr. and Mrs. Irvin B. Berd, Arden, Delaware; BMA, by purchase, 1972

86. TALL CASE CLOCK (1796–1800)

Baltimore, Fells Point
Clockmaker: William Elvins
98⅛ × 21¾ × 10⅞ in. (249.3 × 55.3 × 27.6 cm.)
Collection of Rossetta A. and Sadie B. Feldman, Baltimore:
Promised Gift to The Baltimore Museum of Art

Of unusual height, even with a flat topped rather than scroll pedimented hood, this tall case clock belongs to a group of Baltimore clocks, by various makers, with a design of grape vine and clusters at the sides of the tympanum arch.[1] And some clocks, as in this example, also have bellflower inlays at the outer sides of the arch.[2] Another shared decoration is the inlaid line frieze at the waist below the hood and above the case door. Here intersecting half circles of line inlay form intersecting diamond patterns. The maker of the works was William Elvins, a watch and clockmaker and silversmith, who worked from 1796–1841, at various locations in the Fells Point section of Baltimore.[3] His name and location are painted on the front of the enameled dial, and on the back, with its separate phases-of-the-moon polychrome enameled dial and a painting of a British-flagged ship, is stamped Wilson Birm, indicating that the dials were imported from England.[4] The front colonnettes of the hood have vertical line inlays;

86

86

87. SHELF CLOCK (1792–1820)

Newburyport, Massachusetts
Clockmaker: David Wood
35¾ × 11¹⁵⁄₁₆ × 5⅞ in. (90.8 × 30.3 × 14.9 cm.)
case h.: 33¼ in. (84.5 cm.)
The Baltimore Museum of Art: Gift of Mrs. Francis
White, from the Collection of Mrs. Miles White, Jr.
(BMA 1973.76.232)

The works of this shelf clock were made by David
Wood (1766–ca. 1824) of Newburyport, Massachusetts. Wood set up his clockmaking shop in 1792
and is believed to have worked as a clockmaker
into the third decade of the nineteenth century.[1]
From the evidence of surviving numbers, shelf
clocks seem to have been his specialty, although
some fine tall case clocks by him have survived.
A variety of his clocks can be found in the collection
at Winterthur,[2] the Garvan Collection at Yale,[3]
and the Metropolitan Museum,[4] as well as in many
private collections. No records have survived to
reveal who made the cases for the many Wood
shelf clocks, but perhaps it was a cabinetmaker
employed in his shop. The wide range of clock
cases, from simple to elaborate, doubtless reflects
the tastes as well as pocketbooks of his clients. As

the rear colonnettes do not. The block inlay of
light and dark woods outlining the tympanum arch
above the glass door also borders the inlaid frieze
at the top of the waist. The mirror veneered base
is inlaid with a smaller version of this light and
dark wood block inlay. The mahogany veneered
case door has an applied beaded edge.

NOTES:
1. These clocks are identified and well described in bibl.
   84, p. 126, no. 82, ill. Obviously a number of Baltimore
   clockmakers employed the same cabinetmaker to make
   their cases. Although there are some variations in the
   inlaid grape vine and cluster motifs (some are more
   detailed and sophisticated in design than others), all are
   derived from the same local source.
2. Bibl. 84, p. 127, no. 83, ill. and bibl. 4, p. 145, no. 93,
   ill.
3. Elvins' addresses were 32 Thames Street until a move
   in 1799 to 10 Bond Street, and from 1802 to 1808 at 12
   Fell Street; bibl. 65, p. 119. He may also have worked
   in Charleston, South Carolina from 1801–1806; bibl.
   36, p. 251.
4. Bibl. 36, p. 51.

MATERIALS: Primary: mahogany, mahogany veneers, light
and dark wood inlays. Secondary: tulip wood (backboards),
yellow pine. Wooden escutcheons (not original). Eight-day
movement with recoil escapement

PROVENANCE: Collection of Samson Feldman, Baltimore;
Rossetta A. and Sadie B. Feldman

REFERENCES: Bibl. 84, p. 126, no. 82, n. 2

87

in this example, nearly all of Wood's clocks have painted metal dials believed to be English imports. To a wide variety of clock face designs David Wood then added his name and sometimes Newburyport. Many inscriptions about the care and repair of the works are found on the inside of the case door, the earliest being G G Brewster with the date April 10 1820 inscribed in the same hand below the signature. This is probably George Gaines Brewster (1797–1872), a watchmaker in nearby Portsmouth, New Hampshire.[5] Originally the clock was fitted with three brass finials; the one remaining is a replacement.

NOTES:
1. Bibl. 60, p. 313.
2. Bibl. 56, pp. 211–212, no. 169, ill.; p. 213, no. 170, ill. p. 212; and p. 213, no. 171, ill.
3. Bibl. 7, pp. 78–81, no. 15, ill. and pp. 168–171, no. 37, ill.
4. Bibl. 24, p. 94, fig. 192.
5. In red pencil below this signature is the name Wm Butterfield, the address New Boston, New Hampshire, and the notation cleaned Nov 1857. Another inscription on the door records that the shelf clock was cld [cleaned] by H. McAllister/June 14, 1895/629 Broadway. Mr. McAllister's city and state are unknown at the present time. For information on George Gaines Brewster, see bibl. 46, p. 402.

MATERIALS: Primary: mahogany, mahogany veneers, light and dark wood inlays. Secondary: white pine. Brass finial and escutcheon; thirty-hour movement with anchor recoil escapement; two winding holes plugged and overpainted
PROVENANCE: Mrs. Miles White, Jr., Baltimore; Francis White; Nancy Brewster White (Mrs. Francis)
REFERENCES: Karen M. Jones, "Museum accessions," *Antiques*, May 1974, p. 1010; bibl. 55, vol. 2, p. 958, no. 1920, ill. p. 960

88. SHELF CLOCK (1815–1825)

Boston
Clockmaker: Aaron Willard
34⅞ × 13⅜ × 6 in. (88.6 × 34 × 15.2 cm.)
case h.: 29⅛ in. (74 cm.)
The Baltimore Museum of Art: Gift of Mrs. Francis White, from the Collection of Mrs. Miles White, Jr. (BMA 1973.76.233)

Aaron Willard (1757–1844) was born in Grafton, Massachusetts, the youngest of four clockmaking brothers. He probably learned the trade from his older brothers Benjamin and Simon; together they were to become the most recognized names in American clockmaking. Aaron Willard moved to Roxbury in 1780, about the same time as Simon. By 1798 he had purchased land and a house on Washington Street in Boston "on the Neck," with a factory connected to the house by a row of

88

buildings rented to various craftsmen. Some of these artisans would seem to have been directly connected to the clockmaking industry.[1]

This shelf clock is typical of the clocks mass-produced in the Willard factory. Because it is painted white, the example here is commonly called a "bride's" clock. That such clocks were produced only for brides cannot be substantiated by any nineteenth-century documentation, but the claim is not entirely implausible because white cases are unusual and suggest that they were probably made only on special order. The mass production of such clocks trained and prepared other artisans to imitate the Willard products. The extent of this industry is revealed in a shelf clock made by a Daniel Hubbard of Medfield, Massachusetts.[2] Since Aaron Willard produced shelf clocks in large number in what he called a clock factory, the clock case makers and the decorators of the painted glass panels were presumably also on the premises. Aaron Willard, Jr. (b. 1783) is known to have done much of the reverse painting on glass for his father. There survives an Aaron Willard wall clock whose reverse painted rectangular panel at the base is signed A. Willard, Jr. and Spencer Nolen.[3] Another ornamental painter, Charles Bullard, rented space from 1816–1844 from Aaron Willard between Willard's house and his clock manufactory.[4]

The Willard shelf clock is comprised of three separable units—the bonnet, the case, and the removable lower front églomisé panel. The bonnet door is signed Aaron Willard/BOSTON in gilt in a red oval surrounded by gold leaf foliage and shells. The glass surrounding the dial is decorated with gold lyres and scrolled foliage with green and red highlights on a black ground. The same foliage motif, but with stars rather than lyres in each corner, is repeated on the enframed scene painted on the bottom glass panel of a young girl and a garlanded sheep in a pastoral landscape. The same subject is found on another Willard shelf clock and on a clock by a student of the Willard school, William King Lemist (see cat. no. 89).[5] The gilded, cushion-molded clock base sits on pressed-brass front feet and cast hollow ball rear feet. The carved pineapple finial and flanking balls at the top are original. The white painted dial with black Roman numerals has been retouched but not completely repainted. The case has been repainted and regilded in the past.

Of the numerous inscriptions found on the clock's interior, the earliest would seem to be that in pencil below a groove cut to receive the clock works. In flourishing script, it reads Made at Willards/Roxbury/Boston.[6]

NOTES:
1. This and other information on the Willards is found in bibl. 86, pp. 85–89.
2. Bibl. 24, p. 100, fig. 208.
3. Bibl. 21, p. 22, ill. p. 23, pl. 6. Spencer Nolen was the brother-in-law of Aaron Willard, Jr.; they worked together as clock dial and sign painters from 1805–1809 under the name of Nolen and Willard. He was probably the Nolen of Nolen and Curtis (Samuel) who were listed in both Boston and Philadelphia (1809) and are known to have been ornamental painters. See bibl. 60, p. 251 and bibl. 7, pp. 194–195.
4. Charles Bullard (1794–1871) is said to have been trained in the art of glass painting by an anonymous English artist who worked for Simon Willard. He frequently advertised his services as an ornamental painter and probably worked for many Boston clockmakers.
5. Bibl. 24, p. 104, fig. 217.
6. Other interesting inscriptions, all in pencil script are, in order of date, as follows: Cleaned by John Holden/ Quincy Dec 7. 1846/EOR; Bought [. . .] Old Bryant Newcomb Auction/at Braintree Neck Oct, [. . .] 1847; Cleaned By Jonathan S. Johnson/February 9th 1874/ Cleaned and oiled/Nov 29 Thanks Giving Day/By J.S. Johnson/Quincy; found on the base section behind the églomisé panel the following list, all in the same hand: HB Ellis./M Ellis./ME Ellis./LF Ellis./PW Ellis./CF Ellis.; next to the list is written Feb 9th 1874./splendid sleigh-

ing; on a printed label pasted in the bonnet: Cleaned and Repaired/BY/E.L. Fisher,/New-Boston, N.H.; and handwritten on this label: No. 355 and Aug. 25 1880/ Nov. 4, 1887. Elsewhere on the clock's interior the number 164 appears many times. No. 4 is also marked on the inside of the backboard of the case.

MATERIALS: Primary: cherry painted white and gilded. Secondary: white pine. Reverse painted glass panels. Eight-day movement with recoil escapement
PROVENANCE: Mrs. Miles White, Jr., Baltimore; Francis White; Nancy Brewster White (Mrs. Francis)
REFERENCES: Bibl. 55, vol. 2, p. 959, no. 1922, ill. p. 961

89. SHELF CLOCK (1815–1825)

Philadelphia
Clockmakers: William King Lemist (1791–1820) and William B. Tappan (working in Philadelphia, 1818–1820)
32⅛ × 13 × 5¾ in. (81.6 × 33 × 14.6 cm.)
case h.: 31⅛ in. (79.1 cm.)
The Baltimore Museum of Art: Bequest of J. Gilman D'Arcy Paul (BMA 1972.27.10)

This shelf clock with beautifully painted églomisé glass panels, one surrounding the concave painted iron dial and the other at the base of the clock, bears the names of Lemis & Tappan,/Philad[A] on the painted glass below the dial. William King Lemist was born in Dorchester, Massachusetts, April 18, 1791.[1] His family was acquainted with the Willards and he is said to have learned clockmaking as an apprentice to Simon Willard. A wall clock, inscribed on the dial, made by William Lemist, 1812, and given as a wedding present to his sister in that same year, was long thought to have been his only work.[2] However, the Museum's shelf clock was apparently made by Lemist and William B. Tappan during their brief partnership in Philadelphia.[3] Tappan was listed as a clockmaker in 1818 at 49 North Third Street in Philadelphia.[4] For the next two years, 1819–1820, Tappan joined Lemist as a clock and patent timepiece maker at 3 South Third Street. After the latter's death in 1820, the listing for Tappan stops as well[5] so it would seem he chose not to continue his trade, at least not in Philadelphia.

The clock is constructed of three basic units in the same manner as the Aaron Willard shelf clock. The reverse painted glass of the Philadelphia clock is also related to Willard and the Roxbury school, for the pastoral scene is much like that of cat. no. 88. Lemist and Tappan obviously transported in toto the Willard shelf clock to Philadelphia and indeed may have imported elements such as the églomisé panels from a New England source.

The scrolls of the pediment have been replaced and the brass finial is not original. Since the clock

89

MATERIALS: Primary: mahogany, mahogany veneers. Secondary: white pine, cherry (case), tulip wood (bracket support). Reverse painted glass panels. Painted iron dial; brass finial (not original); eight-day movement with recoil escapement
PROVENANCE: J. Gilman D'Arcy Paul, Baltimore
EXHIBITIONS: Bibl. 12, p. 116, no. 99, ill.
REFERENCES: Bibl. 55, vol. 2, pp. 1004–1006, no. 2044, ill.

90. WALL CLOCK (1805–1820)

Baltimore
Clockmaker: Nathaniel Monroe
38½ × 10¾ × 3¾ in. (97.8 × 27.3 × 9.5 cm.)
case h.: 36¾ in. (93.4 cm.)
The Baltimore Museum of Art: Bequest of Mary Graham Basshor (BMA 1947.132)

The name N. Monroe appears in gold leaf on the églomisé throat panel of this wall clock. Notwithstanding the variant spelling of his name, N. Monroe is certainly Nathaniel Munroe (1777–1861), a New England-born and trained clockmaker and silversmith who is known to have worked in Baltimore between 1817 and 1840.[1] It is believed that by 1800 Munroe was working in Concord with his older brother Daniel, who had apprenticed with Simon Willard in Boston.[2] By 1805–1806 he was in Virginia where he advertised in the *Norfolk Gazette and Public Ledger*, although those ads indicate that he was chiefly a retailer, and probably not making clocks.[3] Upon returning to Concord, Munroe formed a partnership with Samuel Whiting.[4] A clock carrying their names shares many features with the Museum's example including the bracket base with gold balls and an acorn pendant, identical pierced-brass side arms, and the same style of arabic numbers on the dial.[5]

By 1818, one year after Munroe had moved to Baltimore, he was advertising "elegant eight day Clocks and Willard's patent time pieces" from his "Clock and Time Piece Warehouse."[6] The Museum's clock could be described as a Willard timepiece, for Willard patented this form, now commonly known as a banjo clock, in 1802. It is impossible to know whether Munroe made the clock imitating a design well known to him, or imported it from Willard's Boston manufactory. In assigning a place of manufacture the two églomisé panels on the throat and base offer contradictory evidence as to the clock's origin. The thermometer inset in the throat panel is an unusual feature; in addition to the normal degree markings are temperature descriptions such as Blood ht, 90°, spirits boil, 176°, Sumʳ ht, 76°. The latter hardly describes

never had feet, the bracket support may be original. Much of the visual impact of the clock is due to the brilliant red backgrounds of its painted glass panels. V is stamped on the inside of the lower rail of the bonnet door, on the front upper edge of the bottom, and on the inside lower rail of the painted glass panel at the base. Scratched on the lower left rear plate of the clock works are the initials, E.W. Jr., an early twentieth-century Baltimore repairman who also marked another Museum clock (cat. no. 90).

NOTES:
1. Bibl. 86, pp. 113–114.
2. Bibl. 86, pl. 36.
3. Bibl. 26, p. 182.
4. Bibl. 26, p. 194.
5. A young man with poor health, Lemist went to sea, hoping to improve his constitution; sadly and ironically, he died in a shipwreck off the coast of Africa in October of 1820.

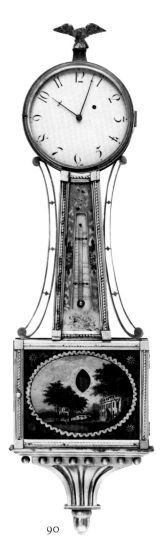

90

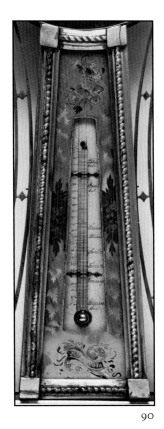

90

William Watts' *The Seats of Nobility and Gentry*.[7] The views in both the engraving and on the clock are very close except that as a result of reverse painting on the glass, the view on the clock is a mirror image of the original. The majority of early nineteenth-century shelf and wall clocks with églomisé painting have simple geometric or trophy patterns; where there is a scene it is most often pastoral, romantic, or mythological, so that depiction of an identifiable view is, like the thermometer, very rare. This suggests that the clock was a commission, and that the order may have come from someone familiar with Watts' book. What is most interesting to note, however, is that Baltimore's first significant art collector, Robert Gilmor II, owned a watercolor of the same subject.[8]

XVI is chisel-marked on the inside lower rail of the throat panel and on the inside top rail of the base panel. There are many inscriptions by late nineteenth and early twentieth-century Baltimore repairmen on the interior.[9] There has been some restoration to the painting on the base panel and the upper left throat panel, and the painted dial numbers have also been retouched. The cast copper eagle finial appears to be original.

NOTES:

1. Dates for Munroe's first appearance in Baltimore have been variously reported as 1811, 1815, and 1817. His advertisements in the city begin in 1817 (*Federal Republican and Baltimore Telegraph*, 10 Oct. 1817). The spelling of his name as marked on his silver was always Munroe (bibl. 36, p. 272); the "o" variant appears in advertisements and city directories where such misspellings were common.
2. Bibl. 60, p. 248.
3. *Norfolk Gazette and Public Ledger*, 21 Apr. 1806.
4. Bibl. 60, p. 248.
5. N. Hudson Moore, *The Old Clock Book* (New York: Frederick A. Stokes Co., 1911), fig. 93.
6. *American and Commercial Daily Advertiser*, Baltimore, 27 May 1818.
7. William Watts, *The Seats of Nobility and Gentry* (1783; reprint, New York: Grammercy Publishing Co., 1982), pl. LX.
8. The Gilmor watercolor is in the Charles J.M. Eaton Collection of The Johns Hopkins University, P.I.11.32.
9. The earliest is by C. Nuitz dated 1875, who worked in the city 1856–1889 (bibl. 36, p. 273). "E W Jr" inscribed the clock in 1906 and 1911; he also repaired the clock by Lemist and Tappan (cat. no. 89).

MATERIALS: Primary: mahogany. Secondary: white pine. Painted iron dial. Eglomisé glass panels. Eight-day movement with anchor recoil escapement. Mercury thermometer

PROVENANCE: Mary Graham Basshor, Baltimore

REFERENCES: Jane Webb Smith, "Clock and Watchmaking in Maryland," in bibl. 36, p. 57, fig. 12

summer heat in the Baltimore area. Despite this suggestion of a New England origin, the base panel picture raises the possibility that the clock was a product of Munroe's Baltimore shop. The view can be identified as Carshalton House, Surrey, England, an engraving of which was published in 1783 in

Tables

91

91. DROPLEAF TABLE (1720–1740)

Mid-Atlantic states
28¼ × 57¾ × 47⅝ in. (71.8 × 146.7 × 121 cm.)
top with leaves down: 18½ in. (47 cm.)
The Baltimore Museum of Art: Gift of Mrs. Francis
White, from the Collection of Mrs. Miles White, Jr.
(BMA 1973.76.223)

Oval-topped gatelegged tables, a seventeenth-century furniture form that persisted well into the eighteenth century, were popular along the entire Atlantic seaboard. There are repeated references in eighteenth-century inventories to "walnut oval tables." Gatelegged tables of the middle colonies, notably those of Pennsylvania, are usually larger with bolder, more pronounced turnings on their legs and stretchers. The large vase-turning on each of the four fixed legs and the shortened vase turnings of the gatelegs are more typical of the middle Atlantic and southern colonies than of New England. The drawers at each end appear to be nineteenth-century additions. The legs terminate in ball feet. The vase, reel, spool, and ball design of the legs is repeated in the turned stretchers of the base. The table was purchased by Mrs. Miles White near Port Deposit in Cecil County. No other provenance is known.

MATERIALS: Primary: walnut. Secondary: red oak (framing), tulip wood (drawer framing, rail of gatelegs). Brass pulls (not original)

PROVENANCE: Mrs. Miles White, Jr., Baltimore; Francis White; Nancy Brewster White (Mrs. Francis)

92. DROPLEAF TABLE (1750–1780)

Maryland or Pennsylvania
28⅝ × 56¾ × 49⅞ in. (72.7 × 144.2 × 126.7 cm.)
top with leaves down: 17⅜ in. (44.1 cm.)
The Baltimore Museum of Art: Bequest of J. Gilman
D'Arcy Paul (BMA 1972.27.9)

Dropleaf tables like this example were regularly used as dining tables and called such by the 1760's.[1] When the two leaves are raised, they form an oval top with the stationary center which has rounded ends. The table may have originated in Maryland, Philadelphia, or the adjacent Delaware Valley area. Queen Anne-style dining tables were made in considerable number in mid- to late eighteenth-century Philadelphia but usually show certain elements of design and decoration that are not found on the Museum's table. For instance, the cabriole legs have a more inward curve than the outward stance found in the legs of comparable Philadelphia tables. The carved shell on the knees of the Museum's table legs is rather unusual, the carving

92

being almost three-dimensional. It differs sharply from the somewhat standardized flatter five-lobed Philadelphia shell. At the base of these shells are rather coarsely carved bellflower drops. Also, Philadelphia tables of the period usually have a thumbnail-molded edge on the inner edge of the stile of each leg which is not found here. One swing rail has been replaced, the other is of beech. The use of mahogany is unusual in a table of this style, walnut being more common. According to the last owner the table came from Maryland's Eastern Shore.

NOTES:
1. Bibl. 39, p. 177.

MATERIALS: Primary: mahogany. Secondary: true poplar, beech

PROVENANCE: Edward Gibson, Baltimore; J. Gilman D'Arcy Paul

92

93

93. DROPLEAF GAMING TABLE (1790–1810)

Annapolis or Baltimore
28⅝ × 43¾ × 31¾ in. (72.7 × 111.2 × 80.7 cm.)
top with leaves down: 20⅞ in. (53 cm.)
The Baltimore Museum of Art: Anonymous Gift
(BMA 1982.142)

Dropleaf gaming tables are a great rarity in American furniture of the Federal period, although there were numerous English prototypes.[1] Because of its known provenance, secondary woods, and construction, this dropleaf table with a sliding and reversible top would seem to have been made in Maryland, although whether in Annapolis or Baltimore cannot be determined. The table's basic form and simple inlay lack the sophistication shown in the fully developed Baltimore Pembroke tables of the period. There is a visual link between this table and the conservative English-influenced furniture made by John Shaw and other Annapolis cabinetmakers in the late eighteenth century.[2] When inverted the inner side of the plain sliding table top is inlaid with light and dark woods to form a checker or chess board. Removal of the top reveals a recessed two-section inlaid backgammon board with tills at each end having sliding lids.

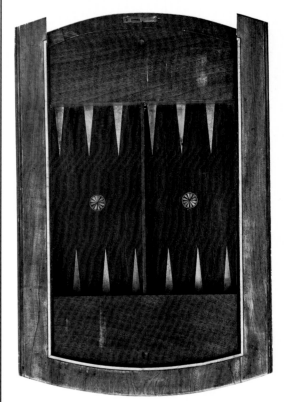

93

The bowed end aprons are inlaid and mounted with hardware to simulate drawers, with a lock at one end to secure the sliding top. The present bail pulls are replacements that reproduce the original hardware. The last owner purchased the table at the estate sale of Miss Liza Ridgely of Baltimore, a descendant of the Ridgely family of Hampton.[3] Although many of her possessions came from that house, it is not possible to ascertain whether or when this table was at Hampton.

NOTES:
1. Other tables of the period incorporating inlaid gaming boards include one in The Museum of Fine Arts, Houston, illustrated in bibl. 83, p. 82, no. 156; a Boston example owned by the Kaufman Americana Foundation illustrated in bibl. 32, p. 248; and two examples illustrated in bibl. 2, vol. 2, p. 316, no. 784 and vol. 5, p. 1247, no. P4100.
2. See bibl. 30.
3. Hampton National Historic Site, Towson, Maryland. This house, begun in 1773, remained in the Ridgely family until it was acquired by the National Park Service in 1947.

MATERIALS: Primary: mahogany, mahogany veneers, light and dark wood inlays. Secondary: yellow pine (interior side rails), tulip wood (end rails), oak (hinge rail, leaf supports). Brass hardware (not original)

PROVENANCE: Ridgely family of Hampton, Baltimore County; by descent to Miss Liza Ridgely, Baltimore; Private Collection

REFERENCES: Bibl. 19, nos. 578 and 579, ill.; bibl. 20, p. 633, no. 3, ill.

94. DROPLEAF SOFA TABLE   (1830–1840)
Baltimore
Maker: John Needles
27 × 64 × 22⅛ in. (68.6 × 162.6 × 56.2 cm.)
top with leaves down: 45⅜ in. (115.3 cm.)
The Baltimore Museum of Art: Gift of John O. Needles, in Memory of Mrs. William A. Dixon (BMA 1953.226.1)

In 1953 a great-grandson of the Baltimore cabinet-maker John Needles (1786–1878) presented eleven pieces of Needles' furniture to The Baltimore Museum of Art in memory of Needles' granddaughter Mrs. William A. Dixon, nee Emma Needles of Baltimore.[1] The dropleaf sofa table, according to Mrs. Dixon, had been made for William Moale of Baltimore[2] who refused it when finished, thinking a price of $60 excessive.[3] The table was then given to Needles' daughter Mary when she married in 1837[4] and, since it is in the Gothic-Revival style which in Baltimore would date to about 1830–1860, the family tradition is plausible. The rectangular top and side drop leaves are richly cross-banded and veneered with striped walnut. The drop leaves when extended are supported by slides. The molded apron is actually a drawer front on one of the long sides and made without a pull, in order not to break up the expanse of handsome veneer. It can be opened by grasping the lower edge through cutouts in the drawer rail.

94

94

NOTES:
1. The other Needles pieces are a wardrobe given by the wife of this donor, cat. no. 72, and a labeled secretary-bookcase, cat. no. 81. The gift also included a mirror (BMA 1953.226.2), marble-topped wash stand (BMA 1953.226.3), dressing table (BMA 1953.226.4), chest of drawers (BMA 1953.226.5), two work tables (BMA 1953.226.6&.8), bedstead (BMA 1953.226.7), side table (BMA 1953.226.9), youth's bed (BMA 1953.226.10), and dressing glass (BMA 1953.226.11).
2. Probably William Armistead Moale (1800–1880).
3. Bibl. 57, p. 295.
4. Bibl. 57, p. 295. The date of 1857 for the marriage of Needles' daughter Mary is incorrect. She was married in 1837.

MATERIALS: Walnut (top, stiles, drawer, feet), walnut veneers, yellow and white pine (apron, base below stiles)

PROVENANCE: Mary Needles Roberts, Sandy Spring, 1837; by descent to John O. Needles, Baltimore

REFERENCES: Bibl. 63, p. 48; bibl. 55, vol. 2, p. 752, no. 1426, ill. p. 751; bibl. 19, no. 610, ill.; bibl. 57, p. 295, ill.

95

95. CARD TABLE (1765–1780)

Boston or Salem
28⅝ × 32 × 15⅝ in. (72.7 × 81.3 × 39.7 cm.)
The Baltimore Museum of Art: Gift of Mrs. Howard R. McPeck (BMA 1945.20)

Made in either Boston or Salem ca. 1770, this small card table is superbly proportioned, with slender cabriole legs and shallow scalloped apron characteristic of Massachusetts card tables of this period. Also in the Massachusetts mode are the pronounced boldly carved ball-and-claw feet with two side claws slightly turned back. The star punch decoration above the leaf carvings on the knees is found on another Massachusetts table (cat. no. 131), and is often considered characteristic of Salem rather than Boston. The table when open originally revealed a red baize playing surface. Four recessed oval dishes are carved at each corner. The drawer may have been added in the early nineteenth century when the piece underwent extensive repairs due to damage by fire. A table of similar design and proportion is in the collection of the Milwaukee Art Museum.[1] Family history records that the table has been in Maryland from at least the middle of the nineteenth century when it belonged to Judge Peter W. Crain in whose family it descended until given to the Museum.[2]

NOTES:
1. Karen M. Jones, "American furniture in the Milwaukee Art Center," *Antiques*, May 1977, p. 979, fig. 8.
2. Registration files, The Baltimore Museum of Art. Crain was a judge of the First Judicial District Court.

MATERIALS: Primary: mahogany. Secondary: white pine, birch. Leaves reversed top for bottom; knee brackets (not original). Baize (not original). Brass knob (not original)

PROVENANCE: Peter W. Crain, Charles County and Baltimore; Robert Crain; Mrs. Robert Crain (Mrs. Louis R. Cheney), Hartford, Connecticut; Eleanor Crain McPeck, Washington, D.C.

EXHIBITIONS: Bibl. 12, p. 100, no. 72, ill.

96. CARD TABLE (1760–1790)

New York
26⅛ × 34¼ × 16⅞ in. (66.4 × 87 × 42.9 cm.)
Collection of Dorothy McIlvain Scott, Baltimore: Promised Gift to The Baltimore Museum of Art

An exuberant and bold expression of the card table form was developed in New York City during the latter part of the eighteenth century. While the most fully realized type was the five-legged card table with serpentine-front and ball-and-claw feet, variants of the characteristic design having four

96

legs, as in this example, are also known. Morrison H. Heckscher has identified two types, each with distinctive characteristics, and while this table shares certain elements, it does not correspond exactly to either Type I or Type II as specified by Heckscher.[1] Like them, however, it is made of mahogany; features a serpentine front skirt with attached molding below and semi-serpentine side skirts; large projecting square corners on either side of the front supported by cabriole legs with carved knees and ball-and-claw feet; and a double top with serpentine sides. The top is fitted with a conforming baize playing surface and is cut around square candlestick corners and oval counter dishes. Although the gadrooned molding here is less vigorously carved than on most Type I examples, other elements such as the deep serpentine skirt, the foliate acanthus carving on the knees of the front legs and exposed part of the back legs, and the high ball-and-claw feet closely resemble the Type I group. A definite link to either of the two New York shops that produced the distinctive types cannot be confirmed. In construction, the Museum's table is most closely allied to a four-legged card table lacking gadrooned ornament and knee carving now in The Metropolitan Museum of Art.[2] Both have deep serpentine fronts faced with veneers; thick serpentine-shaped outside rails, straight on the inside; similar pegging of the rails to the rear legs; and a similar four-part finger-joint hinge dividing the outer rear rail. Shaped glue blocks are behind each knee bracket and there are three glue

blocks along the back rail. The top is attached with two screws through the front and rear rails and one through each side rail.

NOTES:
1. Morrison H. Heckscher, "The New York serpentine card table," *Antiques*, May 1973, pp. 974–983.
2. Bibl. 39, pp. 168–169, no. 101, ill.

MATERIALS: Primary: mahogany, mahogany veneers. Secondary: chestnut (back rail), white oak (fly rail), ash (inside rear rail). Baize (not original)

PROVENANCE: David Stockwell, Inc., Wilmington, Delaware; Dorothy McIlvain Scott, Baltimore

96

97. CARD TABLE (1800–1810)

Annapolis
Maker: John Shaw
29½ × 36¼ × 17¾ in. (75 × 92.1 × 45.1 cm.)
The Baltimore Museum of Art: Purchased as the Gift of Mr. and Mrs. Francis C. Taliaferro (BMA 1967.3.1)

The design and inlay of this card table are atypical of John Shaw's work, but the table has been attributed to this well-known Annapolis cabinetmaker because, except for a different string inlay on the bottom edges of the front and side aprons, it is identical to a card table bearing Shaw's label.[1] The

97

97

tulip wood tops of both tables are veneered with matching grain woods cut from the same piece of mahogany; likewise the veneers on the front and side aprons. The Museum's card table has no known early Maryland provenance and was found about twenty-five years ago in Omaha, Nebraska. The other privately owned table has remained in Maryland. It is conceivable that the two tables were made as a pair, so minor are their differences. The only serpentine card tables known to have been made by Shaw, their elegantly curved form is more advanced than his usual square card table.[2] The inlaid motifs on the front stiles of a vase of flowers on a wall bracket set against a satinwood background stained green are unusual and not found on any of Shaw's other known works. The rounded edge, with a slight bead, of the top and the line inlays on the apron are perhaps the only recognizable exterior Shaw characteristics. However, certain construction details are repeated again and again by John Shaw: the stationary back rail and hinged fly rail of white oak; the inner frame and backings of the top and leaf of yellow pine and tulip wood respectively. The playing surface is covered with its original light green baize.

NOTES:
1. John Shaw (1745–1829) working in Annapolis by 1771. Bibl. 30, pp. 155–158, no. 57, ill.
2. Bibl. 30, pp. 55–56, no. 4, ill. and pp. 80–82, nos. 18 and 19, ill.

MATERIALS: Primary: mahogany (legs, leaves), mahogany veneers (apron), satinwood, light, dark, and stained wood inlays. Secondary: tulip wood, yellow pine (three horizontal laminations of apron, fixed rear rail), white oak (rear fly rail)

PROVENANCE: Purchased in Omaha, Nebraska by Berry B. Tracy; Israel Sack, Inc., New York, 1965; BMA, by purchase, 1967

EXHIBITIONS: Bibl. 30, p. 155, no. 56, ill. p. 156; *Washington Antiques Show: "John Shaw & Cabinetmaking in Annapolis,"* The Shoreham-Americana Hotel, 7–11 Jan. 1977, n.p., ill.; bibl. 41, pp. 175–176, no. 56, ill. p. 177

REFERENCES: Bibl. 6, p. 375, ill. p. 373, pl. IX

98. CARD TABLE (1790–1810)

Baltimore
29⅜ × 35⅞ × 17¾ in. (74.6 × 91.2 × 45.1 cm.)
Collection of Rosetta A. and Sadie B. Feldman, Baltimore: Promised Gift to The Baltimore Museum of Art

In its design, construction, and decoration this is a classic example of a Baltimore card table of the Federal period. Demi-lune in shape when closed and with a circular playing surface when opened, the table is supported by four taper legs with spade feet cut from the solid. The back legs have oak fly rails, hinges, and stationary fly rails, as is customary in Annapolis and Baltimore card tables; the back rail is of yellow pine. Although the card table does not have the usual medial brace under the top, the front and side skirts are composed of

98

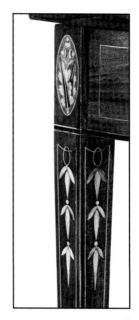

98

horizontal laminates, in this instance of three pieces of wood faced with mahogany veneers. The top has a molded edge and there is a similar thumbnail molding under the top. The baize-covered playing surface is edged with mahogany veneer. Most characteristic of Baltimore cabinetmaking of the period are the placement and design of the oval inlays of oak leaves and acorns on the stile of each leg. The half-round inlay on the top leaf (when folded) is somewhat stylized and simpler when compared with more complex finished inlays similarly placed on other Baltimore card and pier tables (see cat. nos. 99 and 120). Light wood line inlays form rectangular panels in the veneered skirt; there is also a banded inlay of both light and dark woods along the skirt. The bellflowers on the legs, descending from an oval inlaid hoop, are one of the most characteristic forms found in the decoration of Baltimore Federal furniture (see cat. no. 21).

MATERIALS: Primary: mahogany, mahogany veneers, light and dark wood inlays. Secondary: oak, yellow pine, tulip wood. Baize (not original)

PROVENANCE: Collection of Samson Feldman, Baltimore; Rosetta A. and Sadie B. Feldman

99. CARD TABLE (1790–1810)

Baltimore or Annapolis
29¼ × 34⅞ × 17⅜ in. (74.3 × 88.6 × 44.1 cm.)
Collection of Dorothy McIlvain Scott, Baltimore: Promised Gift to The Baltimore Museum of Art

This demi-lune card table shares the same provenance as a pair of side chairs (see cat. no. 25). Possibly made en suite with an original set of chairs, the card table has similar tapered legs terminating in spade feet cut from the solid; inlaid bellflowers on the front legs identical to those on the back splats and front leg stiles of the chairs; and a conch shell inlay related to a shell inlay on the chairs' back splats. The card table design is further enriched by the choice, richly grained mahogany and mahogany veneers used respectively for the hinged and fixed leaves, and on the table's skirt. The mahogany veneered top of the demi-lune card table when closed is banded at its outer edges with lighter mahogany veneers. The chevron-line inlay on the inner edge of this band repeats to form rectangular panels on the skirt. The inlaid conch shell in a large fan on the table top is beautifully executed. The yellow pine and tulip wood backing of the skirt is composed of three pieces of horizontally laminated wood. A characteristically Baltimore yellow pine and tulip wood medial stretcher runs under the table top from front to back. The two rear legs have oak hinge rails typical of Maryland construction.

99

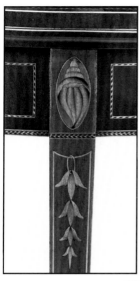

99

99

MATERIALS: Primary: mahogany, mahogany veneers, light, dark, and dyed wood inlays. Secondary: yellow pine, tulip wood (laminated apron), oak (fixed and fly rails)

PROVENANCE: Samuel Chase (1741–1811) of Annapolis and Baltimore; by descent to William Edward Steele; David Stockwell, Inc., Wilmington, Delaware; Dorothy McIlvain Scott, Baltimore

EXHIBITIONS: Bibl. 11, p. 75, no. 59, ill.

100. CARD TABLE (ONE OF TWO) (1785–1800)

Baltimore
29¼ × 30¾ × 15 in. (74.3 × 78.1 × 38.1 cm.)
The Baltimore Museum of Art: Gift of Mrs. Harry B. Dillehunt, Jr., in Memory of her Husband (BMA 1978.60.2)

Exquisitely proportioned and detailed, this card table is one of the finest products of Baltimore cabinetmaking in the Federal period. Its modified half-moon shape and small size are unusual features not often found in contemporary Baltimore card tables. The front and outer sides of each leg have carved rather than inlaid decoration, with beautifully carved bellflower or husk drops below the carved half rosettes at the top of the legs. These carvings are like those found on the legs of side chairs (see cat. no. 33) that according to tradition belonged to Charles Carroll (1737–1832) of Annapolis and Doughoregan Manor, Howard County.[1] The carved rosettes and quartered fan designs on the stile of each leg are repeated in reduced scale on the front and outer sides of the front leg stiles on the chairs. A band of light wood inlay, framed by two string inlays of dark wood at the table skirt's bottom edges, is also found along the bottom of the chair's seat rails. The card table, and the related card table given to the Museum in 1978, may belong to one set of furniture and therefore could have had the same original owner.[2] The tables seem to have been owned in the early nineteenth century by a William E. Hooper of

100

100

Baltimore, a contemporary of Charles Carroll of Carrollton.[3] Closely related leg carvings of half-flower rosettes and bellflowers can also be seen on two Baltimore side chairs in the collection of the Maryland Historical Society.[4]

The five-section skirt is veneered with choice mahogany, inset with thin line and diagonal block inlays that form ovals. The upper face of the top leaf is edged with light wood veneers as are the inner edges of both the leaf and the top. Three horizontally laminated pieces of oak make up the veneered skirt. Characteristic of Baltimore cabinetry is the medial brace dovetailed into the front and rear rails. The use of oak in the two rear hinged legs as well as the side and front rails is another common feature of Baltimore card tables. The spade feet are cut from the solid. The related card table has suffered fire damage and some of its original inlays and veneers have been replaced.[5] A third similar card table with the same provenance is privately owned in Baltimore.

NOTES:
1. Bibl. 51, no. 717, ill.; bibl. 17, p. 158, no. 542, ill. p. 159; bibl. 4, p. 95, no. 58, ill. (This chair is included in the present catalogue, cat. no. 23.)
2. Bibl. 4, pp. 33 and 95; William Voss Elder III, "The Carroll Family: An English Lifestyle in America," in bibl. 82, p. 284, ill. p. 283.
3. Bibl. 4, p. 33. At the time of her gift to the Museum in 1976, the donor confirmed that the tables had been owned by William E. Hooper, a great-grandfather of her husband.

4. Bibl. 4, p. 96, no. 59, ill.; bibl. 84, p. 102, no. 44, ill. p. 103.
5. See bibl. 41, p. 174, no. 54, ill.

MATERIALS: Primary: mahogany, mahogany veneers. Secondary: tulip wood, oak, mahogany (single original glue block)

PROVENANCE: William E. Hooper, Baltimore; by descent to Harry B. Dillehunt, Jr.; Mrs. Harry B. Dillehunt

EXHIBITIONS: Bibl. 4, p. 33, no. 7, ill.

REFERENCES: Bibl. 87, p. 179, fig. 7; bibl. 19, no. 554, ill.

101. CARD TABLE (1800–1810)

Baltimore
Makers: attributed to John and Hugh Finlay
30⅜ × 38¾ × 17³⁄₁₆ in. (77.2 × 98.5 × 43.7 cm.)
The Baltimore Museum of Art: Friends of the American Wing Fund (BMA 1977.83)

In the Federal period card tables were usually made in pairs, and the mate to this example of Baltimore painted furniture is in the collection of the Winterthur Museum.[1] Both tables repeat in their rounded ends and hollow front the design of a pier table (cat. no. 122), also part of the original set of sixteen pieces of painted furniture made for the Buchanan family of Baltimore (see also cat. nos. 30 and 40). Sawtooth bands with vermiculation framing the panels on the table skirts and repeated on the edges of the table's top are a trademark of the Finlay shop. The house painted on the table was a summer retreat mentioned in family reminiscences as the

101

family's country house in the Green Spring Valley, north of Baltimore.[2] The detailed architectural views on the furniture are thought to have been done by landscape artist Francis Guy (1760–1820), who is credited with similar views on another set of furniture owned by the Museum (cat. nos. 29, 39, and 121).[3]

The aprons of the card table are composed of three horizontal laminations of maple. The characteristic Baltimore medial brace tenons into the front and rear rails. The hinged top leaf is peculiarly constructed of four crosswise joined boards secured with deep cleated ends and the fixed leaf is a single board. Both leaves have mahogany veneer on the interior playing surface. The single fly leg with rounded hinge knuckle is cut out at the top to fit against and under the left rear corner of the apron, acting as a support.

NOTES:
1. Bibl. 56, p. 451, no. 456, ill.
2. Bibl. 13, p. 269. However, a letter in the Museum's files from a former owner and Buchanan family descendant, Reverend S. Janney Hutton, states that according to family tradition the building shown on the Museum's card table was a summer house built by William Buchanan (1732–1804) in the Ruxton area north of Baltimore, which later burned. The Winterthur card table shows a large double residence, the left half of which was occupied by James A. Buchanan, son of William, who continued the family's shipping business. About 1795 he "had built himself a fine house with a great ball room," the scene of a banquet for General Lafayette in 1824. Bibl. 13, p. 266. In the Baltimore City Directory of 1810 Buchanan's residence is described as "N. Calvert st. next the Court-House"; in 1822, after the Battle Monument was erected, it is described as "NW Corner of East and Calvert, Monument Square." The table is

useful in dating this set because the architect Robert Mills oversaw the addition of a portico to James Buchanan's house in October 1816. (Robert Mills, *Pocket Memorandum Book or Daily Journal for the Year 1816*, Library of Congress Manuscript Division). The view of the house painted on the table was executed pre-1816, before addition of a portico. That both entrances were different after Mills' work is confirmed by an engraving of Battle Monument Square drawn after 1825 and first published in 1834. The engraving shows clearly two different doors with the Buchanan (left) half under a roofed structure with triangular pediment supported by freestanding columns. The right entrance is simpler and flush with the building façade. Lois B. McCauley, *Maryland Historical Prints, 1752–1889* (Baltimore: Maryland Historical Society, 1975), L115, p. 126.
3. Bibl. 18, pp. 84–85.

MATERIALS: Yellow pine with mahogany veneer (top), maple (legs, apron, medial brace), oak (fly rail), yellow pine (rear fixed rail); painted black with polychrome and gilt and bronze decoration

PROVENANCE: William Buchanan, Baltimore; the Misses Sydney and Margaret Buchanan; by descent to Reverend S. Janney Hutton, Miles, Virginia; BMA, by purchase, 1977

EXHIBITIONS: Bibl. 27, p. 31, no. 8, ill.; bibl. 18, p. 84, F18, ill.

101

102

102. CARD TABLE (1800–1820)

Baltimore
29⁹/₁₆ × 36⅛ × 17½ in. (75.1 × 91.8 × 44.5 cm.)
The Baltimore Museum of Art: Gift of Gertrude Morrow
Chambliss, Baltimore, in Memory of her Mother, Amanda
Howser Morrow (BMA 1980.168)

Another painted Baltimore card table (BMA 1960.45)
owned by the Museum is of this same form, as are
a pair of Baltimore card tables in the Winterthur
collection.[1] The front aprons are of serpentine
shape; the side aprons and each leaf are half-
serpentined, unfolding to a full serpentine when
in use. The front legs form ovolo projections on
the apron which are repeated in the shape of the
leaves. All four tables use mahogany for the upper
leaf as well as having the same form and dimensions. The wood surface is exposed on top but
painted on the interior, an interesting contrast to
the Baltimore card table in cat. no. 101 on which
the interior surface is veneered and the outside
painted.

Of the four serpentine examples, the two owned
by the Museum are most closely related in decoration though all differ in this aspect. Both Museum
tables are black with gilt decoration; the Winterthur pair are red with elaborate floral designs. In
this example, the design is lighter, more Adamesque, than that of the other Museum table which
has large gilt leaves and an undistinguished landscape on the center front apron.

A card table long owned by a Boston family is
identical to this entry. No other history is available
to indicate how or when it came to be in Boston,

or whether the two are actually a pair.[2] When the
Museum's card table was acquired, it underwent
much needed restoration. A thorough cleaning
eliminated accumulated dirt and layers of varnish.
Black paint covering the guilloche banding on the
leaf edges was removed. The insides of both leaves
had lost their original painted surfaces which were
restored on the basis of the untouched playing
surface of the Museum's other related card table.
This included a gilt blossom on each of the ovolo
projections. (The Boston-owned card table does not
have an eight-point gilt blossom painted on the
ovolo corners and may represent the way this entry
should have been restored.) The front legs are
attached to the ovolo corners from the rear with
screws. The front and side aprons and ovolo corners
are cut from the solid, with interior faces cut
straight. The characteristic Baltimore medial brace
is half dovetailed to the front apron and interior
rear rail. The hinge has a rounded knuckle. There
is a single leaf edge tenon.

NOTES:
1. Illustrated in bibl. 27, p. 40, no. 17. Winterthur's example
   is found in bibl. 56, p. 455, no. 464, ill.
2. A letter on file at the Baltimore Museum from the firm
   of Shreve, Crump & Low Co., Boston, dated 1 July 1975,
   with accompanying photographs.
MATERIALS: Tulip wood (legs, apron, lower leaf), mahogany
(top leaf), oak (rear fixed and fly rails); painted black with
gilt stenciled and freehand decoration
PROVENANCE: Howser and Morrow families of Baltimore;
Amanda Howser Morrow; Gertrude Morrow Chambliss

103. CARD TABLE (1815–1820)

Philadelphia
29¼ × 34¹⁵/₁₆ × 17⁷/₁₆ in. (74.3 × 88.8 × 44.3 cm.)
The Baltimore Museum of Art: Gift of Mr. and Mrs.
Bernard Trupp (BMA 1964.51.1)

When purchased by the donor's father in the 1932
auction of the Louis Guerineau Myers Collection,
this lyre-base card table was identified as New
York in origin.[1] However, similar tables with strong
Philadelphia provenances are now known in sufficient numbers to suggest that this form of a
centrally supported table was also made in that
city.[2] In addition there are lyre-base card tables
that were produced in Boston which are readily
distinguished from the New York or Philadelphia
type.[3] The northern versions are generally plainer
and lack the Philadelphia types' exquisite proportions and visually appealing interplay of light wood
veneers, many ormolu mounts, and dark mahogany. Philadelphia had long exerted a strong influence over design in Baltimore, as a comparison of

103

104

this card table with a work table (cat. no. 132) belonging to the Museum makes clear. There are turned ivory knobs on the roll knees of each leg and brass rods form the stringing of the lyres.

NOTES:
1. Bibl. 17, p. 70, lot 344, ill. p. 71.
2. A pair of card tables at Cliveden National Historic Site, Germantown, Pennsylvania are illustrated in Hope Coppage Hendrickson, "Cliveden," *Antiques*, Aug. 1983, p. 260, pl. II. A table from the collection of Mrs. John Thompson Spencer, Philadelphia, was sold by Parke-Bernet Galleries, 23 Apr. 1938, sale no. 35, p. 32, lot 149, ill. A group of related work tables with Philadelphia histories is discussed in bibl. 81, p. 76, no. 20, ill. p. 43.
3. New York tables are illustrated in bibl. 56, pp. 340–342, nos. 319 and 320; Boston examples are illustrated in bibl. 66, pp. 140–141, nos. 104 and 105.

MATERIALS: Primary: mahogany, mahogany, satinwood, and maple veneers. Secondary: ash (pedestal base). Ivory and ormolu mounts

PROVENANCE: Louis Guerineau Myers, New York, 1932; Manuel Hendler, Baltimore; Florence Hendler Trupp (Mrs. Bernard)

104. CARD TABLE (ONE OF TWO) (1820–1830)
Boston
Maker: attributed to Timothy Hunt and Company
29⅝ × 36⅜ × 18 in. (75.3 × 92.4 × 45.7 cm.)
The Baltimore Museum of Art: Gift of Dr. and Mrs. Curt P. Richter, Baltimore (BMA 1984.117)

This card table, one of a pair, is almost identical to a card table bearing the label of Timothy Hunt and Company, cabinetmakers of Boston.[1] The brass

103

104

feet on the Museum's example are cast with leaf designs while those on the labeled example are of the more usual animal paw type. The labeled card table also has a half-round applied molding at the bottom edge of its apron rather than the flat profiled molding seen on this example. The dimensions of all three tables vary by only half an inch. Timothy Hunt, in business in Boston by 1819, entered into partnership with a Simon Hunt that lasted until 1826. That city's directories show the label address to be that of Timothy Hunt and Company from 1823–1824, so it is probable that the Museum's card tables also date from that period.

This table retains its original folding swivel top; the other matching table has a replaced top leaf. The beautifully figured veneers on the inside of the leaves mirror each other. The veneer of the front apron is seamed at the center and is also of mirrored grain. The turned vase-shaped pedestal support is boldly and skillfully carved with acanthus leaves. Equally well carved leaf decoration is found on the knees of the klismos-shaped legs. The carved design on the base, especially the broad, flattened leaves, suggests the Boston vernacular of the period and was not confined to any one shop.[2] Oversized gadrooning surrounds the base of the pedestal. There is a storage compartment under the swivel top. The table has no secondary woods; a lesser grade of mahogany was used for unseen construction.

NOTES:
1. Page Talbott, "Boston Empire furniture Part II," *Antiques*, May 1976, pp. 1004–1013, ill. p. 1008, fig. 7 and p. 1009, pl. III.
2. *The American Heritage Auction of Americana*, sale cat., Sotheby Parke-Bernet, New York, 28–31 Jan. 1981, sale no. 4529Y, lot 1563, ill. A candlestand labeled by the Boston shop of George Croome has similar carving.

MATERIALS: Mahogany, mahogany veneers

PROVENANCE: Colburn and Tilden families of Boston; Jane Colburn Darley; Leslie Tilden Bidwell; Leslie Bidwell Richter (Mrs. Curt), Baltimore

105. CARD TABLE (1832–1840)

Baltimore
Maker: Anthony H. Jenkins
29⁵⁄₁₆ × 39¹⁄₁₆ × 19½ in. (74.5 × 99.3 × 49.5 cm.)
The Baltimore Museum of Art: Friends of the American Wing Fund (BMA 1980.522)

Mahogany pedestal-base card tables like this example were obviously made in quantity in Baltimore in the first three decades of the nineteenth century, because they have survived in great number when compared to other furniture forms pro-

105

duced in the same period. They reflect a lavish use of materials—usually solid mahogany leaves (as here) on a rectangular top richly veneered with mahogany, all supported by an urn, pedestal, and four klismos legs of solid mahogany. The reeded edges of the top leaves, the fillet molding at the base of the top's skirt, the turned rings of the pedestal, the shaping of the vase urn, as well as the rather heavy reeding of the klismos legs, are all characteristic of such Baltimore card tables. All that is missing is the spiky reeding (see cat. no. 106) that might have been carved on the base swelling of the urn support.

Lightly incised with a chisel in the lower face on the right side of the skirt molding are the initials AHJ, and on the outside bottom face of the interior till ∧ H JENKINS. Anthony Hearn Jenkins (1814–1884), the eldest son of Michael Jenkins who was a cabinetmaker and undertaker in Baltimore from 1799–1832, probably learned cabinetmaking from his father.[1] On September 25, 1832, after Michael Jenkins' death, Anthony advertised that he was continuing his father's business at "the old stand No. 16 Light St."[2] Stylistically this table could have been one of the earliest productions of the newly organized shop. However, these card tables, almost always produced and sold in pairs, were probably produced in Baltimore as late as the 1840's. Anthony Jenkins worked alone until 1837, when his brother Henry Worthington Jenkins joined the firm. In turn this partnership was dissolved in 1857. In the collection of the Maryland Historical Society there are five side chairs, one of which bears the paper label of A.H. Jenkins, that are of comparable date to the Museum's card table.[3]

NOTES:
1. For complete information on the successive generations of Jenkins family cabinetmakers in Baltimore, see John H. Hill, "Furniture Designs of Henry W. Jenkins & Sons Co.," *Winterthur Portfolio 5* (Charlottesville: University Press of Virginia), 1969, pp. 154–187.
2. The undertaking firm, which was carried on by Anthony and Henry, is still in business in Baltimore.
3. Bibl. 84, pp. 119–120, no. 72, ill.

MATERIALS: Primary: mahogany, mahogany veneers. Secondary: black ash (pedestal block), black walnut, tulip wood (medial brace), yellow pine (till)

PROVENANCE: Joseph Cornett, Antiques, Gettysburg, Pennsylvania; BMA, by purchase, 1980

106. CARD TABLE (ONE OF TWO) (1820–1840)

Baltimore
29½ × 35⅝ × 17⁷⁄₁₆ in. (75 × 90.5 × 44.3 cm.)
The Baltimore Museum of Art: Middendorf Foundation Fund (BMA 1972.26B)

One of a pair, this card table is closely related to its Philadelphia counterparts from the first three decades of the nineteenth century. The three-legged pedestal base with ring turnings above the legs and drop pendants on the skirt, as well as the use of yellow pine and maple as secondary woods, are shared Baltimore and Philadelphia characteristics. However, the heavy reeding of the pedestal and legs is distinctly Baltimore. The reeding is sharp-

106

edged and has spiky tops. Similar reeding can also be seen on the legs of a work table (cat. no. 133) and Baltimore sofas of the period.[1] The block at the top of the pedestal base is tenoned into the front and back apron of the table skirt. The interior till, revealed when the top is swiveled, is of maple coated with a pink-red wash. The tables have in the past been attributed to Baltimore cabinetmaker John Needles (1786–1878), a claim yet to be substantiated.

NOTES:
1. Bibl. 84, pp. 163–164, no. 126, ill.

MATERIALS: Primary: mahogany, mahogany veneers. Secondary: yellow pine, white pine, maple

PROVENANCE: S. Freeman Auctioneers, Philadelphia; Dr. and Mrs. Irvin B. Berd, Ardin, Delaware; BMA, by purchase, 1972

107. SIDE TABLE (1740–1760)

Pennsylvania
base: 28⅞ × 43 × 18½ in. (73.4 × 109.3 × 47 cm.)
marble: 1⅜ × 44¾ × 21½ in. (3.5 × 113.7 × 54.6 cm.)
The Baltimore Museum of Art: Bequest of J. Gilman D'Arcy Paul (BMA 1972.27.8)

Although this table was found by a Baltimore collector more than fifty years ago on the Island of Montserrat in the West Indies, its eighteenth-century Philadelphia origins are obvious. The "straightness" of the cabriole legs, their slipper feet, and the carved five-lobed shells on the front leg knees are very much in the Philadelphia vernacular of the period, frequently found on side chairs as well.[1] The shape of the front and side skirts with ogee curves, pendant lobes, and cusps is related to the similar shape of aprons on Philadelphia Queen Anne-style dressing tables and high chests of drawers. The stiles of the front legs have rounded outside corners. The original marble top with its shaped edge and notched and rounded front corners is of the blue-veined white marble quarried in the eighteenth century near King of Prussia, Chester County, Pennsylvania. There is no medial brace; the heavy marble top is supported by the unusual thickness of the mahogany boards used in the apron. The legs are strengthened by heavy three-piece quarter-round glue blocks.

NOTES:
1. For examples of Philadelphia chairs of the period, see bibl. 39, pp. 82–87.

MATERIALS: Primary: mahogany. Secondary: tulip wood (rear rail, glue blocks). King of Prussia, Pennsylvania, marble top

PROVENANCE: Found on the island of Montserrat, West Indies; J. Gilman D'Arcy Paul, Baltimore

EXHIBITIONS: Bibl. 12, p. 109, no. 87, ill.

107

108. SIDE TABLE (1760–1780)

Philadelphia
base: 31¾ × 41¼ × 22 in. (80.7 × 104.8 × 55.9 cm.)
marble: ⅞ × 42 × 23⅛ in. (2.2 × 106.7 × 58.8 cm.)
The Baltimore Museum of Art: Bequest of Mabel Frances
Reeder (BMA 1964.37)

The carving on the knees and knee brackets of this marble-topped side table is closely related to similarly placed carving on two well-known examples of Philadelphia cabinetmaking now in the Winter-

thur collection, one a card table and the other a side chair.[1] Knee carvings of a central cabochon surrounded by scrolled foliage extending halfway down the leg and the knee brackets with strongly modeled crossed-scroll foliage on this table and the Winterthur card table are almost identical and would appear to be by the same hand. The carved corner brackets of the Winterthur side chair legs are also closely related in design and execution to the Museum's table, but the knee leaf carvings are dissimilar in overall design. Both the Winterthur

108

108

card table and side chair have hairy paw rather than the claw feet found on the Museum's side table.[2]

The heavy gadrooning, very much in the Philadelphia style, is applied under the front apron only. Two original diagonal braces from the front to the back rail were removed when repairs were made to the marble top early in this century.

NOTES:
1. The table is illustrated in bibl. 25, no. 345; the side chair is illustrated in bibl. 89, pp. 196–199, fig. 3.
2. The Winterthur card table has long been considered to be part of the household furniture ordered by John Cadwalader of Philadelphia between 1769 and 1771, and attributed to the cabinetmaker Thomas Affleck. See bibl. 25 and Nicholas B. Wainwright, *Colonial Grandeur in Philadelphia: The House and Furniture of General John Cadwalader* (Philadelphia: Historical Society of Pennsylvania, 1964), p. 120, ill. p. 121. Two articles, one specifically on Philadelphia carvers, have suggested that the table's body may have been made by Affleck but its decoration by an anonymous carver. See bibl. 89 and bibl. 8, pp. 1120–1133. This card table and side chair have also been related in their carved detail to the well-known set of magnificently carved side chairs made for Cadwalader, presently attributed to Affleck. This most recent attribution is found in bibl. 39, pp. 105–108, no. 59 and also in bibl. 8, p. 1130.

MATERIALS: Primary: mahogany. Secondary: yellow pine (rear rail), white cedar (glue blocks). King of Prussia, Pennsylvania, marble top

PROVENANCE: Clarence Reeder, Baltimore; Mabel Frances Reeder

EXHIBITIONS: Bibl. 12, p. 111, no. 90, ill.

109. SIDEBOARD (1797)

Annapolis
Maker: John Shaw
38 × 71 × 25⁵⁄₁₆ in. (96.6 × 180.4 × 64.3 cm.)
The Baltimore Museum of Art: Gift of the Colonial Dames of America, Chapter 1 (BMA 1932.31.1)

This sideboard is one of two labeled pieces of John Shaw furniture in the collection of The Baltimore Museum of Art.[1] (The other is a linen press of the same date, cat. no. 71; see also cat. no. 97, a card table attributed to Shaw.) From the evidence of surviving numbers, sideboards must have been one of the most numerous furniture forms produced by Shaw's shop. The sideboard, owned by the Randall family of Annapolis and Baltimore until acquired for the Museum, is among the first rank of his work. The five-part division of the case is the standard Shaw format, repeated in four other sideboards either labeled or firmly attributed.[2] The fitting of the right end cupboard with a bottle drawer is a variant feature since some examples have two bottle drawers while others have two plain cupboards. In all examples a door provides access to the center compartment which here conceals three graduated drawers. The other salient Shaw features are the molded face of the top edge, the cross-banded zebrawood ovals on the end and central doors, and the ovoid spade feet cut from the solid. The sides of the bottle drawer as well as those of the two drawers flanking the center com-

109

109

109

109

ill.; bibl. 54, p. 245, ill. p. 244, pl. 232 and p. 245, pl. 233; Ethel Hall Bjerkoe, *The Cabinetmakers of America*, Garden City, New York: Doubleday & Co., 1957, p. 198, no. 2, pl. XXVII; bibl. 75, p. 243, ill. p. 242, fig. 7; Rosamond Randall Beirne and Eleanor Pinkerton Stewart, "John Shaw, cabinetmaker," *Antiques*, Dec. 1960, ill. p. 556, fig. 6; bibl. 6, p. 375, ill. p. 374, figs. 13 and 13a

partment are extended, a characteristic and practical construction feature. Such extended sides not only act as a drawer stop but help to prevent the drawer from tipping out of the case when opened too far. Even the three small drawers of the center compartment have extended sides. On all drawers the backboard tenons through the drawer sides. White oak is used as the secondary wood in the three large drawers, tulip wood in the smaller. The beautifully grained mahogany veneers on the faces of each compartment are laminated to mahogany. The vertical partitions between the end bays and the center section are tenoned through the back, whereas the partitions in the center section abut the backboard and are nailed, not tenoned, in place. Shaw's label, affixed to the inside center compartment door, is inscribed in ink [I] 1797 [H]. The knobs are early nineteenth-century additions. Probably the drawers and doors of the sideboard were originally opened by a key.

NOTES:
1. Bibl. 30, pp. 88–90, no. 24, ill.
2. Bibl. 30, pp. 76–78, no. 16, ill.; pp. 78–79, no. 17, ill.; pp. 84–85, no. 21, ill.; and pp. 153–154, no. 55, ill. A Shaw sideboard of similar design is privately owned, bibl. 30, p. 115, figs. A and B.

MATERIALS: Primary: mahogany, mahogany veneers, light and dark wood inlays. Secondary: tulip wood, yellow pine, white oak. Brass and glass knobs (not original)

PROVENANCE: According to family tradition, John Randall, Annapolis; Alexander Randall; Blanchard Randall; BMA, 1932

EXHIBITIONS: Bibl. 4, p. 72, no. 41, ill. p. 73; bibl. 30, pp. 112–115, no. 38, ill.

REFERENCES: Dr. James Bordley, Jr., "A Study of Baltimore Furniture—Period 1785–1815," (Paper presented at the Maryland Historical Society, n.d.); W.M. Hornor, Jr., "John Shaw of the Great Days of Annapolis," *International Studio*, Mar. 1931, ill. p. 46, fig. 8; bibl. 55, vol. 1, p. 537, no. 971,

110. SIDEBOARD TABLE (1790–1810)

Maryland
$37\frac{7}{8} \times 68\frac{3}{8} \times 23\frac{5}{8}$ in. (96.2 × 173.7 × 60 cm.)
The Baltimore Museum of Art: Gift of Mrs. Francis White, from the Collection of Mrs. Miles White, Jr. (BMA 1973.76.220)

It is believed that the last owner of this sideboard table, Mrs. Miles White, Jr., purchased it from the same member of the Carroll family from whom she acquired two side chairs also included in this catalogue (see cat. no. 22). According to family tradition the table was said to have belonged to Charles Carroll of Carrollton (1737–1832) and thought to have been used at Doughoregan Manor west of Baltimore, rather than in his Annapolis house. The table (and chairs as well) could have also belonged first to Charles Carroll of Homewood (1775–1825) and been taken to Doughoregan by his son Charles Carroll of Doughoregan (1801–1862). It is probable that the table was made in Baltimore rather than Annapolis. By the late eighteenth century the Carrolls and other Maryland families who had earlier been Annapolis-oriented turned toward the fast-growing new metropolis on the Patapsco. The only possible Annapolis maker would have been John Shaw (1745–1829).[1] The eagle inlay is of a type generally confined to Maryland, and found on both Baltimore and Annapolis furniture.[2] The bellflower inlays, suspended from an inlaid loop, with elongated center petals, and diminishing in size, are perhaps the most typical and repeated element of decoration in Baltimore furniture of this period. However, this same bellflower inlay is used on one occasion on a monumental piece of Annapolis furniture attributed to John Shaw, a billiard table made about 1797 for the Lloyd family of Maryland and now in the Winterthur collection.[3] The thick table top with its canted front corners is related to another Maryland sideboard top (see cat. no. 111). Such corners continue the serpentine curve of the front of the top and serve the practical purpose of minimizing the otherwise sharp front corners of a sideboard table. The inlay at the base of the skirt is a late nineteenth-century replace-

110

ment of the original. The spade feet are formed with four applied faces which are butted rather than mitred.

NOTES:
1. Bibl. 30.
2. Bibl. 56, p. 39, no. 119.
3. Bibl. 30, pp. 147–150, no. 52, ill.

MATERIALS: Primary: mahogany, mahogany veneers, light and dark wood inlays. Secondary: yellow pine (rear rail, vertical medial brace), tulip wood (four-piece laminated front apron, solid side and rear rails, battens around edge of top)

PROVENANCE: Charles Carroll of Carrollton; by descent to Charles Carroll of Homewood, Howard County; by descent to Charles Carroll of Doughoregan; Mrs. Miles White, Jr., Baltimore; Francis White; Nancy Brewster White (Mrs. Francis)

EXHIBITIONS: Bibl. 4, p. 56, no. 29, ill. p. 57; bibl. 82, p. 295, no. 136, ill. p. 284

REFERENCES: Bibl. 55, vol. 2, p. 764, no. 1455, ill. p. 763

III. SIDEBOARD (1790–1810)

Baltimore
39¼ × 77⅞ × 26⅛ in. (99.7 × 197.9 × 66.4 cm.)
The Baltimore Museum of Art: Gift of Mrs. Francis White, from the Collection of Mrs. Miles White, Jr. (BMA 1973.76.221)

The sideboard is over six feet long and unusually deep, providing an extra large top surface. The side and front edges of the top are cross-banded by mahogany veneers and line inlays. The front canted corners of the top are often seen in Baltimore side tables (see cat. no. 110). Oval inlay design at the top of the stiles of the front legs resembles somewhat the cross section of a tulip bulb; although not a motif commonly found in Baltimore furniture, it is seen again in a demi-lune sideboard also owned by the Museum (cat. no. 114). The mitred veneers of the drawer fronts and the center banded oval veneers are reminiscent of the work of John Shaw of Annapolis (see cat. no. 109). The bellflower inlays on the legs are a characteristic Baltimore design. Light wood string inlay is used on each end of the sideboard in rectangles with hollow corners. The two interior vertical partitions are tenoned through the back. The hardware is not original, and the piece was refinished when acquired by the Museum in 1973. An almost identical sideboard is privately owned. Of almost exactly the same dimensions the only minor differences between the two sideboards are found in the shape of the bellflower petals and in the pattern and grain of the veneers.[1]

Sideboards are among the finest examples of the exceptional classical-style furniture produced in Baltimore. In the late eighteenth and early nineteenth centuries Baltimore was the fastest growing

111

111

city in America. Baltimore's population of 6,755 at the time of the Revolution had by 1800 reached more than 20,000 persons. Furniture made in Baltimore from about 1790–1815 is in its style, design, and decoration some of the finest produced in America at the time. Despite the burgeoning of its population, Baltimore was still a small city compared to Philadelphia, New York, or Boston, so that the quite large quantity of still-existing Baltimore classical-style furniture when compared to Philadelphia production is noteworthy.

NOTES:
1. *Antiques*, Jan. 1962, p. 42.

MATERIALS: Primary: mahogany, mahogany veneers, light, dark, and stained wood inlays. Secondary: yellow pine, tulip wood. Brass hardware (not original)

PROVENANCE: Mrs. Miles White, Jr., Baltimore; Francis White; Nancy Brewster White (Mrs. Francis)

EXHIBITIONS: Bibl. 4, p. 68, no. 39, ill. p. 69; bibl. 11, p. 76, no. 60, ill.

REFERENCES: Bibl. 55, vol. 1, p. 528, no. 950, ill. p. 526; Sarah B. Sherrill, "Current and coming," *Antiques*, May 1974, p. 978, ill.

112. SIDEBOARD (1790–1810)

Baltimore
$40\frac{3}{8} \times 72\frac{1}{2} \times 25\frac{1}{4}$ in. (102.6 × 184.2 × 64.2 cm.)
The Baltimore Museum of Art: Bequest of Dr. William
H. Woody, Baltimore, in Memory of Anne Mellier Woody
(BMA 1985.112)

During the Federal period sideboards with serpentine fronts and rounded ends, now often referred to as kidney-shaped, seem to have been produced in greater numbers in Baltimore than in other cabinetmaking centers.[1] This example, although its inlaid decoration is not typically Baltimore, is in size and proportion like other Baltimore sideboards of similar design, which usually have four rather than the customary six legs. The curved front edge of the top becomes serpentine at the center of the sideboard, the drawer front and cupboard doors below repeating its reverse curve shape. The quarter-round ends are divided into two panels of branch mahogany veneer, each edged with a light wood string inlay and inset with a circle of chevron inlay. The inner panel is hinged and provides access to the entire case end while the outer panel is a false door. To complete the illusion,

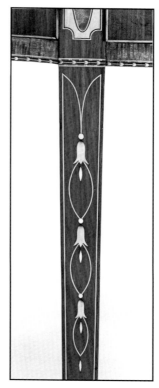

112

112

both panels have an ivory escutcheon; originally both were equipped with an oval drawer pull as were all the other doors. The post holes were probably plugged during nineteenth-century repair work. The two central cabinet doors are veneered like the end doors with the chevron inlay set in an oval appropriate to their proportions.

The line inlay forming a long ellipse on the drawer front is composed of light and dark diagonals. The string inlay inside the ellipse has pinched ends that reverse the rounded ends of the outer inlay, with the point of the inner string punctuated by a black dot and a light leaf.[2] The motifs on the stiles and legs were used in other cabinetmaking centers, particularly the bellflowers pendant between string inlaid ovals which are often found on New York table legs.[3] However, this pattern was also employed by Baltimore cabinetmakers, for it (or designs very similar to it) can be found on tables with Baltimore provenances and design and construction features.[4] The backing of all the doors is composed of horizontally laminated mahogany strips with cleated ends. The backing of the veneered drawer front is similarly laminated. The satinwood cuffs appear to be replacements for the missing originals. The interior partitions tenon through the backboard. This sideboard and a secretary-bookcase (cat. no. 80) were among the furnishings in an estate sale held in Baltimore in 1942.[5] No earlier history of the piece is known.

NOTES:
1. For other examples of kidney-shaped sideboards with Maryland provenances, see bibl. 55, vol. 1, pp. 538–540, nos. 972–974, ill.
2. A desk with similar indented inlay was exhibited with this sideboard in the Baltimore Museum's 1947 exhibition *Baltimore Furniture: The Work of Baltimore and Annapolis Cabinetmakers from 1760 to 1810* (bibl. 4); the sideboard is no. 43, p. 76, ill. p. 77; the desk no. 70, p. 108, ill. p. 109.
3. There are two sideboards with the labels of William Whitehead, one at the High Museum, Atlanta, the other illustrated in Barry A. Greenlaw, "American furniture in Houston collections," *Antiques*, Sept. 1979, p. 553, pl. XIV.
4. A card table descended in the family of Major General Isaac Ridgeway Trimble (bibl. 4, p. 36, no. 10, ill.); in the catalogue a card table of the same shape as this sideboard employs similar inlays on the apron and stiles as well as on the legs. See also bibl. 41, pp. 171–173, no. 52, ill.
5. Bibl. 31, p. 48, lot 265, ill. p. 47.

MATERIALS: Primary: mahogany, mahogany veneers, light and dark wood inlays. Secondary: tulip wood, yellow pine. Brass hardware (not original); ivory keyhole escutcheons (five not original)

PROVENANCE: Edyth Johns Cotten, Baltimore, by 1942; John Schwarz, Antiques, 1942; purchased at the sale of the Estate of Edyth Johns Cotten; Dr. and Mrs. William H. Woody, by 1947
EXHIBITIONS: Bibl. 4, p. 76, no. 43, ill. p. 77
REFERENCES: Bibl. 31, p. 48, lot 265, ill. p. 47

113. SIDEBOARD (1795–1810)
Annapolis or Baltimore
38⅝ × 73½ × 26¼ in. (98.1 × 186.8 × 66.7 cm.)
Private Collection, Baltimore: Promised Gift to The Baltimore Museum of Art

This sideboard with center drawer and flanking side cupboards displays choice mahogany veneers and intricate inlays. The oval-banded and line inlays on the drawer and door fronts surrounding the oval veneers are repeated in the spandrel arches of the apron. Light wood string inlays with hollow corners frame panels of cross grain mahogany veneers on the stiles of the front legs. A light wood string inlay also defines the front and sides of the top. The face edges of the top are veneered. The lower edges of the case front and sides are defined by a three-part line inlay of dark and light woods. The four bellflower drops of diminishing size on

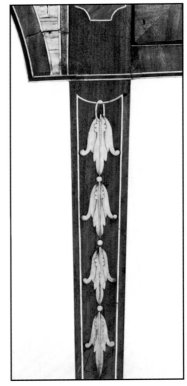

113

113

each of the front legs, elaborately formed of numerous pieces of wood, are of the same high quality as those found on another sideboard (cat. no. 114) and differ from the simpler, more usual, Baltimore type (see cat. nos. 98 and 110). However, the bellflowers are suspended from a line inlay loop and separated by a dot inlay in the customary Baltimore manner. At the bottom of each leg below the horizontal cuff inlays is a different grain of mahogany from that used above the cuff and suggests a restoration of height. The top overhangs the case sides by more than two inches and the case back by just under two inches, which allowed the sideboard top to reach the wall surface over the customary eighteenth-century chair rail projection. The lobed half-oval inlay in the center skirt shows vestiges of an original green-shaded background. The interior partitions are tenoned through the one-piece backboard. The original pulls were knobs with a single central post and a round back plate. In overall design the sideboard is related to another Maryland example included in an exhibition held at the Baltimore Museum in 1947.[1]

NOTES:
1. Bibl. 4, p. 80, no. 45, ill. p. 81.
MATERIALS: Primary: mahogany (top, sides, legs, stiles, doors, drawer face), mahogany veneers. Secondary: chestnut (rails, apron), tulip wood. Brass hardware (not original)

PROVENANCE: Joseph Kindig, Jr., Antiques, York, Pennsylvania; Private Collection, Baltimore
REFERENCES: Helen Comstock, *The Looking Glass in America, 1700–1825*, New York: Viking Press, 1968, p. 45, ill.

114. SIDEBOARD (1790–1810)

Baltimore or Annapolis
39¼ × 58⅞ × 25¼ in. (99.7 × 149.6 × 64.2 cm.)
The Baltimore Museum of Art: Purchased as the gift of Mr. and Mrs. Kenneth S. Battye, Baltimore (BMA 1972.32.1)

Obviously made to order for an architectural space, this small Maryland sideboard has a rounded back. Only the front of the sideboard was intended to be visible, for the canted sides of the case are of unfinished secondary wood. American houses of the Federal period, like their English prototypes, often featured walls with half-round niches, sometimes on either side of a fireplace.[1] The central cupboard recessed below the top center drawer is flanked by side cupboards whose top sections are mock drawers matching the center drawer. Imitating the drawer form, the cupboards' locks are placed at the top rather than on the inner sides. The elaborate oval inlays at the top of the stiles (the inner right inlay being a replacement), display a

114

stylized design that resembles the cross section of a tulip bulb or tulip tree seed pod, and are similar to the oval inlays on another Maryland sideboard (cat. no. 111). The leaf and tendril inlay on a field of shaded satinwood placed on the stiles at cupboard level and below the drawers is unusually archaic when compared with the other more sophisticated inlays on this piece. The contrast is particularly evident when the bellflower drop inlays on the front legs are closely examined for they are of intricate design and shape, composed of numerous pieces of shaded wood.[2] The inlaid and veneered border on the edge of the top only extends across the top and its canted corners. Each of the two side boards and the backboard are made of one piece of tulip wood. The stiles of the two back legs have been crudely notched out, obviously to fit over a chair rail in the niche.

When acquired by the Museum, the sideboard was restored and refinished. The hardware is of the period but not original to the piece. According to a notebook kept by Nellie Whittaker, Georgetown antique dealer, the sideboard was purchased "from a private family in Sandy Spring."[3]

114

NOTES:
1. A serving table with a curved back was included in the exhibition of Maryland furniture held at the Baltimore Museum in 1947, bibl. 4, p. 65, no. 36, ill.
2. See also bibl. 4, p. 70, no. 40, ill. p. 71.
3. The notebook recording her purchases and acquisitions became the property of Sotheby Parke-Bernet in 1972 but cannot now be located. The Sandy Spring provenance of the sideboard was stated in the auction catalogue.

MATERIALS: Primary: mahogany, mahogany veneers, light, dark, and dyed wood inlays. Secondary: tulip wood (drawers, sides and back partitions, bottom), yellow pine (top battens). Brasses (not original)

PROVENANCE: Estate of Nellie Whittaker, Georgetown, D.C.; Prevost Hubbard, New York; Sotheby Parke-Bernet; BMA, by purchase, 1972

EXHIBITIONS: Bibl. 3

REFERENCES: *Important American Furniture* (sale cat.), Sotheby Parke-Bernet, Inc., New York, 19–20 May 1972, sale no. 3371, pp. 98–99, lot 432, ill.; bibl. 21, pp. 207–208, fig. 240

115. SIDEBOARD (1790–1810)

Probably New York
Maker: attributed to the shop of William Whitehead
40⅞ × 83⅝ × 27⅞ in. (103.9 × 212.5 × 70.8 cm.)
Collection of Dorothy McIlvain Scott, Baltimore: Promised Gift to The Baltimore Museum of Art

Almost seven feet long and twenty-eight inches deep, this massive yet graceful sideboard has been attributed to a New York cabinetmaker, William Whitehead, who is recorded as working at 75 Pearl Street for about seven years, beginning in 1792. A visual comparison with one of his two labeled sideboards reveals a similar division and shaping of the front of the case: outwardly curved end drawers; their shape repeated in the doors below; two serpentine center drawers with recessed serpentine doors below.[1] Between the stiles of the two front inner legs and the central storage compartment, convexly curved panels angle inward resulting in an overhang of the center drawers. However, this sideboard also has two fitted bottle drawers each with small drawers above, between the stile of the legs and the curved panels. Thus the span between the two front inner legs is correspondingly increased. Some New York sideboards as well as those made elsewhere make use of two additional interior front legs.[2] While the second labeled Whitehead sideboard, now in the High Museum in Atlanta, shares inlay motifs and veneer and line inlay patterns with the other labeled example,[3] none of these elements are repeated by correspondingly placed inlays on this sideboard. Instead of oval paterae near the top of the leg stiles, here there are oval inlays of Adamesque urns. Instead of oval veneers edged with light

115

115

example in a private midwestern collection.[4] The back of the sideboard is composed of one white pine board with the vertical case dividers all tenoned through this backboard. Each bottle drawer is fitted for the storage of four bottles. The original blown glass bottles which have miraculously survived have etched markings measuring three pints. The hardware is of the period but not original to the piece.

NOTES:
1. Wendy A. Cooper, *In Praise of America, Masterworks of American Decorative Arts, 1650–1830: A Guide to the Exhibition* (Washington, D.C.: National Gallery of Art, 1980), p. 14, ill. p. 15, fig. 7.
2. For examples see bibl. 19, no. 512, ill. and bibl. 32, p. 235, ill.
3. Bibl. 2, vol. 5, pp. 1254–1255, no. P4286, ill.
4. Bibl. 69, p. 82, no. 37, ill. p. 83.

MATERIALS: Primary: mahogany, mahogany veneers, light and dark wood inlays. Secondary: tulip wood (drawers' sides horizontal dividers), white pine (backboard, top, inner frame, bottom board, vertical dividers, drawer bottoms). Brass handles (not original)

PROVENANCE: Israel Sack, Inc., New York, 1974; Dorothy McIlvain Scott, Baltimore

REFERENCES: Bibl. 2, vol. 4, 1974, pp. 871 and 968–969, no. P3744, ill.

wood line inlay, the front leg stiles are inlaid with panels of satinwood edged with black and light line inlays. This same inlay is used on the legs instead of the bellflower drops found on the two labeled examples. The only similar inlay decoration on all three sideboards is the striped motif at the very top of the stiles. The mahogany veneer of the top is of one piece of wood, supported by a pine backing of fielded panels. The same kind of elaborately constructed backing for the top is found in the High Museum's sideboard and in an attributed

116. SIDEBOARD (1800–1810)

Boston
Maker: possibly shop of John and Thomas Seymour
41⅛ × 79 × 26⅝ in. (104.5 × 200.7 × 67.7 cm.)
The Baltimore Museum of Art: Gift of Joseph Hennage; Gift of Mrs. Henry Homlet; Bequest of Eleanor M. Lehr; Bequest of Robert Tucker; Bequest of William A. Tuerke, Sr.; and Bequest of Lucy Ridgely Seymer, by exchange (BMA 1974.6)

The possible origin of this sideboard has long been the subject of discussion. Over fifty years ago Homer Eaton Keyes wrote about it as "A Perplexing Sideboard" in his column in *Antiques*, recording that "John Ware . . . has long been accepted as the proud maker of the piece."[1] This attribution had been based on inscriptions on three bottom boards of the case which were deciphered to read John Ware; unfortunately, it is no longer possible to make out anything except faint chalk shadows. However, Keyes dismissed Ware as the maker, in part because his name does not appear in the Boston City Directories until 1818, and then he is listed as housewright or carpenter. A second set of inscriptions on two drawer bottoms repeats the name Mrs. Mary Wood four times and Boston April the 12th 1810 written once in the same hand. The date led Keyes to speculate on an earlier Boston cabinetmaker, and he suggested John Seymour because

115

116

the sideboard's drawer and cabinet interiors are painted a characteristic light blue-green.[2] Keyes also mentioned that the sideboard's stiles and carved blossoms are related to those on the important Derby commode, now in the Museum of Fine Arts, Boston.[3] His association of this commode and the Museum's sideboard was more prescient than he could know, for a bill documenting the commode to the shop of Thomas Seymour in 1809 was discovered, negating Fiske Kimball's 1931 attribution of the work to the Salem architect Samuel McIntire.[4]

The sideboard was published by Vernon Stoneman as definitely attributed to the Seymours in his 1959 catalogue raisonné of their work.[5] Attempts to document the sideboard through its provenance and the Mary Wood inscription have proved fruitless. No bill survives and, although the provenance Keyes recorded gives the last known private owner as Townsend H. Soren, a native of Dorchester, Massachusetts, who claimed Mary Wood as his great-grandmother, research did not find her name among Soren's antecedents.[6] Mary Wood's signature is of the period, and records indicate the presence of at least two married women by this name in Boston in 1810.[7]

Because the sideboard was owned in Boston in 1810, it is probable that it was made there. While

116

there are few documented Boston-made pieces of this kind for comparison, the Derby commode provides some parallels. Both make use of fine materials with beautifully figured veneers and mahogany drawer sides. Both the commode and sideboard stiles have a carved blossom at the top, and, below, a ring of beads is carved at the top of the leg. Furthermore, two chests of drawers with attached mirrors which share the commode's provenance have legs that are like this sideboard's in having foliage carved below a ring of beads atop reeded legs that terminate in an inverted bulb-shaped foot.[8] Two sideboards similar to this piece are also illustrated in Stoneman's work on the Seymours.[9] The survival of three such similar sideboards may indicate that their source was a single shop with large production. Given the evidence of design parallels and inscriptions, the Seymours are as likely a source for the Museum's sideboard as any other large Boston cabinetmaking firm.

NOTES:

1. Bibl. 48, p. 182. In Keyes' article the date is incorrectly given as 14 April 1810.
2. Bibl. 78, pp. 27 and 159.
3. The commode in the Museum of Fine Arts, Boston, is a half-round chest of drawers with cabinet ends and is an important element for understanding Boston Federal furniture. It is as renowned for its provenance (made for Elizabeth Derby West, daughter of the Salem merchant Elias Hasket Derby) as for its extraordinary appearance, including the shell-painted top.
4. Fiske Kimball, "Furniture Carvings by Samuel McIntire: V. Case Pieces," *Antiques*, Mar. 1931, pp. 207–210. Bibl. 67, pp. 103–113. Illustrated in bibl. 78, p. 248, pl. 159. The bill is made out to Elizabeth Derby, who dropped the name West after her divorce in 1806. (Mabel M. Swan, "Where Elias Hasket Derby Bought His Furniture," *Antiques*, Nov. 1931, p. 282).
5. Bibl. 78, pp. 158–159, no. 85, ill. Sure of his attribution, Stoneman was mainly concerned with "how much of the carved work was attributable to John Seymour as distinguished from Thomas."
6. Index of Marriages in Massachusetts, 1856–1860 (Vital Records, Massachusetts State Archives), vol. 136, p. 228. *Harvard College Class of 1893, 25th Anniversary Report* (Cambridge, Massachusetts: Crimson Printing Co., 1918), p. 261.
7. *Thirtieth Report of the Record Commissioners: Boston Marriages 1752–1809* (Boston: Municipal Printing Office, 1903). Daniel Wood married Mary Lewis 29 November 1804; Elishai Wood married Mary Gammell 10 May 1802.
8. One is in the collection of the Essex Institute of Salem, Massachusetts (bibl. 78, pp. 262–264, no. 169, ill.) and the second belongs to the Museum of Fine Arts, Boston (bibl. 32, p. 251, ill.).
9. Bibl. 78, pp. 157–158, no. 84, ill. and bibl. 79, p. 38, no. 23, ill.

MATERIALS: Primary: mahogany, mahogany and light wood veneers and inlay. Secondary: white pine (bottle drawers), maple (backs), mahogany (drawer sides). Glass knobs with brass mounts

PROVENANCE: Townsend H. Soren, Hartford, Connecticut; Peter Tillou, Antiques, Litchfield, Connecticut, 1974; BMA, by purchase, 1974

EXHIBITIONS: Bibl. 12, p. 106, no. 82, ill.

REFERENCES: Bibl. 48, pp. 181–182, ill.; *BMA Record*, Summer 1974, ill. on cover; Karen M. Jones, "Museum accessions," *Antiques*, May 1976, p. 888; bibl. 78, pp. 158–159, no. 85, ill. and pp. 247 and 249

117. SIDEBOARD (1815–1830)

Baltimore
46¾ × 82³⁄₁₆ × 27½ in. (118.8 × 208.8 × 69.9 cm.)
The Baltimore Museum of Art: Purchased as the gift of The Jacob and Anita France Foundation; Gift of Robert Freedman, Bequest of Eleanor M. Lehr, and Bequest of Lucy Ridgely Seymer, by exchange (BMA 1974.18)

While the side table discussed in cat. no. 118 has been attributed to either Baltimore or Philadelphia, this sideboard because of its decorative elements, is surely the work of a Baltimore cabinetmaker. *The New York Book of Prices for Manufacturing Cabinet and Chair Work* of 1817 refers to caryatid supports as "tapered therms with mummy heads and feet," mummy being interpreted in a number of ways not necessarily of the familiar Egyptian type.[1] On this sideboard (and on other related pieces of furniture), the heads on the four tapered therm supports are bearded, mustachioed, and wear a Turkish or Middle Eastern headdress with tassels.[2] A cylinder desk in the collection of the Maryland Historical Society, recently attributed to the Baltimore cabinetmaker William Camp (1773–1822), has almost identically carved heads complete with tasseled headdresses.[3] Another sideboard, present whereabouts unknown, with even more closely related carved heads but with hairy paw rather than ring turned feet was sold in the famous Crim Sale in Baltimore in 1903.[4]

Features repeated in marble-topped pieces owned by the Maryland Historical Society[5] and The Baltimore Museum of Art (BMA 1972.56.3) as well as in the lost Crim sideboard include: two end cupboards, a recessed center two-door cupboard, all with Gothic-arch paneled doors; obliquely angled panels on each side of the central compartment with similarly inset Gothic arches over quatrefoils; and small intaglio panels on the stiles at the top of each column or caryatid support. The four examples are so similar in appearance and close in dimensions as to suggest that all were the product

117

of the same cabinetmaking shop. As was usual in Baltimore cabinetmaking of the period, the drawer fronts, sides, and backs were all made of mahogany, only the bottoms being of tulip wood. The Maryland Historical Society's sideboard is constructed in one piece, while this sideboard neatly disassembles into five separate units. On the platform base sit three independently constructed sections: two end storage compartments with attached figures and doors which lift off their hinges; a central compartment with similar doors; and the galleried top. The tops, bottoms, and sides of the three storage sections, where not normally visible, have nevertheless been coated with a red stain for a neatly finished appearance. The right storage compartment is fitted with a wooden revolving bottle-holder.

NOTES:
1. Bibl. 84, p. 141, no. 100, ill. p. 140.
2. Curiously enough in the Crim Sale catalogue the heads were called "Egyptian Mummies," apparently the generic term for such heads.
3. Bibl. 84, p. 141.
4. *Dr. William H. Crim Collection*, sale cat., Baltimore, 22–24 Apr., 27–30 Apr., 1 May, 4–5 May 1903, lot 107, ill.
5. Bibl. 84, p. 159, no. 120, ill.

117

MATERIALS: Primary: mahogany, mahogany veneers. Secondary: tulip wood, yellow pine. Brass and glass knobs (not original)

PROVENANCE: Purchased at public auction in Baltimore by Peter Hill, Antiques, Washington, D.C.; BMA, by purchase, 1974

118. SIDE TABLE (1815–1830)

Baltimore or Philadelphia
45¾ × 73⅛ × 23¼ in. (116.3 × 185.8 × 59.1 cm.)
The Baltimore Museum of Art: Gift of Mrs. Bennett Darnell, and Bequest of Elsie A. Hyatt, by exchange; and Decorative Arts Fund (BMA 1976.77)

Carved caryatid heads, often turbaned and bearded and best described as Turk's heads, are found on the legs of a group of sideboard tables and sideboards that are the work of Baltimore or Philadelphia cabinetmakers.[1] This piece is not as distinctly Baltimore in character as the preceding example (cat. no. 117), for it has acorns and oak leaves carved down the front legs, ending in acanthus-leaf carved bulbous feet. More typical Baltimore examples often have reeded leg faces and stand on ring turned feet. This example's bulbous feet are

118

118

repeated without carving on the rear legs. The heavily reeded columnar rear legs are each bundled with a carved ring marking the top third of their length. The rectangular top is recessed in the center in the manner of related Baltimore sideboards and the two front ends of the top railing are cut and scrolled in the same fashion as the railing on cat. no. 117. As in the drawers of that sideboard, here the drawer fronts, sides, and backs are of mahogany, the bottoms of tulip wood. Such a seemingly lavish use of mahogany was a customary practice of many cabinetmakers of this period who employed a lesser grade of the wood for secondary purposes than that used for the fine figured veneers. A similar sideboard table, with a long Baltimore history, is privately owned on Maryland's Eastern Shore.

NOTES:
1. Philadelphia examples include two chests (*English & American Furniture & Decorations*, sale cat., Parke-Bernet Galleries, Inc., New York, 18–20 May 1950, p. 120, lot 608, ill. p. 121; bibl. 2, vol. 7, p. 1822, no. P5039, ill.) and a sideboard in the Hill-Keith-Physick House in Philadelphia. Baltimore examples include cat. no. 117 of this catalogue and others discussed in that entry.

MATERIALS: Primary: mahogany, mahogany veneers. Secondary: tulip wood, yellow pine. Cut glass and brass knobs (not original)

PROVENANCE: Peter Kohn, Antiques, Adelphi, 1976; BMA, by purchase, 1976

119. SIDE TABLE WITH ETAGERE (1850–1857)

New York
Maker: Alexander Roux
85⅛ × 79⅛ × 29 in. (216.3 × 201.1 × 73.7 cm.)
The Baltimore Museum of Art: Gift from the Estate of Margaret Anna Abell (BMA 1977.42.11)

This etagere bearing the label of the French-born New York cabinetmaker Alexander Roux (1813–1886) is, except for slight variations in certain carved passages, identical to a labeled example in the collection of The Metropolitan Museum of Art and another unmarked example at the High Museum of Art in Atlanta.[1] The printed paper label (fig. 119a) on one of the backing boards of the mirror depicts Roux's place of business at 479–481 North Broadway. He had first appeared in the New York directory of 1837 as an upholsterer, but by 1844 he was advertising himself as a French cabinetmaker.[2] In 1850 Alexander Roux leased 481 Broadway and in 1857 the firm's name was changed to Roux & Company. Therefore, this label, which is also found on the Metropolitan Museum's eta-

119

gere and on a slipper chair, would have been in use only from 1850–1857.[3]

The Roux shop in the mid-nineteenth century produced a quantity of furniture in various styles—Renaissance and Gothic Revival as well as the Louis XV Rococo Revival style of which this is an excellent example. The quality of the carving is masterful, perhaps the finest produced in American Rococo Revival furniture. The construction is equally fine. In the manner of the best French cabinetry, even secondary areas are finished, as where the underside of the table top is veneered with bird's-eye maple.

The following provenance is partially conjectural. The etagere was given to the Museum in 1977 by descendants of Arunah S. Abell (1806–1888), the founder and publisher of the *Baltimore Sun*. In 1872 he purchased a Baltimore estate known as Guilford from the widow of William McDonald, inheritor of a transportation and real estate fortune.[4] When the Abells purchased Guilford, they also acquired its contents which probably included the etagere, which would have been the height of fashion in the 1850's when McDonald was furnishing his house.[5]

NOTES:
1. *A Bicentennial Treasury: American Masterpieces from the Metropolitan* (New York: Metropolitan Museum of Art, 1976), no. 50, ill. Bibl. 37, p. 25, ill.

119

2. Bibl. 38, pp. 210–217.
3. Bibl. 38, p. 213, figs. 6 and 6a.
4. J. Gilman D'Arcy Paul, "A Baltimore Estate: Guilford and Its Three Owners," *Maryland Historical Society Magazine*, Mar. 1956, pp. 19 and 22. McDonald built the vast Italianate mansion on the estate from plans by the architect Edmund G. Lind.
5. Although the Abells owned another country estate called Woodburne, it was the contents of Guilford which descended through the donor's branch of the family.

MATERIALS: Primary: rosewood (legs, stretchers, apron sides and front, shelf supports, crest), rosewood veneer (table top, shelves). Secondary: ash (table top core, shelves, rear rail of table), mahogany (two braces under table top), tulip wood (backboards), mahogany veneer (inside face of rear rail), maple veneer (underside of top). Mirrored glass

PROVENANCE: Possibly William McDonald (1830–1864), Baltimore; Arunah S. Abell, by purchase, 1872; by descent to Margaret Anna Abell

120. PIER TABLE (1800–1810)

Baltimore
34½ × 39¾ × 20⅛ in. (87.7 × 101 × 51.1 cm.)
The Baltimore Museum of Art: Anonymous Gift
(BMA 1982.143)

A pier table illustrated in Sheraton's *Cabinet-Maker and Upholsterer's Drawing-Book* is, with some variations, the source for the design of this Baltimore table.[1] Although demi-lune card and pier tables are more the Baltimore norm, tables of a modified D-shape, as in Sheraton's design, were produced in some quantity.[2] The most salient reference to the Sheraton design of 1793 is the repetition of the inwardly curved front and side stretchers and the half-round platform connecting

the front and rear stretchers. This table ranks among the finest productions of late eighteenth-century Baltimore cabinetmakers. While there are no other Baltimore pier tables presently known to allow a close comparison, an examination of its parts, especially its inlaid decoration, reveals its Baltimore origin. The half-round blossom inlay at the center back of the top and the platform base conch shell inlay, beautifully shaded and on green stained backgrounds, are both designs found on other examples of Baltimore furniture.[3] The slightly raised inlaid panel of a bowl of flowers on the center apron is somewhat unusual in Baltimore furniture of the period, but an identical design is found in reverse on a pair of Baltimore card tables now in the collection of The White House. The

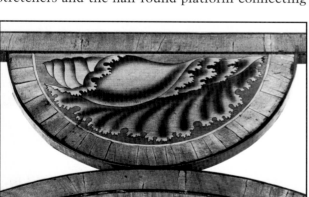

120. PIER TABLE, (1800–1810). Baltimore
The Baltimore Museum of Art: Anonymous Gift (BMA 1982.143)

flowers and bowl on the Museum example are made up of light and dark wood inlays, whereas on The White House tables they are of polychrome inlays on a colored field.[4] The single blossom in a pot inlaid on the stile of each front leg is somewhat atypical of Baltimore. Also following in this style are the four-petaled blossom, bellflower drops, and string inlay forming an ogee arch on the legs. The two curved side aprons of the table are made up of five horizontal laminations, paired thick strips sandwiching a thinner center strip. The rear rail is composed of two boards heavily nailed together in an X-pattern. There is a medial brace characteristic of Baltimore cabinetmaking.

NOTES:
1. Bibl. 73, Appendix, pl. 4.
2. See cat. no. 100 and bibl. 56, pp. 367–368, no. 351, ill.
3. Bibl. 4, p. 40, no. 14, ill. p. 41 and p. 108, no. 70, ill. p. 109.
4. Bibl. 4, p. 42, no. 15, ill.

MATERIALS: Primary: mahogany, mahogany and satinwood veneers, light, dark, and stained wood inlays. Secondary: white pine (rails), tulip wood (medial brace)

PROVENANCE: Joseph Kindig, Jr., Antiques, York, Pennsylvania; Private Collection, Baltimore

REFERENCES: Bibl. 19, fig. 581; bibl. 59, no. 6, ill.; bibl. 20, pp. 632–633, fig. 1; bibl. 77, p. 628, ill.

121. PIER TABLE (1800–1810)

Baltimore
Makers: John and Hugh Finlay
base: 35¼ × 47¼ × 21¼ in. (89.6 × 120 × 54 cm.)
marble top: 1⅛ × 48⅜ × 24⅛ in. (2.9 × 122.9 × 61.3 cm.)
The Baltimore Museum of Art: Gift of Lydia Howard de Roth and Nancy H. DeFord Venable, in Memory of their Mother, Lydia Howard DeFord; and Purchase Fund (BMA 1966.26.13)

This pier table is part of a thirteen-piece set of painted furniture. (For a discussion of the set as a whole, see armchair, cat. no. 29. For a settee from this set, see cat. no. 39.) The table's curved apron is constructed with three horizontal laminations. A medial brace is half dovetailed to the front and rear aprons. Several blocks were screwed to the interior of the apron in this century. The white marble top is original. The architectural view on the front skirt is of an exceptional Adamesque-Federal house called Greenwood, built about 1800 by Phillip Rogers on the then outskirts of Baltimore. Demolished in the nineteenth century, the house stood northwest of the intersection of Hoffman Street and Collington Avenue.

121

MATERIALS: maple (entire frame); painted black with polychrome and gilt and bronze decoration
PROVENANCE: John B. Morris (1785–1874), Baltimore; by descent to Lydia Howard DeFord; Lydia Howard de Roth and Nancy H. DeFord Venable
EXHIBITIONS: Bibl. 4, p. 21, no. 5, ill. and pp. 22–27, ill.; bibl. 18, pp. 76–83, ill.
REFERENCES: Bibl. 54, pp. 238–239, ill.

122. PIER TABLE (1800–1810)

Baltimore
Makers: attributed to John and Hugh Finlay
35⅞ × 45⅛ × 20 in. (91.2 × 114.7 × 50.8 cm.)
The Baltimore Museum of Art: The George C. Jenkins Fund, by exchange (BMA 1969.8.1)

This elaborately decorated and high style Baltimore pier table shares the same provenance as a side chair, window bench, and card table (cat. nos. 30, 40, and 101), which are part of an original sixteen-piece set of painted furniture made for the Buchanan family. The architectural view on the skirt is of two Baltimore row houses built on North Gay Street ca. 1800. The ownership of the houses is discussed in cat. no. 30. The design of the table, especially its arched stretchers, is derived from Sheraton[1] and shares its shape as well as a number of common construction features with the set's card table (cat. no. 101). The ends of the side rails

122

or aprons are dovetailed to an inner rear rail. The medial brace, about half the height of the apron, is half dovetailed into the front apron and inner rear rail. While the use of two rear rails is necessary for card tables, where the outer rail is hinged for the fly leg, it is unusual on a pier table. More usual Baltimore construction features are found in the three-piece horizontal lamination of the front and side aprons.

When acquired by the Museum, the table underwent much needed restoration. The separated and broken stretchers were reassembled and repaired. The painted surface was retouched, and the ringed feet were restored using the matching chair feet as models.

122

122

NOTES:
1. Bibl. 73, Appendix, pl. 4 (bottom).
MATERIALS: Yellow pine (top, rear rails), tulip wood (side, front rails, stretchers), maple (legs); painted black with polychrome and gilt and bronze decoration
PROVENANCE: William Buchanan, Baltimore; the Misses Sydney and Margaret Buchanan; by inheritance and descent to Ulrich O. Hutton, Brinklow
EXHIBITIONS: Bibl. 27, p. 32, no. 9, ill.
REFERENCES: Bibl. 33, p. 135, figs. 220 and 220a

123. PIER TABLE (1815–1830)

Baltimore
base: 37⅜ × 51⅞ × 23¼ in. (95 × 131.8 × 59.1 cm.)
marble: ⅞ × 56¾ × 26 in. (2.2 × 144.2 × 66.1 cm.)
The Baltimore Museum of Art: Gift of A. Hyatt Mayer (BMA 1946.147)

This Baltimore pier table is enhanced by the pleasing combination of mahogany, bird's-eye maple veneer, and a richly veined marble top, a combination characteristic of Baltimore furniture of the period and often found in desks and secretary-bookcases (see cat. no. 81). The simply carved Ionic capitals on the two outside faces of the front legs and one outside face only of the rear legs are

123

123

New York
Makers: Williams and Dawson
base: 35¼ × 41⅝ × 18⅝ in. (89.6 × 105.8 × 47.3 cm.)
marble: ⅞ × 45¼ × 19⅜ in. (2.2 × 115 × 49.2 cm.)
The Baltimore Museum of Art: Bequest of Elizabeth
Curzon Hoffman Wing, in Memory of Hanson Rawlings
Duval, Jr. (BMA 1967.30.11)

This marble-topped pier table has stenciled on its
backboards Williams & Dawson, Cabinet Chair &
Sofa Manufactory, No. 65 Broad Street, New York.

124

Thomas Williams and Jacob H. Dawson were first
listed jointly in New York directories of 1824.[1]
Marble-topped pier tables with mirrored bases were
a common product of East Coast cabinetmaking
centers in the first four decades of the nineteenth

repeated in other examples of Baltimore furniture,
as are its turned columnar legs terminating in large
ball feet.[1] The apron joins the table legs with double
tongued tenons. On the back of the front apron in
black ink the number 59 is inscribed, and repeated
in a chalk inscription on the inside rear apron.
Other inscriptions are: Brantz in chalk on the back
of the front apron; Made by Lewis Brantz/died
1838/Baltimore in black crayon on the inside of
the rear apron; in ink on a manila label on the
inside right apron: Made in Baltimore by/BRANTZ/
Lewis Brantz, died 21 Jan. 1838.

Captain Lewis Brantz (Karl Friedrich Ludwig
Brantz) was born in Stuttgart, Germany in 1766,
emigrated to America in 1785, and at the time of
his death in 1838, was President of the Baltimore
and Port Deposit Railroad. An educated and well
traveled man, his diverse and interesting life is
recorded in files at the Maryland Historical Society.[2] He was a business associate of Christian
Mayer, an ancestor of the pier table's donor. It
seems unlikely that Lewis Brantz actually made
the table himself.

NOTES:
1. Bibl. 84, p. 192, nos. 168 and 169, ill. and p. 142, no.
   102, ill. See also bibl. 55, vol. 1, p. 564, no. 1013, ill. p.
   562, and vol. 2, p. 834, no. 1651, ill. p. 833.
2. The Maryland Historical Society, Baltimore, The J. Hall
   Pleasants Studies in Maryland Painting, #2591.
MATERIALS: Primary: mahogany, bird's-eye maple veneer.
Secondary: tulip wood, yellow pine. Italian Bardiglio marble
PROVENANCE: Lewis Brantz, Baltimore; Christian Mayer; by
descent to A. Hyatt Mayer

124

124

century. However, the plain carved Ionic capitals of the columns here are typically New York in style and appear in a more elaborate piece of furniture attributed to the shop of Duncan Phyfe.[2] The carved cornucopia and leaf brackets below the shelf as well as the heavy paw feet are found on many New York pier tables of this period. The mahogany veneered skirt of the pier table has stenciled gilt decoration that is also found on the columnar supports and the base. The carved brackets as well as the feet were enriched with bronze and other metallic powders. The pier table had never been repaired or cleaned until recently when missing elements of the capitals were replaced and the gilt stenciling restored. The mirrored glass and black and white marble top are original.

NOTES:
1. Their firm's street number 51 changed the following year to 65, either due to an alteration in the numbering system or a move. The partnership continued until 1832 when Williams is no longer found in the directory. Dawson continued on in the same location until 1835. *Longworth's American Almanac, New York Register and City Directory* (New York: Thomas Longworth, 1824), p. 467.
2. Bibl. 54, p. 124, pl. 107.

MATERIALS: Mahogany (base shelf), mahogany veneer (base shelf, apron), cherry (rear stiles, columns, pilasters, rear rail), white pine (apron, front and rear base rails, all carving), ash (side base rails), with stenciled, gilt, and bronze decoration. King of Prussia, Pennsylvania, marble. Mirrored glass

PROVENANCE: John Hoffman, Baltimore; by descent to Elizabeth Curzon Hoffman Wing, Charleston, South Carolina

125. PIER TABLE (1820–1830)

Baltimore
base: 36½ × 44 × 23⅛ in. (92.7 × 111.8 × 58.9 cm.)
marble: ¾ × 45 × 22¼ in. (1.9 × 114.3 × 56.5 cm.)
The Baltimore Museum of Art: Bequest of Elizabeth Curzon Hoffman Wing, in Memory of Hanson Rawlings Duval, Jr. (BMA 1967.30.13)

Lion-headed metal monopodia, also called trapezophorons, serve as the front supports of this marble-topped pier table believed to have been made in Baltimore about 1820. According to family tradition, the pier table was part of the original furnishings of an important Classic Revival house designed by Robert Mills for the Baltimore merchant prince, John Hoffman, and built ca. 1817 on the northeast corner of Franklin and Cathedral Streets.[1] The table was bequeathed to the Museum by his descendant Elizabeth Curzon Hoffman Wing. The mirror surround and part of the rectangular base retain the original painted rosewood grain surfaces. The stenciled and freehand gilt decoration of an urn and flowers on the mirror stiles appears to have been executed upside down, but possibly the mirror surround was incorrectly assembled. Gilt decoration and simulated rosewood grain are very much in the Baltimore painted furniture vernacular.[2] The front and side aprons are ornamented with a gilt frieze of applied plaster anthemions. The monopodia are copied from a classical source by way of Thomas Hope's *Household Furniture*

125

125

and Interior Decoration, but the ultimate source of the apron frieze design is a marble relief on the architrave of a doorway on the 4th-century B.C. Erechtheum in Athens.[3] A portrait of the Baltimorean Robert Patterson at the Maryland Historical Society has the same decorative elements on its original gilt frame, probably made from the same molds. The white marble top may be an Italian import, although marble was being quarried in Baltimore County by 1815. The circular ormolu mounts on the front corners are restorations.

NOTES:
1. Thomas Waters Griffith, *Annals of Baltimore* (Baltimore: W. Wooddy, 1833), pp. 250–251. For an illustration of the house, see William Voss Elder III, "Robert Mills' Waterloo Row—Baltimore 1816," *BMA Record*, vol. 1, no. 12, p. 21.
2. For other similar examples see bibl. 27, p. 62, no. 37, ill.; pp. 66–67, no. 41, ill.; and pp. 88–89, no. 59, ill.
3. Bibl. 43, pl. 15, nos. 1 and 3.

MATERIALS: Yellow pine, maple (front stretcher); rosewood grain painting with stenciled gilt decoration. Gilt plaster molding. Hollow cast lead monopodia; ormolu mounts (not original). Mirrored glass (not original)

PROVENANCE: John or George Hoffman, Baltimore; by descent to Elizabeth Curzon Hoffman Wing, Charleston, South Carolina

EXHIBITIONS: Bibl. 27, p. 60, no. 35, ill.

REFERENCES: Bibl. 35, p. 121, fig. VI-23

126

126. TILT-TOP STAND (1760–1790)

Massachusetts
27½ × 17¼ × 17¼ in. (69.9 × 43.8 × 43.8 cm.)
Collection of Dorothy McIlvain Scott, Baltimore: Promised Gift to The Baltimore Museum of Art

Small tables, such as this example with a tilting top hinged to a turned columnar pillar support on a tripod base, were called "stands" and "folding stands" in the eighteenth century.[1] Such tables were made in all of America's major cabinetmaking centers but this particular tilt-top stand is typical of those produced in the urban areas of Boston, Salem, and Essex County for much of the eighteenth century. One key to this geographic attribution is an example owned by the Museum of Fine Arts, Boston, that was made in 1784 by the Salem cabinetmaker Jonathan Gavet.[2] Another closely related example is in the collection of the Society for the Preservation of New England Antiquities.[3] Like these two published examples, the Museum's stand is supported on three cabriole legs that terminate in pad feet, has a similarly turned

pillar, and has a squared top with serpentine-shaped sides. The top edges are rounded and the three cabriole legs are chamfered on the inside. This tilt-top stand has been refinished and the hinge end of the pillar block repaired.

NOTES:
1. Bibl. 46, p. 304.
2. Bibl. 66, pp. 141–143, no. 106, ill.
3. Bibl. 46, pp. 304–305, no. 76, ill.
MATERIALS: Primary: mahogany. Secondary: birch (hinge block, cleats). Iron brace
PROVENANCE: David Stockwell, Inc., Wilmington, Delaware; Dorothy McIlvain Scott, Baltimore

127. TILT-TOP STAND (1750–1790)

Philadelphia
28 in. high (71.1 cm.); 22½ in. diameter (57.2 cm.)
Collection of Dorothy McIlvain Scott, Baltimore: Promised Gift to The Baltimore Museum of Art

All of the accepted characteristics of a Philadelphia tilt-top stand in the Chippendale style are displayed in this example which also has an impeccable provenance. The circular dished top with molded rim is made of one piece of mahogany, supported by a "bird cage" of four baluster turnings joining square mahogany boards above and below. This in

127

turn is attached to a turned pillar of compressed ball and column form set on three cabriole legs which terminate in ball-and-claw feet. The base of the pillar is carved with tiny ogee arches between each leg, and the same carving is repeated on each leg's underside where it joins the pillar. There is the customary triangular iron brace on the undersides of the pillar and the leg tops. One leg has been broken at the ankle and pinned. This tea table and a dressing table (cat. no. 59) were owned by a sixth-generation descendant of the Da Costa and Tallman families of Philadelphia. Both pieces of furniture have long been associated by the family with Captain Joseph Da Costa and his late eighteenth-century house at Front and Margaretta Streets in that city.[1] An inscription found on the dressing table strongly suggests first ownership by members of the Tallman family (see cat. no. 59), but the tea table could have come into the Tallman family through the marriage of George Tallman to Catherine Da Costa, the captain's daughter. Other Da Costa furniture from the house in Philadelphia was inherited by this branch of the Tallman-Da Costa families in the early twentieth century.[2]

NOTES:
1. Five excellent late nineteenth-century photographs of the Da Costa home survive, one of the exterior; the others are interior views. Copies are in the Museum's files courtesy of a Baltimore descendant of the family. Some of the photographs were reproduced in the catalogue of a sale of Da Costa furniture in 1930 (*The John Chalmers Da Costa, III, Collection of Documented Early Philadelphia Furniture*, Wm. D. Morley, Inc., Philadelphia, 15 Dec. 1930). The house according to the sale catalogue was still standing in 1930, but has been razed with the many other eighteenth-century houses for Philadelphia's interstate riverfront highway.
2. The Philadelphia cabinetmaker Jacob Wayne is known to have made furniture for Joseph Da Costa. A bill dated 1796 from Wayne to Da Costa for seventeen pieces of furniture was among the many items sold at the 1930 sale. "Documented Furniture by Jacob Wayne," by W.M. Horner (*International Studio*, June 1930, pp. 40–43) is largely based on this bill from Wayne to Da Costa. What would appear to be one of the two circular card tables itemized therein is owned by a Da Costa family descendant in Baltimore, and is a promised gift to The Baltimore Museum of Art.

MATERIALS: Mahogany. Brass catch on bird cage, iron brace
PROVENANCE: Da Costa family, Philadelphia; Catherine Da Costa, ca. 1930; Catherine Tallman, Philadelphia and Washington, D.C.; Anna Hunt Tallman Hopkins, Washington, D.C.; Elizabeth Beall Hopkins Luttrell; Saidee Luttrell Cousins; Albert H. Cousins, Jr., Baltimore; Dorothy McIlvain Scott

128

128. TEA TABLE (1760–1780)

Maryland or Pennsylvania
28 in. high (71.1 cm.); 32¾ in. diameter (83.2 cm.)
The Baltimore Museum of Art: Bequest of Ethel Hough (BMA 1961.35)

The baluster-shaped pillar of this tea table is related to well-known Philadelphia examples but lacks the multiple ring turnings usually present at the base of such vase-shaped shafts.[1] However, the

128

stance of the table on its low-slung cabriole legs, the blossom carving in a square at the top of each leg from which emanates an acanthus-leaf knee carving, and the shaping of the three ball-and-claw feet are typical of Philadelphia work of the period. The edge of the two-piece top is expertly and crisply shaped in the scalloped design common to Philadelphia tea tables. The four small columns of the tilting and turning mechanism at the top of the pedestal echo its shape in miniature. At some time in the past when the table underwent repairs, three of the columns were replaced upside down. There is the usual Y-shaped iron brace under the pedestal. The table has been attributed to either Maryland or Pennsylvania for the following reasons: Miss Ethel Hough, who bequeathed the tea table to the Museum in 1961, was of a family which had been in Baltimore since the late eighteenth century, and whose members it seems took spouses only from Maryland. Miss Hough left to the Museum and the Maryland Historical Society objects which in her view were of local importance. Our knowledge of Maryland, and specifically Baltimore versus Philadelphia tea tables of the Chippendale period, is indeed still scanty, as there are no documented and but a few attributed Maryland examples. Like the other furniture forms known to have been produced in Baltimore during this period, tea tables would have been imitative of or strongly influenced by the Philadelphia example.

NOTES:
1. Bibl. 39, p. 191, no. 119, ill.

MATERIALS: Primary: mahogany. Brass latch, iron brace
PROVENANCE: Edmondson and/or Hough families, Baltimore; by descent to Ethel Hough

129. TEA TABLE (1760–1780)

Maryland or Pennsylvania
29 in. high (73.7 cm.); 35⁵⁄₁₆ in. diameter (89.7 cm.)
Private Collection, Baltimore: Promised Gift to The Baltimore Museum of Art

As mentioned earlier (cat. no. 128), Chippendale tea tables that can be definitely ascribed to Maryland are exceedingly rare. This table, included in the 1968 exhibition of *Maryland Queen Anne and Chippendale Furniture* held at the Museum, was once owned by an authority on Philadelphia cabinetry, Joseph Kindig, Jr. who suggested that the table was produced in Maryland because he found it in Frederick, and it did not conform to his standards for tea tables made in or near Philadel-

129

129

phia.[1] The table certainly is characteristic enough of Philadelphia design to establish that it was not made in New York or Massachusetts but, without a comparable example, it is not possible to differentiate between a Philadelphia table and one made in Maryland, where the cabinetmakers were so strongly influenced by furniture from the populous and prosperous neighboring state.

The turning of the table's columnar support does not display the characteristic flattened ball at its base, but not all Philadelphia tea tables display this feature.[2] The ring turning is of Philadelphia origin, as is the construction of the bird cage turn and tilt mechanism, the pedestal's ring collar, and scalloped edge of the top. What is more common in Maryland is the lighter stance of the legs, thinner less articulated carved ball-and-claw feet, the deep acanthus-leaf carvings on the knees of the three cabriole legs, and the carved gadrooning under the legs at the base of the columnar support. This separate wooden member, heavily nailed to the underside of the legs, takes the place of the usual metal brace. The knuckles of the claws or talons of the feet are less defined than those on more characteristic Philadelphia pieces. In addition to the three visible claws, there is a fourth shortened claw on the inside of each foot.

The corners of the bottom platform of the bird cage are concave. The leaf carving on the knees of each leg is in three stages, reduced in size from top to bottom with the carving done more loosely nearest the pedestal. The top of the table is made up of four pieces of wood, their glued joints further strengthened by original pairs of wooden "dutchmen" or butterfly-shaped joints. The latch for the tilt top is a simple design in wrought iron, rather than the usual brass.

NOTES:
1. An apparently identical (if not the same table) was sold at Parke-Bernet Galleries, Inc. in 1950, with a previous New York ownership and origin from a New York dealer. If it is indeed the tea table described in this catalogue entry, it may still have been found in Frederick a few years after this sale. Parke-Bernet Galleries, Inc., New York, *The American Collection of Mr. & Mrs. Norvin H. Green*, sale no. 1202, 29–30 Nov. 1950, p. 111, no. 491, ill. The catalogue states that the table had been acquired from C.W. Lyon, Inc., New York.
2. Bibl. 42, p. 108, no. 58, ill. p. 109.

MATERIALS: Mahogany
PROVENANCE: Unknown source, Frederick; Joseph Kindig, Jr., Antiques, York, Pennsylvania; Private Collection, Baltimore, by 1962
EXHIBITIONS: Bibl. 29, p. 43, no. 26, ill.
REFERENCES: Bibl. 20, p. 634, no. 7, ill.

130. WORK TABLE (1790–1820)

New England
30⅝ × 18¾ × 15¼ in. (77.8 × 47.6 × 38.8 cm.)
The Baltimore Museum of Art: Gift of Mrs. Merrell Langdon Stout, in Memory of her Husband, Dr. Merrell Langdon Stout (BMA 1969.46.1)

This rectangular lady's work table, painted red with gilt decoration, is believed to have been made in Massachusetts because of its provenance and the woods used in its construction. It shares the same East Lexington provenance as two other pieces of furniture (cat. nos. 2 and 5). A hinged lid allows access to the interior of the suspended sewing bag, instead of being opened by the painted trompe l'oeil slide with brass knobs. The top edge is banded with a painted gilt design of vines and blossoms, similar to that found on painted tinware of the period. The central decorative motif—a painted eagle carrying in its beak a banner reading "Be Just and Fear Not"—is enclosed in a painted oval floral wreath.[1] Leaf and tendril swag designs are painted on the side and front aprons of the table and at the top of each leg. The bottom three inches of each leg are painted gold with black stripes. All of the decorative painting in gold is highlighted with black, brown, green, red, and white paint. The brown and blue striped and patterned chintz sewing bag is original. The table lid

130

130

card table owned by the Museum (cat. no. 95).[2]
While turret-cornered work tables like this were made in other East Coast cabinetmaking centers in the early nineteenth century, the combination of design elements points to an eastern Massachusetts origin, probably Boston or Salem. In addition to carving and star punch work, the ring turnings at the top of each leg and the turned feet are characteristic of work of the period in the Boston-Salem area. The upper drawer was once fitted with partitions. The pressed brass knobs are replacements.

131

has cleated or breadboard ends. The apron does not tenon into the tops of each leg as usual; rather these rails are lap joined to each leg and secured with nails and interior glue blocks. The survival of the table with its original cloth bag is remarkable especially considering that the thin legs are made of pine. The whole table weighs no more than three pounds.

NOTES:
1. The motto appears in William Shakespeare and John Fletcher's *Henry VIII, III* (1613), *A New Dictionary of Quotations on Historical Principles from Ancient and Modern Sources*, selected and edited by H.L. Mencken (New York: Alfred A. Knopf, 1942), p. 625, and is also used with the coat of arms of certain English families.

MATERIALS: White pine (legs, apron, cleats), maple (top); painted red with gilt and polychrome decoration. Cotton chintz sewing bag

PROVENANCE: Robbins family, East Lexington, Massachusetts; by descent to Dr. Merrell Langdon Stout, Baltimore; Helen Scarlett Stout (Mrs. Merrell)

131. WORK TABLE (1805–1820)

Eastern Massachusetts, possibly Salem
28¼ × 21 × 17⅝ in. (71.8 × 53.4 × 44.8 cm.)
The Baltimore Museum of Art: Bequest of Alice Morawetz (BMA 1942.112)

This small mahogany work table is distinguished by excellent rosette and leaf carving at the top of each leg. Similar carving in the same location, perhaps by the same hand, appears in a work table believed to have been made in Salem about 1815, now in the Essex Institute.[1] The punched-star background of the rosette and leaf carvings on both tables is a design element characteristic of Salem furniture and also found on a Salem Chippendale

NOTES:
1. Bibl. 19, no. 594, ill.
2. For star punch work on Salem pieces, see bibl. 56, p. 82, no. 23, ill. and bibl. 66, pp. 132–137, no. 100, ill.

MATERIALS: Mahogany (top, legs), mahogany veneers (on white pine drawers and apron). Brass knobs (not original)

PROVENANCE: Alice Morawetz, Baltimore

132. WORK TABLE (1815–1830)

Maryland or Pennsylvania
30⅝ × 22⅜ × 16 in. (77.8 × 56.9 × 40.7 cm.)
The Baltimore Museum of Art: Bequest of Eleanor M. Anderson, Maplewood, New Jersey (BMA 1979.73)

Both the Maryland Historical Society and The Baltimore Museum of Art own work tables that are closely related to two other examples in Penn-

132

the collection of the Philadelphia Museum of Art has been attributed to the Philadelphia cabinetmaker Michael Bouvier (1792–1874).

2. For a discussion of lyre base card tables with many of the same features, see cat. no. 103.

3. Bibl. 84, p. 189.

MATERIALS: Primary: mahogany (legs, lyre arms, corner turrets, knobs), bird's-eye maple veneers (top, drawer fronts, lower lyre), mahogany veneers (case sides, drawer dividers, top banding). Secondary: mahogany (drawer sides and backs), tulip wood (case bottom, upper lyre collar), white pine (drawer bottoms and dividers, top), yellow pine (case sides), ash (pedestal block). Writing surface (not original)

PROVENANCE: Oliver J. Anderson, Baltimore; by descent to Eleanor M. Anderson, Maplewood, New Jersey

133. WORK TABLE (1816–1821)

Baltimore
Maker: Ralph E. Forrester
29¼ × 26¾ × 17 in. (74.3 × 68 × 43.2 cm.)
The Baltimore Museum of Art: Bequest of John M. Glenn, by exchange (BMA 1967.1)

This lady's work table was made in Baltimore between 1816 and 1821, years when the cabinetmaker Ralph E. Forrester worked at 61 St. Patrick's Row (the address, along with Forrester's name, is inscribed on the bottom of the second drawer).[1] Forrester's full name first appears in the Baltimore City Directories in 1814 as a cabinetmaker working at 32 Water Street. The name Forrester alone is listed in the partnership of Forrester and Wheeler

sylvania collections.[1] All four have similarly shaped lyre bases, saber legs, turned colonnettes at the four corners, and combine mahogany and bird's-eye maple for decoration.[2] The Maryland Historical Society example has recently been attributed to the Baltimore cabinetmaker William Camp (1773–1822) based on a comparison of construction details with documented Camp pieces. Camp's work is said to be closely related to Philadelphia examples, and there was much interchange between Philadelphia and Baltimore cabinetmakers in this period.[3] The mahogany veneer of the table's top frames a center panel of bird's-eye maple veneer. The bases of the two solid mahogany lyres with brass rods as well as the drawer fronts are also veneered with bird's-eye maple. The top drawer has a hinged and ratcheted writing surface, two compartments for ink bottles, and a hollowed mahogany block to serve as a pen tray.

The inscription of Oliver Anderson on the bottom drawer indicates that the table was in the Baltimore area in this century.

NOTES:

1. Bibl. 84, pp. 189–190, no. 164, ill. The table owned by the Philadelphia Museum of Art is illustrated in bibl. 81, no. 20, pp. 43 and 76; that owned by the Historical Society of Pennsylvania is illustrated in James E. Mooney, "Furniture at the Historical Society of Pennsylvania," *Antiques*, May 1978, p. 1041, pl. VI. The table in

133

133

at Water Street in Old Town, that area of Baltimore just east of Jones Falls, while the city directories for 1827 and 1829 place Ralph E. Forrester on North Howard Street near Richmond Street.

The gracefully shaped urn support of the pedestal base is reeded in the spiky Baltimore manner and sits on a triple-ring turned collar, a design element found in other early nineteenth-century Baltimore pedestal base tables in the Museum's collection.[2] The top drawer was originally partitioned, and the two half-round side sewing compartments retain the original green baize lining. The hinged lids on the ends and both drawers are fitted with steel locks. The four pendant drops at each corner of the central case have been restored.

An unusual construction feature of this table is the weak attachment of the drawer sides to the face using only one and one-half dovetails, in contrast to Forrester's use of two dovetails attaching the drawer sides to its backboard.

NOTES:
1. The working dates and addresses of Ralph E. Forrester have been taken from two sources: bibl. 27, p. 107 and bibl. 84, p. 281.
2. These include a lady's writing/work table (BMA 1964.51.2), and a drum top table (BMA 1950.80.4).

MATERIALS: Primary: mahogany (pedestal, legs, stiles, drawer dividers). Secondary: oak (pedestal collar), yellow pine, tulip wood (lower drawer bottom)

PROVENANCE: Stoll Kemp Antiques, New Market; BMA, by purchase, 1967

134. CORNER TABLE (1800–1810)

Baltimore
base: 35⅞ × 26¼ × 19⅜ in. (91.2 × 66.7 × 49.2 cm.)
marble: ¾ × 27⅝ × 19⅞ in. (1.9 × 70.2 × 50.5 cm.)
The Baltimore Museum of Art: Anna Campbell Ellicott Bequest Fund, in Memory of her Husband, William M. Ellicott (BMA 1951.34)

At present eight Baltimore marble-topped corner tables are known: two matching tables at the Maryland Historical Society,[1] two at Winterthur,[2] one privately owned in Baltimore,[3] a greatly altered pair at Blair House, Washington, D.C., and one in

Charleston, South Carolina.[4] With the exception of different painted églomisé panels and the variant of a platform base versus arched stretchers, the corner tables are identical in construction and decoration, and are almost certainly products of the same shop. In the past they have been attributed to Joseph Barry of Philadelphia and to the brothers John and Hugh Finlay of Baltimore.[5] A recent publication suggests a possible attribution to William Camp, another important early nineteenth-century Baltimore cabinetmaker.[6] However, the decoration of the tables is most closely related to work by the Finlays who, even if hired to do only the painted work, had the capability within their shop to produce the frame as well.[7]

A number of pier tables obviously made to be used en suite with these corner tables are known. The Museum's corner table has the same first ownership as a matching pier table privately owned in Washington. Both tables have a classical subject, Diana and Endymion, painted on the églomisé panel set into the center skirts, a design which is a slavish imitation of Plate 11 of Thomas Sheraton's *Accompaniment to the Cabinet-Maker and Upholsterer's Drawing Book* (London, 1802). The same scene is depicted on the two corner tables and a

134

134

Baltimore Painted Furniture," *The Decorator* (Journal of the Historical Society of Early American Decoration), Fall 1972, pp. 8–10, figs. 4 and 5; "Accessions, 1951," *BMA News*, Jan. 1952, pp. 1 and 4

135. CENTER TABLE (1825–1830)

Philadelphia
Maker: attributed to Anthony Gabriel Quervelle
29⅜ in. high (74.6 cm.); 47⅞ in. diameter (121.7 cm.)
The Baltimore Museum of Art: Bequest of R. Elisabeth Arens and Adelaide Arens Morawetz, from the Estate of Henry Arens; Bequest of Caecilia H. Norton; Bequest of Anne Hepburn Rolando; and Gift from the Estate of Ellen M. Schaeffer, by exchange (BMA 1974.12)

The French-born Philadelphia cabinetmaker Anthony Gabriel Quervelle (1789–1856) was listed as a cabinetmaker in the Philadelphia City Directories from 1820 until his death in 1856.[1] In 1825 he had opened a "cabinet Ware House." Quervelle emerges as one of the most important early nineteenth-century Philadelphia cabinetmakers who produced a wide range of furniture forms of quality and in quantity. His work was heavily influenced by George Smith's *Collection of Designs for Household Furniture* (London, 1808).

pier table at Winterthur, and a Baltimore writing desk.[8] Unlike the tables at the Maryland Historical Society and that privately owned in Baltimore, which have elaborately arched stretchers, this corner table and the pair of corner tables and pier table at Winterthur have platform bases which serve to strengthen the legs. When acquired by the Museum in 1951, the legs of the table had been cut off about two inches. Restorations were made based on the examples at Winterthur.

NOTES:
1. Bibl. 84, pp. 178–179, no. 149, ill.
2. Bibl. 56, pp. 369–370, no. 354, ill.
3. Bibl. 27, p. 19, no. 2, ill.
4. Recorded in the Southern decorative art survey files of the Museum of Early Southern Decorative Arts; the authors are grateful to Research Associate Bradford Rauschenberg for bringing it to their attention.
5. Bibl. 56, pp. 369–370 and bibl. 27, pp. 18–19, nos. 1 and 2, ill.
6. Bibl. 84, pp. 178–179.
7. The gilt rosettes on the stretcher blocks and bundled leaves on the stiles are also found on two tables illustrated in bibl. 27, p. 35, no. 12 and p. 39, no. 16, where they are attributed to the Finlays. High-scrolled stretchers reminiscent of those found on some of this group of corner tables are found on a similarly attributed pier table which is part of the Buchanan family set of painted furniture (cat. no. 122).
8. Bibl. 4, p. 124, no. 78, ill. p. 125.

MATERIALS: Primary: mahogany (legs, shelf), mahogany veneers and light wood inlays (apron and front legs). Secondary: yellow pine (rear apron rails, braces), tulip wood (three horizontal laminations of front apron); freehand gilt decoration. Eglomisé panel with foil backing. King of Prussia, Pennsylvania, marble

PROVENANCE: Catherine Clemm Brengle, Frederick; Olivia Brengle Shriver; J. Alexis Shriver, Baltimore; BMA, by purchase, 1951

EXHIBITIONS: Bibl. 4, p. 61, no. 32, ill.

REFERENCES: "The Editor's Attic," *Antiques*, Sept. 1952, p. 224, ill.; Mildred Ayers, "The Verre Eglomisé Ovals in

135

135

Pedestal tables like this example were part of Quervelle's stock in trade. The circular tilt top has a bird's-eye maple veneered center from which radiate wedge-shaped branch mahogany veneers, characteristic of Quervelle's work.[2] The table top is encircled by a border of black painted wood, and a similar border frames the central bird's-eye maple veneer. The pedestal is columnar at the top and hexagonal on its lower half, with gadrooning at its base, thus incorporating design elements found in whole or part on other pieces of furniture attributed to his shop.[3] The triangular platform base with concave sides is supported by three carved paw feet. These feet, the most characteristically idiosyncratic design element of Quervelle's work, are carved with a distinctive upswept leaf curl above the paw and scrolling foliate carved brackets, and are found on many other tables attributed to him.[4]

The table is solidly built and beautifully finished with veneer on the underside of the top so that it can be viewed from both sides when tilted up. The top is secured in a horizontal or vertical position with two brass sliding tongue latches connected by a heavy brass handle to release them simultaneously.

NOTES:
1. Bibl. 76, "Part I: The pier tables," May 1973, pp. 984–994; bibl. 76, "Part II: The pedestal tables," July 1973,

pp. 90–99; bibl. 76, "Part III: The work tables," Aug. 1973, pp. 260–268; bibl. 76, "Part IV: Some case pieces," Jan. 1974, pp. 180–193; bibl. 76, "Part V: Sofas, chairs, and beds," Mar. 1974, pp. 512–521.
2. Bibl. 76, July 1973, p. 90, fig. 1 and p. 91, fig. 3.
3. Bibl. 76, July 1973, p. 92, fig. 7; Robert C. Smith, "Philadelphia Empire Furniture by Antoine Gabriel Quervelle," *Antiques*, Sept. 1964, p. 308, fig. 9.
4. Bibl. 76, July 1973, p. 91, fig. 4; also p. 96, fig. 13 and p. 99, pl. III.

MATERIALS: Primary: mahogany, mahogany and maple veneers. Secondary: tulip wood, maple, cherry

PROVENANCE: Mrs. Charlotte Stafford, Baltimore; BMA, by purchase, 1974

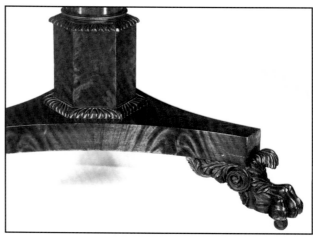

135

Miscellaneous

136

136. BED (1790–1810)

Charleston
91⅝ × 66 × 80½ in. (232.8 × 167.7 × 204.6 cm.)
rail h.: 19¼ in. (48.9 cm.)
The Baltimore Museum of Art: Gift of Mrs. Francis White, from the Collection of Mrs. Miles White, Jr. (BMA 1973.76.271)

Although it lacks that most characteristic Charleston rice carving on the upper urn-shaped section of the two end posts, this bed exhibits nearly all the other characteristics of a South Carolina high post bed of the Federal period.[1] That the bed is made of mahogany is not surprising in view of the Carolinas' proximity to the Caribbean source. The headboard and headposts were meant to be covered by bed hangings. The side rails are heavily notched for slats; the foot posts turned above the rails have

tapered squared bases terminating in spade feet. The headboard is removable, sliding in slots formed by wood strips nailed to the tapered square headposts. There is carved fringing at the base of the end posts' reeding, typical of beds associated with Charleston.[2] The sparely veined leaf carving on the lower urn of the foot posts is also related to Charleston examples.[3] The carving on the upper urn combines a chain and tassel motif with tendril and leaf carving. The squared foot posts have inlaid oval veneers above the bed rails framed with line inlays, and below the rails a tapered rectangle of line inlay of alternating light and dark diagonals.[4]

Virginia Bonsal White purchased the bedstead from Howard Sill of Baltimore.[5] Both she and Sill were among Baltimore's earliest collectors of American furniture. How Sill acquired the Charleston bed is not known.

NOTES:
1. Bibl. 14, p. 42.
2. Bibl. 14, figs. 19–21 and 29.
3. Bibl. 14, figs. 22 and 29.
4. Bibl. 14, figs. 20 and 21.
5. For other pieces of furniture from Mrs. White's collection now in the collection of The Baltimore Museum of Art and included in this catalogue, see cat. nos. 11, 12, 22, 69, 87, 88, 91, 110, 111, and 137. For another piece of furniture originally owned by Howard Sill, see cat. no. 50.

MATERIALS: Mahogany, light and dark inlays; headboard (not original)

PROVENANCE: Howard Sill, Baltimore; Mrs. Miles White, Jr.; Francis White; Nancy Brewster White (Mrs. Francis)

EXHIBITIONS: BMA, "The White Collection," 19 Mar.–2 June 1974

136

137. CELLARETTE (1815–1840)

Baltimore
21⅜ × 27¾ × 19⅜ in. (54.3 × 70.5 × 49.2 cm.)
The Baltimore Museum of Art: Gift of Mrs. Francis White, from the Collection of Mrs. Miles White, Jr. (BMA 1973.76.230)

Cellarettes of this basic form exist in sufficient numbers in Baltimore to establish that they were manufactured in the area from about 1810 to 1840. The octagonal shape is based ultimately on classical Roman sarcophagi, a form of sepulchral sculpture that had been perpetuated from the Renaissance to the eighteenth century. In the Classical Revival of the early nineteenth century both in England and in France, such ancient designs and forms were often applied to furniture. In his *Cabinet Dictionary* of 1803, Thomas Sheraton illustrates a wine cooler which he actually calls a sarcophagus.[1] In the collection of the Maryland Historical Society, there is a cellarette, the case of which is nearly identical to the Museum's example. The Maryland Historical Society example is raised on a pedestal base while the Museum's cellarette sits directly on four feet just a few inches above the floor.[2] Other closely related cellarettes still in use in Baltimore houses are known to the authors. Two edges of the octagonal coffered lid are finished with an ebonized quarter-round molding that is repeated in the base section defining the two-inch thick tulip wood bottom. The mahogany veneers of the top and base are superbly figured with striped and branched graining. The side veneers are of an equally rich plum pudding grain. The interior has a lead liner with six partitions and cylindrical center fitted with a drain. The cellarette was restored and refinished in 1974.

According to notes made by Mrs. Miles White, Jr., she purchased the cellarette from J. Latimer Hoffman, Jr. of Baltimore, in the auction of the contents of his house on May 31, 1910.[3] However, the sale catalogue lists primarily porcelain, silver, prints, paintings, and very few pieces of furniture, none of them cellarettes.[4] Presumably Mrs. White made her purchase before Hoffman's sale in 1910.

NOTES:
1. Bibl. 72, pl. 68, as quoted in bibl. 84, p. 98.
2. Bibl. 84, p. 99, no. 38, ill. p. 98. A similar cellarette, still privately owned and with a long history of ownership in Maryland, was also included in the 1984 catalogue of the Historical Society's Maryland furniture. Bibl. 84, p. 98, no. 37, ill.
3. Typed manuscript of notes on provenance of furniture in the collection of Mrs. Miles White, Jr. and given to her son, Francis White. A copy of the notes is in the Museum's files.

4. *Collection of J. Latimer Hoffman, Jr., Esq.*, sale cat., Pattison and Gahan, Auctioneers, Baltimore, 31 May 1910.

MATERIALS: Primary: mahogany, mahogany veneers. Secondary: tulip wood

PROVENANCE: J. Latimer Hoffman, Jr., Baltimore; sale, 31 May 1910; Mrs. Miles White, Jr.; Francis White; Nancy Brewster White (Mrs. Francis)

137

137

138. MIRROR (1810–1830)

Baltimore or New York
Maker: possibly Peter del Vecchio
23¹¹/₁₆ × 23⁹/₁₆ × 9½ in. (60.2 × 59.9 × 24.1 cm.)
frame d.: 3½ in. (8.9 cm.)
The Baltimore Museum of Art: Gift of Mrs. Henry V. Ward (BMA 1934.56.15)

Thomas Sheraton described a mirror like this example as a "circular convex glass in a gilt frame, silvered on the concave side, by which the reflection of the rays of light are produced."[1] In the conventional form these mirrors are set in conforming circular frames. The Museum's looking glass is set, however, in an almost square gilt frame. Its decoration of shells on diapered backgrounds with floriate scrolls and leaves in the four spandrels is made of cast plaster. The gilt metal candle arms, bronze candle sockets, pressed brass bobeches, and crystal drops are all original and typical of the form. The ornate candle branches, called girandoles, have given their name incorrectly to this convex mirror form.

P. del Vecchio in a neat flowing black ink script on the mirror's backboard probably stands for Peter del Vecchio who lived in Baltimore from about 1797 until his death in 1837. A carver, gilder, picture frame maker, del Vecchio also specialized in scientific instrument-making and also dealt in English and French prints, pianofortes, Spanish "segars," and even "Platina lightning rods." He sold and may well have manufactured looking glasses, such as this one.[2]

However, there are two pieces of newspaper backing the mirror, the bottom layer without a name or date, but indicating New York City from such interior evidence as the names of Fulton Street and Broadway. The upper layers of newsprint refer to Baltimore sites, including a mention of Calvert Street on a fragment dated 1871.

There was a firm of looking glass makers active in New York between 1813 and 1854, which was founded by Charles del Vecchio, and carried on by his sons, Joseph, James, and Charles, Jr.[3] Whether there was any connection between the Baltimore craftsman and entrepreneur and the New York firm is a matter of conjecture.

NOTES:
1. Bibl. 72, p. 271, as quoted in bibl. 56, p. 275.
2. Del Vecchio's obituary is in the Maryland Historical Society Diehlman-Hayward file of Maryland residents. He lived in Baltimore from ca. 1797 to 1837. His instrument-making talents were advertised in the *Federal Gazette and Baltimore Daily Advertiser*, 27 June 1804.
3. Bibl. 56, p. 480.

138

MATERIALS: White pine with gilt gesso. White metal candle arms, gessoed and gilded; brass bobeche and candleholder. Cut glass prisms; mirror glass (not original)

PROVENANCE: Mrs. Henry V. Ward, Baltimore

EXHIBITIONS: Bibl. 81, p. 76, no. 25, ill.; bibl. 11, p. 80, no. 63, ill.

138

139. PIANOFORTE (1820–1830)

Baltimore
Maker: Lovering Ricketts
35⅝ × 67⅞ × 32 in. (90.5 × 172.5 × 81.3 cm.)
The Baltimore Museum of Art: Gift of Mrs. Henry V. Ward, by exchange (BMA 1973.31)

The maker of this pianoforte, Lovering (Levering) Ricketts, whose name L. Ricketts appears with the word Baltimore on the inset panel above the keyboard, worked in Baltimore as a cabinetmaker at 68 French Street in Old Town from 1814–1818 and on the west side of Bond Street, in Fells Point from 1822–1823. He is first listed as a pianoforte maker in 1824, having moved his place of business to the south side of Lovely Lane. He relocated to 51 Center Market Space by the next year where he seems to have remained until at least 1830.[1]

Ricketts was one of more than twenty pianoforte makers working in Baltimore in the first four decades of the nineteenth century.[2] Many had short-lived productions. Since Ricketts is first recorded as a cabinetmaker, it can be assumed that he made or supervised the construction of his piano cases. This rectangular case with canted front corners is veneered with choice grained mahogany and highlighted with panels of maple veneer in the manner typical of Baltimore Empire-style furniture. Bird's-eye maple is used along the lower case front and above the keyboard, and a strip of tiger maple veneer is under the keyboard. The two complex applied ormolu strip moldings that extend around three sides of the lower case are unusual in Baltimore furniture of the period. The pianoforte is supported at each end by heavy saber-legged pedestal supports, whose fine carving avoids the overstatement common to much design of the period. A mahogany panel above the keyboard has gilt decorations, the sort of surface embellishments done by specialists in decorative painting. Ricketts' gold leaf embossed red leather nameplate may have been the work of a bookbinder; it is an unusual treatment not seen on other Baltimore pianofortes.[3]

On the back of the panel above the keyboard is the following inscription: Henry Hull[...]n No 1 March the 1[0] 183[4] which may refer to a repairer, a tuner, or even the fabricator of the piano's action. On the right corner of the sounding board is the name L. Ricketts in gold letters in an outward curving arc. Above his name is a stenciled name Bernard Hanson and Custom Rebuilt.

The white pine bottom boards of the pianoforte run diagonally. The pedestal legs are threaded at the top to facilitate moving.

NOTES:
1. In the newspaper *The Baltimore American* on 6 February of that year, Ricketts advertised both his piano factory and a music store. Bibl. 84, p. 311.
2. Bibl. 27, pp. 96–129. Some of the other pianoforte makers were James Stewart, William Bartlett, George Huppman, and Joseph Hiskey. See bibl. 84, pp. 147–151, for illustrated examples and a thorough discussion of their work.
3. Another Ricketts pianoforte with an identical case but mounted on four turned and carved legs was owned privately in Charlotte, North Carolina in 1967. That piano retains its original lyre-shaped pedal board which is also veneered with maple. Letter and photograph from owners, BMA files.

139

139

MATERIALS: Primary: mahogany (top, legs), mahogany veneer (sides), maple veneer (lower front, keyboard area, case interior), stained poplar (cross-banding). Secondary: white pine (sounding boards, case sides, bottom), yellow pine (back). Gilt brass molding and roundels, brass feet and casters. Ivory, ebony keys.

PROVENANCE: Purchased from a dealer in Northern Virginia; BMA, by purchase, 1973

Exhibitions and References

1. "Accessions of American and Canadian Museums, July–September 1960." *Art Quarterly*, Winter 1960, pp. 398–407.
2. *American Antiques from Israel Sack Collection*. 7 vols. Washington, D.C.: Highland House Publishers, 1957–1983.
3. BMA, "Decorative Arts Accessions, 1968–1973." 27 Feb.–15 Apr. 1973.
4. *Baltimore Furniture: The Work of Baltimore and Annapolis Cabinetmakers from 1760 to 1810* (exhibition cat.). The Baltimore Museum of Art, 1947.
5. *BMA News Quarterly*. Fall 1961.
6. Lu Bartlett. "John Shaw, cabinetmaker of Annapolis." *Antiques*, Feb. 1977, pp. 362–377.
7. Edwin A. Battison and Patricia E. Kane. *The American Clock, 1725–1865*. Greenwich, Connecticut: New York Graphic Society, 1973.
8. Luke Beckerdite. "Philadelphia carving shops, Part I: James Reynolds." *Antiques*, May 1984, pp. 1120–1133.
9. Luke Beckerdite. "A Problem of Identification: Philadelphia and Baltimore Furniture Styles of the Eighteenth Century." *Journal of Early Southern Decorative Arts*, May 1986, pp. 21–64.
10. Robert Bishop. *Centuries and Styles of The American Chair, 1640–1970*. New York: E.P. Dutton and Co., 1972.
11. Arthur R. Blumenthal, ed. *350 Years of Art and Architecture in Maryland* (exhibition cat.). College Park: The Art Gallery and The Gallery of the School of Architecture, University of Maryland, 1984.
12. John B. Boles, ed. *Maryland Heritage: Five Baltimore Institutions Celebrate the American Bicentennial* (exhibition cat.). Baltimore: Maryland Historical Society, 1976.
13. "Buchanan Family Reminiscences." *Maryland Historical Society Magazine*, Sept. 1940, pp. 262–269.
14. E. Milby Burton. *Charleston Furniture, 1700–1825*. 1955. Reprint. Columbia: University of South Carolina Press, 1980.
15. *Charles Carroll of Carrollton (1737–1832) and His Family* (exhibition cat.). The Baltimore Museum of Art, 1937.
16. Thomas Chippendale. *The Gentleman and Cabinetmaker's Director*. 1762. Reprint. *A New Edition of Thomas Chippendale's The Gentleman and Cabinetmaker's Director*. London: The Connoisseur, 1957.
17. *The Collection of Louis Guerineau Myers: American Furniture of the XVIII–XIX Century* (sale cat.). Anderson Galleries Inc., New York, 7–9 Apr. 1932, sale no. 3963.
18. Stiles Tuttle Colwill. *Francis Guy, 1760–1820* (exhibition cat.). Maryland Historical Society, Baltimore, 1981.
19. Helen Comstock. *American Furniture: Seventeenth, Eighteenth and Nineteenth Century Styles*. New York: Viking Press, 1962.
20. Helen Comstock. "Baltimore furniture in the collection of Mr. and Mrs. Sifford Pearre." *Antiques*, Dec. 1962, pp. 632–633.
21. Wendy A. Cooper. *In Praise of America: American Decorative Arts, 1650–1830*. New York: Alfred A. Knopf, 1980.
22. Marshall B. Davidson. *The American Heritage History of Antiques from The Civil War to World War I*. New York: American Heritage Publishing Co., 1969.
23. Jane B. Davies. "Gothic revival furniture designs of Alexander J. Davis." *Antiques*, May 1977, pp. 1014–1027.
24. William H. Distin and Robert Bishop. *The American Clock*. 1976. Reprint. New York: Bonanza Books, 1983.
25. Joseph Downs. *American Furniture: Queen Anne and Chippendale Periods in the Henry Francis du Pont Winterthur Museum*. New York: Macmillan Co., 1952.
26. George H. Eckhardt. *Pennsylvania Clocks and Clockmakers*. New York: Bonanza Books, 1955.
27. William Voss Elder III. *Baltimore Painted Furniture, 1800–1840* (exhibition cat.). The Baltimore Museum of Art, 1972.
28. William Voss Elder III. "Maryland furniture, 1760–1840." *Antiques*, Feb. 1977, pp. 354–361.
29. William Voss Elder III. *Maryland Queen Anne and Chippendale Furniture of the Eighteenth Century* (exhibition cat.). The Baltimore Museum of Art, 1968.
30. William Voss Elder III and Lu Bartlett. *John Shaw Cabinetmaker of Annapolis* (exhibition cat.). The Baltimore Museum of Art, 1983.
31. *Estate of Edyth Johns Cotten* (sale cat.). Galton, Orsburn Co. Inc. Auctioneers, Baltimore, 28–29 Sept. 1942.
32. Jonathan L. Fairbanks and Elizabeth Bidwell Bates. *American Furniture, 1620 to the Present*. New York: Richard Marek Publishers, 1981.

33. Dean A. Fales, Jr. *American Painted Furniture, 1660–1880.* New York: E.P. Dutton and Co., 1972.

34. Dean A. Fales, Jr. *The Furniture of Historic Deerfield.* New York: E.P. Dutton and Co., 1976.

35. Oscar P. Fitzgerald. *Three Centuries of American Furniture.* New York: Gramercy Publishing Co., 1982.

36. Jennifer Faulds Goldsborough. *Silver in Maryland* (exhibition cat.). Maryland Historical Society, Baltimore, 1984.

37. David A. Hanks and Donald C. Peirce. *The Virginia Carroll Crawford Collection: American Decorative Arts, 1825–1917.* Atlanta: High Museum of Art, 1983.

38. Dianne D. Hauserman. "Alexander Roux and his 'Plain and Artistic Furniture.'" *Antiques,* Feb. 1968, pp. 210–217.

39. Morrison H. Heckscher. *American Furniture in The Metropolitan Museum of Art II, Late Colonial Period: The Queen Anne and Chippendale Styles.* New York: The Metropolitan Museum of Art and Random House, 1985.

40. George Hepplewhite. *The Cabinet-Maker and Upholsterer's Guide.* 1794. Reprint. New York: Dover Publications, 1969.

41. Benjamin A. Hewitt, Patricia E. Kane, and Gerald W.R. Ward. *The Work of Many Hands: Card Tables in Federal America, 1790–1820* (exhibition cat.). Yale University Art Gallery, New Haven, Connecticut, 1982.

42. Edwin J. Hipkiss. *Eighteenth-Century American Arts: The M. and M. Karolik Collection.* Cambridge, Massachusetts: Harvard University Press, 1941.

43. Thomas Hope. *Household Furniture and Interior Decoration.* 1807. Reprint. New York: Dover Publications, 1971.

44. William MacPherson Horner, Jr. *Blue Book: Philadelphia Furniture, William Penn to George Washington.* Philadelphia: Philadelphia Craftsmen of 1935, 1935.

45. "In the Museums." *Antiques,* Oct. 1959, pp. 352–355.

46. Brock Jobe and Myrna Kaye. *New England Furniture: The Colonial Era, Selections from the Society for the Preservation of New England Antiquities.* Boston: Houghton Mifflin Co., 1984.

47. Patricia E. Kane. *300 Years of American Seating Furniture.* Boston: New York Graphic Society, 1976.

48. Homer Eaton Keyes. "The Editor's Attic." *Antiques,* Mar. 1931, pp. 181–183.

49. John T. Kirk. *American Chairs: Queen Anne and Chippendale.* New York: Alfred A. Knopf, 1972.

50. John T. Kirk. "The distinctive character of Connecticut furniture." *Antiques,* Oct. 1967, pp. 524–529.

51. *Loan Exhibition of Eighteenth and Early Nineteenth Century Furniture* (exhibition cat.). Girl Scouts, Inc., at The American Art Galleries, New York, 1929.

52. Luke Vincent Lockwood. *Colonial Furniture in America.* 2 vols. 1913. 3rd ed. New York: Charles Scribner's Sons, 1926.

53. Robert Manwaring. *The Cabinet and Chair-maker's Real Friend and Companion.* London: Henry Webley, 1765.

54. Nancy McClelland. *Duncan Phyfe and The English Regency, 1795–1830.* New York: William R. Scott, 1939.

55. Edgar G. Miller. *American Antique Furniture: A Book for Amateurs.* 2 vols. Baltimore: Lord Baltimore Press, 1937.

56. Charles F. Montgomery. *American Furniture: The Federal Period in the Henry Francis du Pont Winterthur Museum.* New York: Viking Press, 1966.

57. Charles F. Montgomery. "John Needles—Baltimore cabinetmaker." *Antiques,* Apr. 1954, pp. 292–295.

58. Minor Myers, Jr. and Edgar deN. Mayhew. *New London County Furniture, 1640–1840* (exhibition cat.). The Lyman Allyn Museum, New London, Connecticut, 1974.

59. *19th-Century America: Furniture and Other Decorative Arts* (exhibition cat.). The Metropolitan Museum of Art, New York, 1970.

60. Brooks Palmer. *The Book of American Clocks.* New York: Macmillan Co., 1950.

61. Edward C. Papenfuse, Gregory A. Stiverson, Susan A. Collins, and Lois Green Carr. *Maryland: A New Guide to the Old Line State.* Baltimore: Johns Hopkins University Press, 1976.

62. *Philadelphia: Three Centuries of American Art* (exhibition cat.). Philadelphia Museum of Art, 1976.

63. *A Picture Book: 200 Objects in The Baltimore Museum of Art.* The Baltimore Museum of Art, 1955.

64. Pauline A. Pinckney. "George Woltz, Maryland Cabinetmaker." *Antiques,* Mar. 1939, pp. 124–126.

65. J. Hall Pleasants and Howard Sill. *Maryland Silversmiths, 1715–1830.* Baltimore: Lord Baltimore Press, 1930.

66. Richard H. Randall, Jr. *American Furniture in the Museum of Fine Arts, Boston.* Boston: Museum of Fine Arts, 1965.

67. Richard H. Randall, Jr. "Seymour Furniture Problems." *Bulletin of the Museum of Fine Arts, Boston,* vol. 57, no. 310, 1959, pp. 103–113.

68. Elizabeth Rhoades and Brock Jobe. "Recent discoveries in Boston japanned furniture." *Antiques,* May 1974, pp. 1082–1091.

69. Oswaldo Rodriguez Roque. *American Furniture at Chipstone.* Madison: University of Wisconsin Press, 1984.

70. Charles Santore. *The Windsor Style in America, 1730–1830.* Philadelphia: Running Press, 1981.

71. Marvin D. Schwartz, Edward J. Stanck, and Douglas K. True. *The Furniture of John Henry Belter and The Rococo Revival.* New York: E.P. Dutton and Co., 1981.

72. Thomas Sheraton. *The Cabinet Dictionary.* London: W. Smith, 1803.

73. Thomas Sheraton. *The Cabinet-Maker and Upholsterer's Drawing-Book.* 1793. Reprint. New York: Dover Publications, 1972.

74. George Smith. *A Collection of Designs for Household Furniture.* London: J. Taylor, 1808.

75. Robert C. Smith. "Key pieces of Federal furniture." *Antiques*, Sept. 1957, pp. 240–243.

76. Robert C. Smith. "The furniture of Anthony G. Quervelle." *Antiques*, 1973–1974.

77. Barbara Snow. "Living with antiques: The Baltimore home of Mr. and Mrs. Sifford Pearre." *Antiques*, Dec. 1962, pp. 628–631.

78. Vernon C. Stoneman. *John and Thomas Seymour: Cabinetmakers in Boston, 1794–1816*. Boston: Special Publications, 1959.

79. Vernon C. Stoneman. *A Supplement to John and Thomas Seymour: Cabinetmakers in Boston, 1794–1816*. Boston: Special Publications, 1965.

80. Mabel M. Swan. "Newburyport furnituremakers." *Antiques*, Apr. 1945, pp. 222–225.

81. Berry B. Tracy and William H. Gerdts. *Classical America, 1815–1845* (exhibition cat.). The Newark Museum, New Jersey, 1963.

82. Ann C. Van Devanter. *"Anywhere So Long As There Be Freedom": Charles Carroll of Carrollton, His Family and His Maryland* (exhibition cat.). The Baltimore Museum of Art, 1975.

83. David B. Warren. *Bayou Bend: American Furniture, Paintings and Silver from the Bayou Bend Collection*. The Museum of Fine Arts, Houston, 1975.

84. Gregory R. Weidman. *Furniture in Maryland 1740–1940: The Collection of The Maryland Historical Society*. Baltimore: Maryland Historical Society, 1984.

85. Walter Muir Whitehill, ed. *Boston Furniture of the Eighteenth Century*. Boston: Colonial Society of Massachusetts, 1974.

86. John Ware Willard. *A History of Simon Willard, Inventor and Clockmaker*. Boston: E.O. Cockayne, 1911.

87. Alice Winchester. "Baltimore and Annapolis Furniture Of the Hepplewhite-Sheraton Period: on View at The Baltimore Museum of Art." *Antiques*, Mar. 1947, pp. 176–179.

88. Stacy B.C. Wood, Jr. and Stephen E. Kramer III. *Clockmakers of Lancaster County and Their Clocks, 1750–1850*. New York: Van Nostrand Reinhold Co., 1977.

89. Philip D. Zimmerman. "A Methodological Study in the Identification of Some Important Philadelphia Chippendale Furniture." *Winterthur Portfolio 13*. Charlottesville: University Press of Virginia, 1979, pp. 193–208.

American Furniture 1680-1880

FROM THE COLLECTION OF THE BALTIMORE MUSEUM OF ART

Printed in an edition of 3000 copies.

Typography in Trump Medieval by
Monotype Composition Company, Baltimore.

Color separations by Prolith International, Laurel, Maryland.

Text paper is Warren's Lustro offset dull enamel, 100 pound;
cover is 12 pt. Warren's Lusterkote;
end papers are Rainbow Colonial Blueberry text, 80 pound.

Printing by Schneidereith & Sons, Baltimore.

Design by Alex and Caroline Castro, HOLLOWPRESS, Baltimore.

© 1987 The Baltimore Museum of Art

PHOTOGRAPHY CREDITS

All photographs are by Joel Breger & Associates, Kensington, Maryland,
except for the following:

Gilbert Ask Photography, fig. 77a.

Duane Suter, Baltimore, cat. nos. 71, 89;
details, cat. nos. 18, 70, 71, 109, 119; and fig. 50a.

Joseph Szaszfai, Branford, Connecticut, cat. no. 56 and detail.